The Stork and the Syringe

Feminist Perspectives

Series Editor: Michelle Stanworth

Published

Veronica Beechey & Tessa Perkins, *A Matter of Hours*
Seyla Benhabib & Drucilla Cornell (eds), *Feminism as Critique*
Harriet Bradley, *Men's Work, Women's Work*
Pat Carlen (ed), *Criminal Women*
Christine Delphy & Diana Leonard, *Familiar Exploitation*
Felicia Gordon, *The Integral Feminist: Madeleine Pelletier 1874–1939:
    Feminism, Socialism and Medicine*
Su Kappeler, *The Pornography of Representation*
Liz Kelly, *Surviving Sexual Violence*
Judy Lown, *Women and Industrialization: Gender and Work in 19th Century
    England*
Henrietta L Moore, *Feminism and Anthropology*
Naomi Pfeffer, *The Stork and the Syringe*
June Purvis, *Hard Lessons: The Lives and Education of Working Class Women
    in 19th Century England*
Yannick Ripa, *Women and Madness*
Barbara Sichtermann, *Femininity: The Politics of the Personal*
Michelle Stanworth (ed), *Reproductive Technologies*
Julia Swindells, *Victorian Writing and Working Women*
Sylvia Walby, *Patriarchy at Work*

Forthcoming

Christine Griffin, *Representations of Youth*
Susan Himmelweit, *Reproduction*
Joan Scanlon, *Bending the Rule*
Gill Thomas, *Women in the First World War*

The Stork and the Syringe

A Political History of Reproductive Medicine

Naomi Pfeffer

Polity Press

Copyright © Naomi Pfeffer, 1993

The right of Naomi Pfeffer to be identified as author of this work has been asserted in accordance with the Copyright, Designs and Patents Act 1988.

First published in 1993 by Polity Press in association with Blackwell Publishers

Editorial office:
Polity Press
65 Bridge Street
Cambridge CB2 1UR, UK

238, Main Street
Cambridge, MA 02142,
USA

Marketing and production:
Blackwell Publishers
108 Cowley Road
Oxford OX4 1JF, UK

ISBN 0 7456 0821 3
ISBN 0 7456 1187 7 (pbk)

A CIP catalogue record for this book is available from the British Library.

Typeset in 10 on 12 pt Garamond by Best set Typesetters Ltd
Printed in Great Britain by Biddles Ltd., Guildford, Surrey

This book is printed on acid-free paper.

Contents

Acknowledgements

This book has taken many years to complete. I could never have undertaken such an ambitious project without help of various kinds. I am indebted to the Economic and Social Research Council for a Postgraduate Training Award 1983–6, which allowed me to research and write my doctoral thesis on which sections of this book are based. I am also indebted to The Wellcome Trust for a two-year Fellowship, followed by a Research Expenses Grant, which enabled me to enlarge the scope of my thesis.

My work was made far easier by many librarians, archivists and medical records staff who pointed me in the right direction. Special thanks are due to Gervaise Hood and the librarians at the Royal College of Obstetricians and Gynaecologists. I have been fortunate in having had archives and interests in common with Lesley Hall of the Contemporary Medical Archives, Wellcome Institute. Thanks also to Doreen Castle for access to the archives of the Population Investigation Committee at the London School of Economics. Dr Bernard Sandler kindly provided me with material collected during his long career treating involuntarily childless women and men at the Manchester Jewish Hospital.

I am indebted to Professor Ludmilla Jordanova of the University of Essex, my supervisor, for showing me how to be a historian. Special thanks are due to Priscilla Alderson who read, commented on and encouraged me to complete the final draft of this book. To my dear friend Anne Woollett goes the dubious honour of having read every word I have ever written on the subject of infertility over the past decade; her support gave me the courage to write about a deeply personal and painful issue. Of course, I take responsibility for the final form of this work; any omissions and errors are mine.

For many different kinds of help, I would like to record my thanks to Jocelyn Cornwell, Sarah Franklin, Sarah Kent, Susan Kerrison, Aviva Le

Prevost, Clare Moynihan, Alison Quick, Margaret Stacey, Michelle Stanworth, James Swinson and Fedelma Winkler. To my mother Rachel Pfeffer, love and thanks for her support.

N. P.

For Gordon (to be read)

Introduction

There have always been infertile women. Yet nowadays there is an apparently ineluctable tendency to talk about infertility, and ways of treating it, in the present or future tense. When infertility is allowed a history, it is usually located in the dim and distant past; biblical times are especially popular. Indeed, the story of Sarah has come to represent the ways in which women responded to involuntary childlessness up until the introduction of the so-called assisted conception technologies: with an admixture of fatalism and reliance on divine intervention. The impression conveyed is that before 1978, when the first baby conceived in a petrie dish was delivered by a hitherto irremediably sterile woman, doctors could not and did not treat infertility. It is also assumed that involuntarily childless women either suffered their fate in stoic silence, or resolved their childlessness by adoption.

Nothing could be further from the truth. Throughout this century women, and sometimes their husbands, have sought medical help for involuntary childlessness. Yet today the techniques of assisted conception are talked about as if they were new treatments of a new problem. We are led to believe that doctors are developing the technology required to treat another modern malaise attributed severally to sexual promiscuity (which is said to lead to venereal infection and damaged fallopian tubes), women delaying pregnancy until past their fertile peak in order to pursue a career, environmental pollutants which are especially toxic to sperm, and so on. The corollary to this present is a past typified by excess fertility in which sexually continent women, with no ambitions other than to marry young and keep home, reproduced with unenviable ease.

The stork and the syringe is about myths: myths about why some women conceive and become mothers, and others do not. Myths about fertility are usually attributed to ignorance, stories to be contrasted with state-of-the-art science, or compared to beliefs held by the ancient Greeks and people of exotic cultures; or their origins are located somewhere within the Judeo-Christian tradition. In fact, the origins of these myths are on our doorsteps, albeit well hidden from view: they are found in political and economic theory and practice, and medical and scientific professional and commercial ambitions. Indeed, the successful repudiation of their influence on ideas about infertility and its treatment is remarkable, and the reasons for it are explored in chapter 1. The rest of the book documents the response of British medicine to infertility during the twentieth century.

Although the chapters are arranged in chronological order, *The stork and the syringe* is not an exhaustive record of every procedure used by doctors in the investigation and treatment of involuntary childlessness. Rather, it offers a series of slices taken out of the history and laid out in order to emphasize important features. My purpose is to explore a number of different issues relating to involuntary childlessness that have exercised me for some considerable time. The first is why the desire to have a child is not considered of political importance while freedom from unwanted pregnancies is deemed crucial? The second point relates to the exclusion of male fertility from both medical and political discourse around reproduction; indeed, unlike other books which examine the politics of reproductive technologies yet at the same time perpetuate the tendency to overlook the significance of male sterility, *The stork and the syringe* covers exhaustively the history of tests and treatments of the procreative power of semen.

A central argument of this book is that medicine's relationship to involuntary childlessness cannot be understood without an appreciation of the political economy in which it is situated. In Britain, the National Health Insurance Scheme, introduced in 1911, and the National Health Service, which began in 1948, have had a major impact on health care. This point leads on to the third issue examined here: the stubborn refusal of successive British governments to encourage and support effective medical services for the investigation and treatment of involuntary childlessness. The manipulation by politicians of population and health policies is examined in order to explain why this tendency prevails, and why commercial interests have flourished in gynaecology. In effect, this book is not a history of women's experience of infertility, but a description of the context of that experience.

1
Talking about Infertility

There are many histories of fertile women. Modern history books are full of women conceiving, contracepting, aborting, pregnant, in labour, breastfeeding, looking after and even abandoning children. Yet women who wanted to but were unable to become mothers are almost never talked about.[1] The impression conveyed is that the incidence and significance of involuntary childlessness are trivial and not worth mentioning.

Almost without exception, the theme that animates recent histories of women's reproductive lives is a version of the following story. In the 'bad old days', women were imprisoned in their homes, where they not only bore the physical cost of repeated pregnancies, but were also weighed down by heavy maternal duties and arduous domestic responsibilities. In dramatic contrast to the image of woman as victim of 'natural' fecundity stands her late twentieth-century counterpart, who has been liberated by scientific contraception and labour-saving domestic technology. Science has defeated Nature which, in this instance, is represented as wielding a cornucopia overflowing with eggs, sperm, embryos and babies. Modern woman has exchanged her reproductive capacity for consumer durables: a washing machine, a microwave oven and a fridge – freezer. She has escaped domestic and maternal drudgery in order to compete alongside men in the public world.[2]

Nowadays, childlessness is taken as proof that a woman is in control; it is interpreted as a voluntary, temporary, reversible condition that is both desired and self-imposed (although this assumption is a double-edged one: more often than not, married women who are childless are deemed selfish, or 'career women', and not involuntarily infertile). If it is acknowledged, involuntary sterility is attributed to the dark, irrational, vengeful side of 'Nature', the aspect that wreaks havoc and brings forth drought, floods, disease and famine. Little wonder, then, that involuntary childlessness makes women desperate, for it fails to respond to reasonable

entreaties. The improved health status of women in industrialized nations
– a boon of scientific hygiene and nutrition – the high rates of sterility in
some parts of Africa (in some regions, up to two out of every five marriages are involuntarily childless) and the much-publicized new assisted
conception technologies are taken as confirmation that, like unwanted
fertility, involuntary infertility is eradicated by Progress.[3]

Stories of women's fertility and infertility convey a powerful, complex
message which operates at two related levels.[4] The first establishes iden-
tities and norms against which moral judgements about individual women
are made. There are many different kinds of women; however, only
certain aspects of their bodies and their lives – the most significant being
class, race, age, sexuality, marital status and fertility – are deemed crucial
to their social status. In different combinations, these attributes convey
messages about women which are easily understood; we know how
we are expected to respond to the large family of a white, upper-class
woman, and to that of a black woman living in an inner-city high-rise
housing estate. Similarly, involuntary childlessness in a lesbian is represented as right and proper, whereas in a married woman it is a plight
that can play on the heartstrings.

The other message uses women's – and sometimes men's – fertility to
comment on a nation's economic health and political power. Within
political economy, the birth rate is inextricably linked to a nation's economic growth. In the last years of the eighteenth century, Thomas Malthus
famously welded the two together in a theory which proposed that
population grows by geometrical increase while agricultural production
expands arithmetically, and that there is consequently an inbuilt tendency
for the former to outstrip the latter. Malthus' theory became indelibly
etched on the minds of influential thinkers of subsequent generations,
who, whether working within or outside government, have fashioned
policies according to its dictates.

Both messages have been combined in stories about women's (and, to
a lesser extent, men's) fertility which have informed key developments of
the twentieth century: to name two which are considered at length in this
book, the loathsome ideology of National Socialism in Europe between
the two world wars and, since the end of the Second World War, coercive
population programmes in the developing world. Both deem crucial the
exercise of control over reproduction, albeit for different ends: National
Socialism sought to encourage the breeding of so-called desirable Aryan
stock and to get rid of those people – namely Jews, gypsies, the mentally
ill, those with learning disabilities and homosexuals – who, according to
its imperialist, racist ambitions, were undesirable; population planners
want all women to have few babies, in order to save the planet from
political upheavals, famine, war and other epic disasters.

Although nowadays involuntary infertility seems a newcomer among stories about women's fertility, in fact it played a leading part in the first half of the twentieth century. Indeed, it is possible to locate the moment when infertility became a political embarrassment and was repudiated. This is because, throughout the twentieth century, there have been people who have shown a remarkable tendency to respond to whatever they consider the burning contemporary issue by trying to find out why British women are or are not having babies (and sometimes why men are or are not fathering them). These people can be described as enthusiasts of 'facts'; they subscribe to the school of thought which believes that a survey is necessary to assess what is going wrong so that an appropriate policy can be introduced that will achieve the desired results (in contrast to people who proceed regardless of the empirical evidence). Some of the investigations were unofficial, initiated, designed and funded by pressure groups; others were carried out by government departments. Although, no doubt, all such investigators would claim to have been guided by the principles of scientific objectivity, in reality their work is polemical: the surveys were designed and their findings reported in a fashion which was intended to inform and provoke political action. In some cases their purpose was pronatalist, that is, they sought ways of encouraging women to have a child and to have larger families; in others, it was antinatalist, that is, they tried to persuade women not to have children. Although, strictly speaking, the terms pro- and antinatalist imply action on the part of the state, they are also used throughout this book to indicate a climate of opinion.

In the mid-1870s, the birth rate in Britain began to fall; it continued to so do until the 1930s, by which time the average family size had been reduced from just over six children to just under two. Around the turn of the century, this trend began to arouse considerable alarm in contemporary commentators, who saw in it a major threat to national and imperial security. In 1905, the Fabian Society set up a committee under the chairmanship of Sidney Webb to investigate the reasons why women were having fewer babies, and to find out what might encourage them to have more.

Fabianism had emerged in the late nineteenth century. Its sympathizers were committed to imperialism, national efficiency – the replacement of government by rule-of-thumb methods with policies based on science – and the collectivist state. Fabians sought to advance their ideas by influencing politicians and by generally spreading their ideas through the process they called 'permeation'.[5] However, Webb's committee knew that before it could convince politicians that, given the right incentive, women would have more babies, they had to discredit a popular belief that Britain was in the grip of an epidemic of male sterility caused by degeneration, a fearful and untreatable condition.

The existence of degeneration had been indicated by a version of evolutionary theory which proposed that all organisms, individuals, nations, races and cultures undergo change, but that the process of change may take either of two directions, namely progressive or degenerative.[6] What else could explain the strange, infertile, aboriginal peoples discovered by Victorian anthropologists? Like progress, its converse, degeneration could take many forms; but, without fail, it always managed to identify itself with the establishment's judgements of the social pecking order. The large families of weak and diseased children of the urban 'residuum', made up of the insane, alcoholics, syphilitics, prostitutes and victims of tuberculosis, were 'proof' of their degeneracy, while among the civilized, servant-keeping, enfranchised classes degeneration had the opposite effect: it spread sterility through 'hypercivilization', that is, the development of the intellect at the expense of the body. In the servant-keeping classes, the symptoms of degeneration were neurasthenia, lack or perversion of sexual energy, and germinal cells too weak to effect fertilization or form a viable embryo.

Degeneration seemed rife in *fin de siècle* Imperial Britain. The country's economic and political dominance of the world appeared increasingly vulnerable to challenges from enemies both within and outside the pink-coloured territories. Beyond its borders lurked Germany, the United States and Japan, all rising to great power status; inside were the stroppy Boer farmers in South Africa and, at home, the increasingly truculent working classes. Adding insult to potential injury, it looked as though British middle-class masculinity, the bulwark against chaos, was flagging. Male homosexuals and lesbians had come out of the closet and were publicly flaunting their sexual preferences.[7] Their increased visibility made it seem as if Britain was afflicted by decadence similar to that which had infected the last days of the Roman Empire: they were the equivalent of Nero playing while Rome burnt. Some doctors claimed that unmanly men and unwomanly women had merged to form an intermediate, infertile sex, which they called 'androgyne'. Yet the distinctness of the sexes was considered essential to an ordered society. The sensational trial of Oscar Wilde in 1895 served as a warning from politicians of their determination to prosecute and punish 'deviant' sexual behaviour in order to preserve the state.[8]

The moral panic around homosexuality – the enemy within – contributed to fears of widespread emasculation of heterosexual men. An alarming number of men volunteering for military service were being rejected on the grounds that they were too weak and physically deficient to fight.[9] At the same time, the birth rate of the middle classes was going down. Perhaps British manhood was exhausted, which was why male homosexuality, impotence and sterility had become more prevalent.

History demonstrated that all great civilizations sank ineluctably into obscurity. Was the British Empire's demise inevitable, or could destiny be thwarted? If the decline in the birth rate was a symptom of widespread and increasing degeneration, then, as the Fabians admitted, the trend was irreversible and the Empire was doomed. 'But a deliberately volitional interference, due chiefly to economic motives, can at any moment be influenced, and its adverse selection stopped.'[10]

The Fabians focused their attention on middle-class men rather than their wives, not only because they were worried that British manhood was exhausted, but also for the simple reason that Victorian marriage reduced women to a subservient status.[11] Husbands were custodians of their wives' fertility. All women were excluded from the polity. Only men had a right to vote; indeed, it was their 'natural' ability to control themselves that had given them the authority to govern others, both in and outside of the home.[12] Middle-class women were socialized into accepting a helpless and dependent role. There was another reason why policies aimed at encouraging the birth rate had to be directed at men: the principal means of preventing conception then in use was a 'male method' – 'volitional interference' meant withdrawal of the penis before ejaculation. The Victorian 'spermatic economy' had condoned this method by associating it with the accumulation of wealth through a play on the double meaning of 'being careful'. Onanism within the marital sexual relationship, motivated by thriftiness, was a virtue; it was a vice when practised by solitary young unmarried men.[13] Like many of their contemporaries, the Fabians believed that if the low birth rate was caused by careful expenditure of both money and semen, then both nation and Empire were safe: when it was expedient, the government could introduce financial incentives that would encourage responsible men to father more children.

The Fabian tract *The declining birth-rate* suggests that Webb's committee was bent on an exercise that would promote confidence in British manhood; not the type represented by the gentleman or, heaven forfend, the poor and unwashed classes, but that exemplified by the artisan, the shopkeeper and other members of the lower middle classes who, they believed, formed the backbone of Britain and the Empire. The committee felt confident that the birth rate of these exemplary types had fallen because of foresight, prudence and self-control. The evidence came from consideration of lying-in claims (applications for maternity benefits) made over the previous forty years to friendly societies under a type of insurance scheme which would admit as members only men of proven good character and in receipt of a wage of at least 24 shillings each week. In all, one and a quarter million men had joined. And their wives were having fewer babies: lying-in claims had fallen from 2,176 for every thousand members in 1866 to 1,165 in 1904.[14]

Webb sought confirmation that 'volitional regulation' and not degeneration was behind the fall in the birth rate of this section of society. He took a voluntary census of a sample of 'very deliberate and farseeing citizens', who, he believed, were also the sort of chaps who could be relied upon to give frank and truthful answers: skilled artisans, professional men and small property owners.[15] Representatives of the great army of labourers were excluded from the census, as were men whose incomes from investments exceeded £1,000 per annum. Respondents were asked if they had taken steps to render themselves childless or to limit the number of children born, and whether there had been any exceptional cause such as the death or serious illness of husband and or wife – suggestive of degeneration – which had made them unable to have as many children as they had wanted. Three hundred and sixteen out of the 634 men who were sent a schedule replied. Seventy-four said that their marriage was 'unlimited' and 242 'limited'. From this Webb concluded that it was 'volitional interference', and not an epidemic of male sterility caused by degeneration, which was responsible for the decline in the middle-class birth rate. Both nation and Empire were safe; the manhood of the men on whom it depended was intact, and they were managing responsibly their wives' bodies.

During the ten years that separated the publication of the Fabian tract and the instigation of the next investigation into the reasons why women were or were not having babies, anxieties about men's physical decline were supplemented by concern over their moral health: men seemed to have lost control over their sexual appetites and were jeopardizing their authority to govern others. An epidemic of venereal diseases was thought to be sweeping the country because of men's promiscuity. In Britain in the years before and during the First World War, startling numbers of people of all social classes were said to have become infected. At least three million people were said to have syphilis, called 'the great destroyer' of life because it causes miscarriage and stillbirth. The incidence of gonorrhea was said to be far greater. Gonorrhea was known as 'the great preventer of life' because it causes sterility in both women and men.[16] Infection by the gonococci may block the fallopian tubes and the urethra. Many women infected by the gonococci both before and during pregnancy became sterile after delivering their first child, suffering from the condition known then as 'one-child sterility'.[17] An estimate of the contribution of gonorrhea to the decline in marital fertility was given in a report on venereal diseases prepared for the Local Government Board and published in 1913; it claimed that the cause of about half of all childless marriages could be traced to the presence of gonococci in women.[18]

The shocking fact emerged that many women, especially those from the middle classes, were kept in ignorance about the cause of their ill-health and childlessness by their doctors and husbands. The suffragettes made much of this scandal; they protested that only political power could shield innocent women, the family, nation and Empire from this male conspiracy: 'We want the vote to stop the white slave traffic, sweated labour and to save the children.'[19]

Opponents of the suffragettes claimed that giving women the vote would exacerbate the problem: they considered that it was women's neglect of hearth and home in favour of 'selfish' pursuits that was responsible for men's sexual promiscuity. Venereal diseases had reached epidemic proportions because the 'angel in the home', that Victorian ideal of womanhood who deployed her moral purity both to contain her husband's wandering lust and to sanctify family life, had got herself a job. In the Edwardian period, new opportunities for middle-class women had enabled many of them to achieve notable successes in both higher education and employment. While some of them became teachers and shop assistants, the increased demand for clerical workers and typists had greatly expanded women's employment opportunities.

The nation, it was said, was paying a high price for middle-class women's education and employment: their fertility was diminishing in three different ways. First, women's neglect of domestic and marital responsibilities was forcing their husbands to seek sexual favours outside the conjugal home, from prostitutes who were seedbeds of venereal diseases. Second, women intent on selfish modern pursuits considered children encumbrances and were using contraception or illegal termination of pregnancy to limit their family size. Contraception was said permanently to damage fertility, and no doubt in many cases infection resulting from abortion really did make women sterile. Third, educated women and those who worked were suffering from 'virilization', that is, taking on the attributes of men, and thereby making their reproductive organs atrophy.

One obvious way of reversing the decline in the birth rate was to encourage women to return home and engage in womanly 'feminizing' tasks. Yet few people proposed the reinstatement of innocent womanhood; there was a new conviction abroad that neither family nor national health had profited by it. For with Madonnas came Magdalenes. Instead, women had to be equipped with sexual knowledge that would transform them into responsive but chaste sexual partners of their husbands, and enable them to supervise the moral development of their children.

The key propagandists of this message were social hygienists, an influential stratum of middle-class reformers who typically worked in peripheral voluntary organizations rather than at the heart of government.[20]

Emerging in the Edwardian period, social hygienists combined the language of religion and social purity with that of medicine in their efforts to rearm the nation's morals. In their mission, they replaced religious sermons with lectures on medical 'facts' that proved that sexual relationships conducted outside marriage were harmful.[21] Medicine was directed at reversing the moral decline, and not at preventing the venereal diseases that accompanied it; social hygienists opposed prophylaxis – the use of condoms – on the grounds that it encouraged sexual immorality.

During the first half of the twentieth century, social hygienists worked hard at encouraging people to confine their sexual relations within the heterosexual monogamous family.[22] They formed voluntary organizations whose members policed sexuality; on behalf of the government, they disseminated sex education material on the dangers of venereal diseases; they introduced biology – a cover for sex education – into the school curriculum; developed marriage guidance counselling;[23] attacked prostitution; and promoted film censorship.

Not everyone shared the social hygienists' belief that marital fertility would be restored by moral rearmament. Some doctors reported that increasing numbers of married women were consulting them about involuntary childlessness; many appeared to be suffering from a type of sterility that did not respond to medical treatment. Doctors A. K. Chalmers and J. Brownlee, two influential Medical Officers of Health, attributed the epidemic of sterility to diminished germinal vitality: British sperm and ova were too weak to effect conception.[24] Through their work on infectious diseases, they lighted on a plausible explanation of this national malaise. Chalmers and Brownlee proposed that human fertility is subject to processes similar to those which govern the virulence of infectious organisms. Historical data indicated that the toll exacted by these fevers fluctuates considerably: an epidemic is followed by many years during which the disease seems fairly harmless, as had happened, for example, with the bubonic plague. Chalmers and Brownlee attributed this phenomenon to fluctuations in the virulence of the pathogens which cause the disease; their strength is exhausted by an epidemic, and can take many years – even centuries – to recover. They noticed that, looked at over a number of centuries, the natural history of populations exhibits a cyclical pattern similar to that of infectious diseases. From this they concluded that, as with pathogens, the power of germinal cells waxes and wanes. The dramatic increase in the British population that had taken place during the first seventy-odd years of the nineteenth century had exhausted the nation's germinal vitality. However, the two doctors felt confident that, in time, marital fertility would be restored.

As Britain's relationship with Germany deteriorated, settling the controversy over the cause of the declining birth rate became increasingly urgent: once again, the question was: was it involuntary or by design? There were frequent loud demands that the government should act as arbitrator of the competing explanations. Yet although it conceded the inclusion in the 1911 'Fertility Census' of questions that might throw light on the causes of death in young babies of married women, and introduced measures to improve the health of pregnant women and children, the government refused to involve itself in the debate about the causes of and solution to the declining birth rate (I will return to this subject in chapter 4). In 1913, the Public Morality Council, a platform for social hygienists founded in 1899 to combat vice and indecency, set up the National Birth-Rate Commission as a demonstration of its exasperation with the government's refusal to call a Royal Commission.

The Birth-Rate Commission conducted itself as though it had the government's authority to proceed: it called witnesses, heard evidence and commissioned research. The preliminary results of the 1911 Census confirmed suspicions that the decline in the birth rate was exacting its toll where the nation could least afford it: among the middle classes. Indeed, clergymen, teachers and doctors had the smallest families.[25] The Commission felt compelled to investigate why middle-class women were having fewer babies. The answer was deemed to lie in a comparison between the health and reproductive histories of married women who had been to college with those of their sisters or near female relatives who had not had a college education. Informants were recruited by Dr Agnes Savill by what we now call a 'snowball' sample: women were invited to send in the names and addresses of fellow college students so that they too might be sent schedules to complete themselves. The investigators felt confident that educated middle-class women would co-operate willingly in a medical inquiry concerned with the future welfare not only of their class, but also of both nation and Empire. In all, 787 schedules were returned to Dr Savill's Harley Street consulting room. More might have been completed, but the outbreak of war meant that the survey had to be abandoned.

In keeping with the social hygienists' creed of giving sex education to women, the survey was both investigative and instructive: women who were ignorant of the processes of fertility were in sore need of education. Sixty-six questions asked women about their bodies, personal habits, family life, education and work: had they taken regular exercise? What was their experience of menstruation? Had they 'limited' their families? Had they had an abortion? Had they found difficulty in having a child? If so, had they consulted a doctor about it?

The data were inconclusive. Although education did not seem to have an adverse influence on women's fertility, many middle-class women were infertile. Furthermore, no significant difference was found between the average sizes of the families of women who admitted 'limiting' and those of women who did not. Indeed, use of contraception seemed to make no difference to the number of children women had. In their conclusion, the investigators acknowledged that the data were 'open to those who saw the decline in the birth rate as a "biological" phenomenon and little influenced by the popularisation of anti-conceptual methods to claim our results as evidence in favour of their belief'.[26] There was little to discredit the belief that middle-class bodies were in the grip of an epidemic of sterility.

During the 1920s, demographic anxieties turned to fears of overpopulation. Recession, labour unrest and growing unemployment made it seem as though there were too many people in England. The natural increase of the population – the balance between births and immigration on the one hand and deaths and emigration on the other – replaced the birth rate as the signifier of national health. Since registration of births had become compulsory in 1837 the population of England and Wales had always (with the exception of the first six months of 1919) shown an increase. During the 1920s death rates continued to decrease, more than compensating for any fall in birth rates. As a result, despite the persistent fall in the birth rate, the total population continued to grow. Antinatalism predominated. As one man recalled, 'there were two million unemployed at the time he was out of a job; if there had been 1,999,999 fewer people in the country, he might have slipped in'.[27] Little wonder, then, that the first birth control clinics were set up during the 1920s and neo-Malthusians – people who believed in Malthus' theory and who campaigned around making birth control advice and techniques more widely available to the working classes – won small concessions from the government.[28]

   Towards the end of the 1920s, the rise of fascism in Italy and Germany refocused attention on British fertility and brought new, sinister meanings to its decline. The Italian demographer Corrado Gini developed a 'scientific' justification of Mussolini's imperial ambitions which exploited the diminishing British birth rate.[29] Gini proposed that all civilizations pass through a 'parabola of evolution' from birth though youth and maturity to senility; and their reproductive vigour corresponds to their age.[30] The low fertility of peoples such as Eskimos, Redskins, Polynesians and Maoris 'proved' that these races were long past their prime; they were senile, impotent and infertile. They exemplified the fate that awaited old nations. The political message in Gini's law of population was not a subtle one: the birth rate of the recently formed Italian state was well above that of old nations such as France and Britain, which were advised to face up to their inevitable demise and relinquish their dominions to this young and virile people. According to Gini, the contribution of birth control to the decline in marital fertility in Britain and France had been overstated. The reason why people preferred this explanation to a pessimistic, biological alternative was because it 'conceals a secret hope, since a thing which is voluntary may still be remedied; man has always shown great reluctance to admit that he is not the arbiter of his own species'.[31]

In the late 1920s and early 1930s, population statistics experienced a revolution compared then to the impact on physics of Newton's discovery of the laws of gravity: the discovery of reproduction rates. Reproduction rates reveal the extent to which a population is replacing itself. They direct attention to the performance of women of child-bearing age by focusing on how many girl babies women produce as their replacements in the next generation. Reproduction rates are both objective and prescriptive measures: they provide an indication of how seriously women are taking their procreative responsibilities. Both birth rate and natural increase statistics were discredited on the grounds that they described what had happened to the whole population in the past, when what the nation needed was an indication of its procreative prospects.[32] As one demographer put it, using the birth rate and natural increase to assess national health was equivalent to a physician trying to measure fever by counting the pulse.[33] Reproduction rates were crystal balls; unfortunately, what they foretold was a dramatic decline in the size of the British population.

The discovery of reproduction rates transformed the collection and analysis of population statistics into the science of demography. Yet in Britain demographers found it difficult to establish a foothold in an academic institution.[34] In 1930, the London School of Economics and Political Science – established by the Fabian Sidney Webb in 1895 – opened a Department of Social Biology which offered demography a home. Headed by Lancelot Hogben and supported by funds from the Rockefeller Foundation, the department combined the study of biology with empirical investigations into social problems. Six years later, the economic depression forced the Rockefeller Foundation to withdraw its financial support and the Department closed. In the same year demography made headline news when it revealed to the public that Britain was threatened by depopulation.[35]

The British Eugenics Society can claim responsibility for the depopulation scare. Eugenists were enthusiasts of the new science of demography because it combined the study of reproduction and the pursuit of national ambitions in the sort of scientific language which they spoke. The Society sponsored the publication of three books on population which used reproduction rates to draw people's attention to the shrinking and ageing British population.[36] It was a review of these books in *The Times* in 1936 which sparked off the depopulation scare. Vigour, adventure, love and laughter would soon be no more. Too few girls were being born to replenish the nation's numbers; too few youthful spirits to make the wheels of community go round. The British people had better be on their guard; Hitler and Mussolini were simultaneously calling for more children and declaring their territories too small for their existing populations. As economic and political crises deepened, it looked as though there might be truth in Gini's taunt that old nations like Britain became colonies.

The depopulation scare had its greatest impact on the ideas and policies of members of the British Eugenics Society. The Society had been founded in 1907 in order to educate public opinion in the deleterious influence of degeneration on the quality of the nation's breeding stock. What worried eugenists most was differential fertility: the tendency of poorer, less healthy and, according to them, less intelligent sections of society to have larger families than their betters. Eugenists warned that unless draconian steps were taken, the population of Britain would soon consist almost entirely of physical and mental 'defectives'. The problem was a biological one. The solution was negative eugenics: preventing 'defectives' from reproducing by providing them with birth control and encouraging them to volunteer for sterilization.[37]

By the early 1930s, negative eugenics had become an uncomfortable platform because it sounded too much like the racist propaganda of German National Socialism and British fascism. On his appointment as Secretary to the Society in 1931, Carlos Blacker, a psychiatrist, set out to distance it from these unfavourable associations by cleansing its member-ship of its more rabid right-wing members, encouraging a 'progressive' element and pursuing a programme of positive eugenics: the encourage-ment of the reproduction of socially valuable traits. Initially, the Society confined its attention to the better-off classes. However, the depopulation scare made it clear that in the short term, quality had to be sacrificed for quantity. Reproduction rates showed that the nation desperately needed women in the early years of their married lives to make up for the threatened shortfall of girl babies as quickly as possible. Women had to be persuaded of their patriotic duty to have at least three or, preferably, four wisely spaced children (but not to return to the 'quiverful', the large family that was regarded as a blessing in the Victorian age). However, as the eugenists reluctantly acknowledged, if there was to be any significant increase, it would have to come from among the lower, more numerous classes. To save the nation and the Empire, the Society abandoned its campaign of discouraging working-class women from having any babies and decided to try and persuade them to have more children. But before they could encourage them to have more children, they had to find out why they were having so few.

The government seemed unconcerned by the prospect of a world without young British men and women; it refused to take seriously warn-ings of the dire fate that awaited nations – especially imperial powers –

with declining birth rates. The Eugenics Society decided to act on its behalf. In 1936, it set up the Population Investigation Committee (PIC) to investigate the causes and consequences of the increasing infertility of the English.[38] In view of the fascists' manipulation of demographic 'facts' for political ends, the Society went to great lengths to gloss the PIC with scientific objectivity. Its brief was research; another, initially secret, organization was set up in conjunction with Political and Economic Planning (PEP), an offshoot of the Fabian Society, to plan pronatalist policies.[39]

One of the first tasks the PIC set itself was an investigation into the reasons why women – especially working-class women – were having so few babies. Their expedition into the dangerous, dark continent of working-class sexuality took the form of a medical mission. Blacker conceptualized the problem as a medical one; low birth rate was a national disease and women had to be encouraged to seek a cure. A medical subcommittee of the PIC developed a questionnaire which had to be administered, like medicine, by a medically qualified person. The design of the questionnaire owed much to an inquiry carried out in the USA by the biologist Raymond Pearl, because his had proved successful in getting information from recalcitrant working-class women.[40] It went through six drafts, each receiving a 'clinical trial'. The relationship between interviewer and respondents was conceived of as essentially that between doctor and patient. Respondents were to be recruited by doctors from patients whom they encountered in their private practices, hospitals and local authority clinics. Doctors were offered a consultation fee of one guinea for each woman interviewed. In order to maintain the feel of a medical investigation – and also to escape being charged with prurient curiosity about delicate matters – interviewers were told to wear white coats and, at the same time as asking them questions, offer respondents helpful medical advice.

Eugenists suspected that the inchoate and atavistic beliefs and practices of working-class women surrounding fertility were incompatible with a 'scientific' investigation into population problems. Many of these women were too ignorant to explain why they did or did not have babies; most were said to rely on their husbands 'being careful', without fully appreciating what that might entail. A booklet of instructions to interviewers advised them that, 'in dealing with uneducated women with little power of expressing themselves in words, you may find that the knowledge that you have already obtained may enable you to give a more coherent account than she can give'.[41] Indeed, the investigation was predicated on antagonism; hostility and suspicion, and not co-operation, were anticipated. Only an exceptionally agreeable and sensitive man such as Dr Cooper, who had piloted the questionnaire among a group of predominantly lower-class married women, would be able to achieve a good response.[42]

The survey had three aims: first, the data would permit the calculation of the numbers of extra girl babies who might be born as a result of an effective pronatalist programme. This calculation would include babies conceived as a result of successful medical treatment for sterility; by women abandoning birth control; and rescued from an illegal termination of pregnancy. Second, it would indicate what elements an effective pronatalist strategy might contain. Women were to be asked about the physiological, social and economic factors that had encouraged them to have or discouraged them from having more children. Third, the survey would test the claim that the increasingly available contraceptives had caused women to become sterile. If this were the case then the Eugenics Society would have to accept some of the responsibility for Britain's impending depopulation.[43]

The PIC's survey was abandoned when war was declared, but it formed the basis of the investigation later carried out for the Royal Commission on Population. Members of the PIC dominated the Commission, which was set up by the coalition government in 1943 with instructions to examine whether the threat of depopulation was a real one and to offer guidance on postwar reconstruction plans. The medical tone of the Commission's fertility survey was intensified, because although during the war the coalition government had assumed unprecedented powers and purpose that gave it a fully directive role in people's life and labour, none the less it was reluctant to delve into people's sexuality for reasons other than health.[44] Indeed, only the campaign against venereal diseases was exempted from restrictions on talking about sex in public. In 1941 Dr Eustace Chesser had faced prosecution on the grounds that his book *Love without fear* – a handbook on the conduct of sexual relationships within marriage – was an obscene publication. The Commission's investigation was supervised by a committee of the Royal College of Obstetricians and Gynaecologists under the guidance of Eardley Holland (1879–1967), an eminent gynae-cologist who in 1946 became President of the College and was a member of the PIC's medical subcommittee. Although the questionnaire used was essentially the same as that drawn up by the PIC, some additional questions were included to enable evaluation of the impact of the war on women's reproductive histories.

Once again, only medically qualified people were allowed to act as interviewers, although the fee they received was reduced from one guinea to five shillings for each completed questionnaire.[45] Respondents were recruited from among hospital patients, which meant that they were overwhelmingly working-class; better-off women obtained private treatment and were more likely to have their babies at home.[46] Fertile women were sought in maternity wards and infertile women in general hospital wards. The investigation proved unsatisfactory: only 11,000 out of the intended sample of 25,000 respondents were interviewed; and the sample was thought to underrepresent childless and sterile women because too few well-to-do women, the sort the investigators believed were most at risk of involuntary infertility, had been included.[47]

The data indicated that during the twentieth century there had been a steady growth in the use of appliance methods of birth control by married women. Yet the investigators knew that use of birth control did not mean that a woman was fertile (an important factor that seems to have been forgotten since the 1940s). The data also suggested that involuntary child-lessness was common. In answer to the question, 'Are you satisfied with the number of children that you have had?', of all the women who had reached the menopause, 45 per cent stated that they would have preferred more children and 43 per cent that they were happy with the number they had; only 9 per cent would have liked fewer.[48] However, this finding was not interpreted to mean that a large number of women or their husbands had had a fertility problem. Defeat of the fascists and the postwar baby boom had restored confidence in the biology of the British. Members of the Commission declared Gini's theory of 'racial senescence' political rather than scientific. If anything, the vigour of the nation's germinal cells had probably increased. 'The British people of today are on average better fed and fitter than their grandparents were; it would seem unlikely that the capacity to produce children should not have been to some extent favour-ably affected, as other physical powers have been.'[49]

The USA had stayed on the sidelines of the European depopulation propaganda war. But from the 1920s onwards, aroused by the challenge to its hegemony posed by the Japanese in the Pacific, it had begun to express fears about the potential for population growth in Asia. At that time, European demographers were giving scant attention to Asia, Africa and Latin America, except for desultory British interest in the population of India. Even then, few envisaged rapid growth. Indeed, in 1936, in one of the three books that led to the depopulation scare, A. M. Carr-Saunders, a sociologist and leading eugenist, prophesied that in India the growth of population would be slow and fluctuating.[50]

In the interwar period, the new science of demography had established a secure base for itself in the USA, helped by the financial backing of wealthy foundations.[51] Its position was strengthened in 1939, when the League of Nations moved its Department of Population to the three-year-old Office of Population Research at Princeton University. It was there, in 1945, that the American demographer Frank Notestein first expounded the theory that the decline in fertility that had apparently accompanied industrialization in Europe and the USA could and should be engineered in other, non-industrialized parts of the world.[52] The fertility decline in Europe (and especially in England) became the subject of research aimed at discovering why, in the late nineteenth century, women had begun to have fewer children, in order to reproduce it strategically in other countries.

US interests dominated the radical realignment of geopolitics that took place in the postwar cold war climate, and increasingly they determined what constituted a problem of population in other nations, including Britain. Although defeat of the Japanese quelled US anxieties about that country's population, the cold war produced a new potential enemy: the poor, densely populated countries of Asia where, it was feared, communism would find a fertile breeding ground. The late 1940s and early 1950s saw the publication in the USA of several books on world population problems with apocalyptic titles such as *Road to survival, Our plundered planet, Population roads to peace or war* and *The population bomb*. In the 1950s, numerous national and international organizations concerned with countering population growth were set up in the USA with the support of commercial interests and charitable foundations.[53]

At first, the British ignored the US doom merchants. The postwar baby boom – which was taking place in all European countries – was depicted as a temporary phenomenon; people were 'catching up' now that peace had broken out. Indeed, many people continued to see the threat of depopulation hanging over the nation. When Margaret Sanger, the renowned proponent of birth control, arrived in England from the USA in July 1947, and declared a worldwide motherhood moratorium, she met with hostility: what the nation needed was more, not fewer, babies.[54] An article in the *News Chronicle* of June 1949, declared: 'Britain's fate as a world power may be sealed in some 30 years' time unless we revert to larger families – unless, at the least, every fifth couple in the land have an extra baby.'[55] But food rationing and a succession of poor harvests rekindled antinatalism and, by the early 1950s, as the upsurge in the British birth rate persisted and anxieties about the burgeoning populations of non-industrialized countries began to be taken seriously, it was winning influential supporters. Fear of population growth was fed by the antiutopian anxieties which flourished after the war. In the interwar period, according to one calculation, about three hundred 'futuristic tales' had been published, most of them marked by chronic anxieties about the future of mankind; in the postwar era, an incalculably greater number of such tales spelled out, in even more alarming tones, the message of the mushroom-shaped cloud.[56] By 1956, British journalists were convinced that the world's population was in danger of exploding; when President Eisenhower sent a plan to Congress for tackling the 'fearful crisis of abundance', newspapers sported headlines declaring 'every second another mouth to feed' and 'all over the world there's a boom in babies', the latter related to an article which discussed the latest birth statistics issued by the Registrar General.[57]

The postwar baby boom had delivered the *coup de grâce* to the prophetic powers of reproduction rates which, by the late 1930s, had begun to fall into disrepute. Their behaviour proved highly unpredictable. At first, technical reasons were offered for their deficiencies: the formulae needed tinkering with. But soon their logic rather than their arithmetic came under attack: reproduction rates were declared invalid because they ignored the setting in which women had babies.[58] The war had shown that it was pointless considering women's procreative behaviour in isolation from the world in which they were living.

Reproduction rates were replaced as a signifier of national health by 'family building', a concept that had been around since the 1930s. At the heart of family building is the reproductive couple: a husband and wife capable of making harmonious decisions and acting in concert. During their courtship, this couple is purported to reach agreement on the number of children they intend having when they are married. This 'intended' family size will not necessarily be the same as the 'ideal' size – which is derived from a culturally determined norm – because a mature and sensible couple will recognize that it is their responsibility – both personal and social – to have the number of children that is appropriate both to themselves and to the society in which they live. Attitudes towards the fit between 'intended' and 'ideal' depend on whether a pro- or antinatalist climate prevails; in a pronatalist climate, for example, where 'ideal' family size is below replacement level, 'intended' should exceed it. According to family building, couples must 'space' their children's conception in an orderly fashion which ensures that they are born in a sequence that is manageable practically and threatens the least disruption of their sexual relationship. Although in some quarters it was still considered immoral, birth control benefited from the concept of family building, for without it planned families and the sexual pleasure purported to be crucial to marital harmony are impossible.

In the postwar era, family building gained credibility through several complex associations. At first, it drew great strength from the language of postwar reconstruction and the belief in the importance of planning. The idea that people build families implied that techniques analogous to those used in factory management can and should be applied to sexual and marital relationships. However, because the spotlight fell upon family building at a time when antinatalism was gathering strength, it was 'unplanned' pregnancy, and not involuntary childlessness, that came to stand for mismanagement of the human (re)production process. Most of the prestige associated with the concept was gained through the glorification of nuclear families that took place during the 1950s. A great deal was pinned on demonstrating that harmony ruled both marriage and polity. Consensus – marital and political – was erected as a bastion against the evils of communism. Consensus did not mean that everyone was the same; that was a monstrous Marxist goal. Instead, consensus was achieved through 'homogenization' of aspirations and experience, through people putting aside petty personal and factional interests in order to defend democracy in the cold war. The British welfare state contributed to the fantasy of consensus; it had been established in order to reduce inequalities, including those relating to health. The domestic front was purported to be both homogeneous and harmonious: the differential fertility of the social classes had almost disappeared; and the exclusion of women from the workplace was interpreted to mean that they had willingly abandoned paid employment taken up during the war in order to devote themselves to housewifely duties. Husbands and wives were happily acknowledging an equal but different partnership of a male breadwinner and a dependent female housewife and mother in order to achieve marital stability and provide a firm foundation on which to build family life and defend the nation from the threat of communism.

During the war, external factors had been singled out as the most telling constraint on successful 'family building'; of necessity marriages had been disrupted, and couples had been forced to adopt atypical roles. After the war, however, failure to build a family was taken as a sign of personal and conjugal inadequacy. The fit between 'actual' and 'intended' family size became a measure of the quality of marital relationships. Psychoanalytical theories of sexuality and fertility began to intrude into discussion of the reasons why some women did not have children.[59] Under the rubric of 'attitudes', psychological and emotional factors gained a place in the canon of determinants of fertility; and as I shall point out in chapter 5, doctors spoke of them frequently in relation to the lack of success they were experiencing in treating infertility.

It should come as on surprise that the next investigation into the reasons why women did not have children was embedded in the PIC's nationwide 'Marriage survey' carried out in 1959. After the war, the PIC had been given a secure home in the London School of Economics, but it had no income of its own and had to seek funds for the support of its day-to-day existence and research projects. Most of the financial support for the 'Marriage survey' came from the US Rockefeller Foundation, which contributed £10,000; the British Family Planning Association and the Marriage Guidance Council each gave £1,000.

The interests of its backers shaped the design and conduct of the investigation. The Rockefeller Foundation was keen to find out what had transformed British society into an infertile, consensual utopia in order to try to reproduce it in non-industrialized nations and thereby save the world from the twin evils of too many babies and communist revolution. Both the Family Planning Association and the Marriage Guidance Council sought data that would demonstrate the value of their work in promoting happy, planned families, the former through its birth control and infertility clinics, the latter through the provision of counselling and sex therapy. Questions on involuntary infertility were included in the schedule largely because artificial insemination using donated semen (AID) was a burning issue of the day (this subject is addressed more fully in chapter 5).

The survey set out to capture the nation's experience of marriage and measure its success in building planned families. This time, both wife and husband were interviewed about marriage aspirations; choice of partner; factors influencing age at marriage; education for marriage; marital break-down; family size; and voluntary and involuntary infertility. The sample was stratified and random. The interviewers were lay people employed by Social Surveys (Gallup Poll) Ltd, a market research company. The investigators went to considerable lengths in order to minimize the potential for embarrassment. Respondents were interviewed by a married person of the same sex. An 'ordinary home interview' was used because, it was argued, questions on fertility, infertility and contraceptive practice would be less embarrassing when posed in a domestic environment. The interview schedule of 196 questions was structured so that the sensitive topic of birth control followed as a 'natural' sequel to questions on marriage. The interviewer was equipped with a card on which each method of birth control was written alongside a number. Respondents could point to the number of the method they used and thereby avoid speaking it out loud.[60]

Marital harmony was assessed by questioning both wife and husband and then measuring the extent to which their answers were in agreement. They were asked whether they had done anything to limit the size of their family; if so, why, when and what; and finally, if it had worked. Access to advice on contraception was still governed by prewar restrictions which meant that, strictly speaking, it could be offered to married women only on health grounds. Yet willingness to admit using birth control was considered the most important distinguishing characteristic of respondents; they were organized into classes of 'reticent', 'avowed' or 'genuine non-' users. 'Attitudes' towards birth control were sought and organized according to marriage cohorts; it looked as though younger people were using birth control to a substantially greater extent than their elders, thereby confirming the association of contraception with modernization, and reluctance to use it with old-fashioned tendencies. Despite the use of special probing techniques that were supposed to tease out the truth from those who denied using contraceptives, the survey's findings were still considered to underestimate by a small extent the 'real' incidence of family planning in Britain.[61] It looks as though the investigators were intent on demonstrating that infertility in Britain was almost always achieved by design. Questions on involuntary infertility had been included in the schedule; none the less, no special techniques were thought necessary to encourage people to talk about any difficulties they might have experienced in having children. And data collected on involuntary infertility were never analysed fully or published.[62]

In the early 1960s, inexorable population growth in developing countries made it look as though the world was on the brink of a Malthusian disaster. Between 1958 and 1963, comprehensive censuses had been carried out in 157 countries and territories covering about 70 per cent of the world's population. The results were alarming: numbers in less developed countries exceeded all expectations. The developed world was also contributing to the impending disaster; in 1963 the Registrar General forecast 16 million more people in Britain by 2002. During the 1950s, communist and Roman Catholic member states of the United Nations had opposed any policies that smacked of Malthusianism.[63] However, in 1961 the UN Population Commission was mandated to pursue an aggressive antinatalist policy. From then on, its agencies devoted more meetings to overpopulation than to any other topic. Other international non-governmental organizations followed suit.

Science was seen by many as on hand to save the world. In the early 1960s, science was no longer seen as an instrument of tyranny and mass conformity and was viewed instead as a liberator and cornucopian provider.[64] The 'green revolution' promised to boost agricultural productivity; the intrauterine device (IUD) and 'the pill', two new, scientific methods of contraception, offered a totally effective way of controlling the growth of the world's population. A newspaper report on a UN Conference on Population held in September 1965 captures this new faith in technology. Headlined 'Race against disaster', it said that, 'the old, almost comfortable belief that population would be gradually controlled by famines and epidemics has also disappeared with the realization that science which gave us the population explosion can probably save us from pestilence and actual starvation.'[65]

At this point, as one demographer put it, the theory of demographic transition became 'the central preoccupation of modern demography'.[66] The theory purports to describe a historical process through which all nations must pass. According to this theory, a nation's birth and death rates are determined by its economic base. In preindustrial societies, both birth and death rates are high; indeed, death is the principal governor of population growth. As the economy evolves away from a predominantly agrarian one, and food supplies become more regular, death rates fall and the rate of growth of the population takes off. The next stage sees continued economic development sustained through industrialization, an increasingly complex division of labour and a more educated and urbanized society, which combine to lower the birth rate. Birth control takes over from death as governor of population growth; knowledge and availability of effective contraception techniques enable women to have few or no children. In the final stage of the transition, both birth and death rates level off, the population reaches equilibrium, and fertility ceases to threaten social order.

The theory of demographic transition was first outlined in the early 1930s as an explanation of the shift from high to low birth and death rates that seemed to accompany industrialization. At the time, Britain's low birth rates were taken as further proof that the nation was in the vanguard of civilization (although, as was pointed out earlier, the Italian demographer Gini offered a less flattering alternative explanation). After the war, the theory was gradually cleansed of its early jingoistic and racist tendencies.

The importance given to the theory of demographic transition in population programmes afforded historians an influential role in the development of policy, and they responded by 'forgetting' the controversies over the cause of the decline in marital fertility in Britain.[67] Instead, they proclaimed with confidence that obviously the cause was increasing knowledge and practice of birth control.[68] However, in the 1960s the world could not afford to leave history to its own devices in the developing countries, especially as it looked as though the 'green revolution' in agriculture might lead to a spurt in the birth rate. A two-pronged strategy was developed by population programmers.[69] First, a nation's intended family size had to be reduced. Indeed, at this point, intended family size became the signifier of a nation's economic and political status. Nations began to be ranked according to it, so that intended fertility became 'a feature of the national heritage in the same way as the flag, defence of the homeland, respect for the law and so forth. It now represents the number of children the nation wants.'[70] Politicians and religious leaders were recruited by international agencies and instructed to convince the teeming masses of the importance of reducing the size of their intended families. The second part of the strategy sought to provide people with the means of not having children. Non-medical technicians – social scientists and specialists in community development – searched for incentives that would persuade as many people as possible to use birth control methods. 'Action' research was used to evaluate the success of campaigns; by the end of 1965 the Population Council in New York had deployed government and trust funds to support more than twenty surveys into peoples' knowledge, attitude and practices (KAP) with respect to contraception.[71] Their findings were used to fine tune population programmes and make them more effective.[72]

In developed nations approaching the final stage of the demographic

transition, where (for political reasons) governments were loath to associate themselves with population programmers, fertility control was advocated for a somewhat different purpose: to enhance social cohesion.
Resisting contraception began to be cited as a major source of social
problems: broken marriages, divorces, 'latchkey' children and cases of
child neglect were contrasted with the happy children of well-planned
families. In 1966, marking a change in British official attitudes, a Ministry
of Health circular stated that planned parenthood strengthened family life,
and that without it, social chaos in the form of ill-health, marital break-
down and criminal abortion would ensue.[73]

In the late 1960s, the regulations that restricted access to birth control
advice and technology to married women were relaxed. Women now had
no excuse for getting pregnant. Women who resisted contraception were
called feckless for running the risk of an 'accidental' and 'unwanted'
pregnancy. Non- or careless users of contraception were sought out for
re-education. A new philosophy began to be advocated by family planning professionals, expressed by a representative of the Family Planning
Association as follows: 'Instead of concentrating on bringing people to our
services, we can now begin to think about taking our services to people
who need them most.'[74]

The emphasis on programme evaluation in developing countries made
itself felt in the developed world. By the second half of the 1960s, in
Britain, investigations into the reasons why women did not have children
were inseparable from investigations into the adequacy of services offered
by birth control services: not having a baby became a measure of the
effectiveness of family planning services.[75] As one demographer put it,

> family planning programs are meant to deliver products and related services
> that are wanted by customers. Given the intrinsic quality of the products,
> there is no great mystery surrounding what attracts potential customers, and
> what keeps them attached to, a program. It is the quality of the point of sale,
> as it were, or rather – since the service is typically free the quality of the
> service at the point of delivery.[76]

After the completion of the 'Marriage survey', the PIC had been unable
to attract funding for further research into trends in fertility in Britain.[77]
British foundations would not support its work, preferring to seek immortality through paying for buildings which would carry their names. The
University Grants Committee did not favour demography and left it to
compete for funds against other social scientists such as economists, who
usually won.[78] At this stage, it looked as though the only way the science
of demography could survive in Britain was by turning its attention to the

study of populations elsewhere. In 1965 the PIC set up at the London School of Economics a training scheme in demography for postgraduate students from developing countries who were supported by the Ford and Rockefeller Foundations, the Foreign and Commonwealth Office and, later, the Ministry of Overseas Development. Demographers working at the LSE now combined teaching population planners from developing countries with doing research on fertility trends in Britain.

At the end of 1965 the International Planned Parenthood Federation (IPPF) invited the PIC to carry out a national survey of fertility and birth control practice as one of its series of comparative studies in Europe into changes in attitudes and practices around contraception since the introduction of the pill and the IUD. The IPPF gave £15,000 and the Nuffield Trust (UK) £11,500 to the PIC to support the survey. The investigation set out to discover 'the kinds of actions which might help to produce more fully effective access to birth control services and a wider use of modern contraceptive techniques'.[79] The schedule of questions was provided by the IPPF, with a few additions suggested by the Family Planning Association.[80] Women were classified according to their social class, religion, level of education and parity (number of children). They were asked what they thought about contraception; if they made effective use of it; and about the relationship between their practices in relation to birth control and their aspirations in relation to family size. The researchers were also concerned to discover where people had learnt about and obtained advice on birth control, because it was believed that some women were still ignorant of the aesthetic advantages of scientific methods.[81] Questions on infertility were included in order to identify involuntarily childless women, by definition non-users of birth control, remove them from the sample and thereby prevent them from 'contaminating' the data.

Towards the end of the 1960s, fears of global population growth reached a zenith of anxiety exacerbated by the activities of the environmental and ecological movement. 'Spaceship earth' was becoming so overcrowded that it was in danger of imploding.[82] This time, the warnings of impending apocalypse registered on British politicians: legislation restricting immigration was introduced; the rules governing the circumstances under which advice on birth control could be given were relaxed;[83] the law relating to abortion was liberalized; and governments – both Labour and Conservative – began to sponsor an unprecedented number of investigations into women's fertility. *Family intentions*, carried out in 1966, was designed by the Office of Population, Censuses and Surveys (OPCS) to complement the PIC's survey which, because it purported to be an academic inquiry, was able to delve more deeply into birth control practice and its relationship to clinics than an official inquiry could without risking public outrage.[84] In 1970, the Parliamentary Select Committee on Science and Technology, which had taken as its first topic the population of the United Kingdom, berated the government for giving insufficient attention to the dangers of population growth. The lack of government support for demographic research was condemned and the committee urged it to 'act to prevent the consequences of population growth becoming intolerable for the everyday conditions of life'.[85]

As anxieties about the size of the population increased, the government sponsored more and bolder investigations; indeed, a plethora of surveys into women's attitudes and practices around birth control were carried out during the 1970s. In effect, these investigations measured potential demand and how well services – provided since 1974 by the government through the National Health Service – were meeting it. Some looked at ideal and intended family size and how this was achieved;[86] others focused on the type of birth control being used and where it was obtained.[87] These studies complemented commercial reports with titles such as 'The UK contraceptive market' that used manufacturers' sales data to estimate contraceptive usage.[88] The nation's women were classified according to the type of contraceptive they used; in 1975, for example, it was claimed that 30 per cent of all women under 41 years of age were 'on the pill'. A survey carried out on behalf of the Department of Health and Social Security concluded that between 1970 and 1975, all the changes which were thought to be necessary to reduce excess pregnancies had occurred.[89]

Despite the fact that, as one newspaper put it, 'mums were getting scarce' in Britain, the influence of fears of global population growth on these investigations is marked. *Family formations*, for example, opens with the question, 'How can we achieve freedom from unwanted fertility?'[90] Supported by the Department of Health and Social Security, this report was Britain's contribution to the World Fertility Survey (WFS), a massive international research programme sponsored largely by the United Nations Fund for Population Activities, which saw research as a politically acceptable way of spending money on population programmes.[91] Work on the world survey, which started in earnest in 1973, spawned eighty scientific reports, fifty multinational comparative studies, eleven technical bulletins, twelve papers on basic methodology and at least 500 analytical projects based on WFS data.[92]

The investigations carried out during the 1960s and 1970s used women as subjects; no one bothered to ask men about their family intentions or attitudes and practices around contraception. Men's exclusion was justified in methodological terms; they were rarely available at home for interview, and if they were they made poor respondents.[93] However, methodological considerations were not the only reasons why the investigations ignored the centrality of power relations between women and men in determining the type of contraceptive used.[94] Both government and doctors found it expedient to describe the introduction of policies related to fertility control, which in effect were part of a population programme, as promoting the health of individual women. Women were made responsible for procreative behaviour. 'Male' methods of contraception – the condom and withdrawal – were frowned upon because they were unscientific, unaesthetic and, apparently, out of place in a modern society. When in 1974 – World Population Year – the National Health Service began to offer free contraceptives, it did so as a medical service for women. Doctors considered it beneath their professional dignity to prescribe condoms; as one doctor put it, 'so far as condoms are concerned, I did not study medicine with the idea of supplying these articles'.[95] Yet, for a fee, they were prepared to retail birth control to women.[96]

The right of rich developed nations to define and prescribe solutions to global population problems was challenged in 1973 when the Organization of Petroleum Exporting Countries (OPEC) massively increased the price of oil. The political and economic crisis that followed made producers of essential, basic commodities aware that they had muscles. Governments of developing countries began to condemn population programmes sponsored by international agencies; they claimed that the issue needing to be addressed was the division of wealth between nations, and not differential fertility. International agencies began to backpedal on their population programmes, spurred on by the economic recession that had followed the oil price hike and dramatically reduced their available resources. Some developing countries introduced their own family planning programmes, but on health and not population grounds. By the late 1970s, domestic and not international interests determined ways of thinking about fertility in Britain.

Involuntary infertility resurfaced as a live issue in 1978, when the first baby conceived in a petrie dish was delivered by a hitherto irremediably sterile woman. Suddenly, a quarter of a million 'desperate', involuntarily childless women appeared in Britain.[97] Infertility seemed to be a new disease, which, like HIV infection, was rapidly achieving near-epidemic proportions.[98] Explanations of its origin were sought.[99] Women delaying childbirth until past peak fertility in order to pursue a career is probably the most popular theory; it is closely followed by environmental pollutants, which are said to be especially toxic to sperm. Some people claim that it just looks as though more women and men are finding themselves involuntarily childless; they attribute the increased visibility of infertile women and men to the publicity given to the new assisted conception technologies which had encouraged sufferers to come out of the closet in order to seek medical help.[100]

Demands for research into the reasons why so many women seemed unable to have a child intensified as the new technologies made more flamboyant claims about their potential to effect conception in hitherto irremediably sterile women. The plea for more data was taken up by the Warnock Committee on Human Fertilization and Embryology, established in 1982 by the government to consider whether some old and some new solutions to infertility threated the social order. One of its sixty-four recommendations was that government funding should be made available for the collection of adequate statistics.[101] However, it fell on deaf ears. Social research that intrudes into people's personal lives was anathema to the right-wing Conservative government that had appointed the Committee. In 1989, for example, the then Prime Minister Margaret Thatcher personally blocked a Whitehall-funded investigation into the sexual lifestyles of 20,000 adults that had been set up in order to assist in the prevention of the spread of HIV.[102]

The birth rate seems to have lost the power to provoke contemporary commentators. There is broad agreement that developed countries, including Britain, have entered a period of substantial population decline, indicating, perhaps, that they have reached the final stages of the demographic transition (although once again, the evidence is controversial).[103] International conferences have been convened in order to discuss the causes and implications of depopulation, for example by the Council of Europe in 1976, and by the Hoover Institute, Stanford University, in 1985.[104] Yet politicians appear unconcerned by it. This apparent lack of interest in the birth rate should not be interpreted as signifying that demographic factors carry less weight. Rather, the focus of concern has shifted; what is deemed to be wrong with the British population nowadays is its tendency to live for an increasingly long time. The spectre of older people unreasonably demanding health and social care services has replaced procreation as the focus of contemporary demographic anxieties.

The prevalence of involuntary childlessness is considered important nowadays only in terms of enabling doctors to gauge the size of the market for assisted conception technologies. Indeed, almost all recent research into the prevalence of infertility has been initiated by doctors in charge of those technologies.[105] The ease with which the message spoken by involuntary childlessness has been translated into the language of consumerism is in keeping with the politically driven tendency that emerged in the late 1980s, through which all medical encounters are being converted into market transactions: patients are customers now.[106] Involuntary childlessness has been transformed into a shopping opportunity, a definition with echos of the Victorian spermatic economy where expenditure of income was intimately associated with procreative power; although, a century later, it is women and not men who hold the purse strings.

What impact have these changing stories of fertility and infertility had on women's procreative attitudes and behaviour? When commentators, academics and politicians talk about fertility, they usually speak a language that fails to engage with people's everyday experience. In 1945, when the Royal Commission on Population was taking evidence on the threat of depopulation, Mass Observation, an organization that documented everyday life in Britain, sent a team of interviewers to ask a random street sample if they could say whether the birth rate in Britain had been going up or down in the past fifty years. Nearly a quarter had no idea, and one in six thought it had been going up.[107] No doubt a similar survey carried out today would uncover similar levels of ignorance about the population. Nevertheless, as the following chapters demonstrate, ideas about the nation's fertility and women's procreative bodies and behaviour have informed both political policies and medical practice, and have thereby structured women's experience of infertility.

2

Norms and Deviations

Jill Wood, a housewife aged 28, was admitted to the care of Mr Duncan, at the Middlesex Hospital, in 1901, suffering from dysmenorrhea (painful periods) and sterility. Jill had been married for eight years. In the two months prior to her admission to hospital, she had been getting very nervous and irritable especially during her periods, which were regular. On examination under anaesthetic, her cervix was found to look downwards and backwards. Her uterus was considered small and acutely anteflexed. The surgeon treated her by dilating her cervix.[1]

Mary Smith, a London housewife aged 23, complained of sterility in 1909. Soon after her marriage, her periods had become more painful. At Guy's Hospital, she was told that her womb was displaced and was fitted with a ring pessary. She thought that the ring wasn't doing her much good and so she went to the Farringdon Dispensary where the ring was changed. She was advised to go to St Bartholomew's Hospital where, at Mr Griffiths' outpatient clinic, the ring pessary was removed. On examination, nothing abnormal was found except that her cervix was somewhat short. Shortly afterwards, she was admitted to St Bartholomew's to have her cervix dilated.[2]

Edwardian medical texts recognized involuntary childlessness explicitly as a symptom of a disordered being. However, although doctors acknowledged that it takes both a woman and a man to make a baby, medical theory and practice focused almost exclusively on the female body. The impression conveyed is that the processes of procreation dominate women's bodies and their lives, yet leave men virtually unscathed.

Were a woman to have consulted her doctor about her inability to conceive, in the late nineteenth and the early twentieth century, she would have been classified according to the extent of her conformity to a ragbag of commonplace preconceptions about what constituted 'normal' female physical appearance, habits, behaviour and morals; the underlying premise was that only a 'normal' woman can become a mother. Doctors set standards of femininity against which to measure both their female patients and women in general. As the historian Ornella Moscucci has persuasively argued, late nineteenth-century gynaecology was the science of woman and the feminine nature, whereas anthropology was the science of man – meaning both the human species and the male – and his peculiarities. Hence, 'gynaecology was the study of the "whole woman"; it thus fused the physical, the psychological and the moral aspects of femininity'.[3]

The science of gynaecology classified women according to their relationship to physical, psychological and moral norms and distributions. Women who were able to have children were not considered separately from those who could not. Women, fertile and infertile, were a homogeneous group. Every woman was susceptible to the radical instability that afflicted her sex; her body, mind and morals were constantly at risk of derangement. In the class of fertility, a woman who had, say, twins, and a woman who remained reluctantly childless were both considered deviants and victims of abnormal sexual health.

J. Matthews Duncan (1826–90), an eminent and influential Victorian physician *accoucheur*, exemplifies the late nineteenth- and early twentieth-century medical tendency to describe and prescribe every aspect of women's lives. Duncan ascertained the 'natural' circumstances under which a 'normal' woman is found fertile; he was then able to specify the deviations which would render her unable to conceive. Timing was a key factor because, as he put it in 1877: 'The fecundity of the average individual woman may be described as forming a wave which, from sterility, rises gradually to its highest point, and then, more gradually, falls again to sterility.'[4] A woman who attempts to conceive when she is too young or too old deviates from the temporal law governing women's fecundity, hits the wave at the wrong point and, as a result, remains childless. By analysing the registers of births and marriages in Glasgow, Duncan worked out that if a woman has not conceived within the first three years of marriage, then she is probably doomed to childlessness. Duncan put great store on numerical statements of the amount, location, timing and causes of involuntary sterility. He estimated that one in ten was the true rate of sterility of marriage in Great Britain. He had arrived at this figure by taking the average of small-scale surveys of different populations; for example, one in six of the British peerage was sterile, one in ten of the inhabitants of Grangemouth, Scotland, and one in eight of his patients at St Bartholomew's Hospital, London.[5]

Duncan's 'laws' of fertility, fecundity and sterility rang true for doctors for nearly fifty years; he is acknowledged in virtually every medical text on the subject published between the 1870s and 1920 (and, on occasion, is even cited nowadays).[6] However, although his laws are the best known, many others guided doctors in their diagnosis of the causes of a woman's involuntary sterility. On the whole, these 'laws' defined women's sexual health first, by the extent to which it was unlike men's, and secondly, by the extent to which it was unrepresentative of the norm of women. An admixture of elements borrowed from numerous sources – such as classical mythology, folklore, the Bible and ethnography – fed the 'natural laws' that a woman has to respect in order to be a mother. Consulted by a woman because she was unable to conceive, a doctor asked her first: How old are you and how long have you been married? If age and length of marriage did not explain adequately her sterility, he then proceeded to investigate her physical, mental, moral and sexual habits in order to uncover the areas in which she was deviant and thereby compromised her fertility.

In their investigations, doctors were guided by a rich imagery which provided them with a template of what a fertile or infertile woman looked like. The historian Ludmilla Jordanova has shown how during the eighteenth and nineteenth centuries the human body was deemed legible; people saw the body as a bundle of signs which could be 'read' and interpreted. The principle of legibility was formalized in medical theory and practice, where it sanctioned a particular form of inferential thinking that moved from visible indicators on the surface to invisible traits inside the body.[7] Hence signs of masculinity in a woman, such as a moustache or beard, or poorly developed breasts and pelvis, were suggestive of disordered sexual health.[8] Beauty and perfection of physical form – both extremes – were deemed incompatible with fertility. Fat women were also thought less likely to conceive than thin ones because it was well known that women past the menopause, and prostitutes (who were notoriously sterile) tend to put on weight.

Doctors did not confine their 'readings' to a woman's outward appearance; they also perused her genitalia and internal organs of reproduction. The introduction of the speculum in the early nineteenth century had opened up to survey the landscape of women's genitalia, and their topography – size, appearance and disposition – became crucial in the diagnosis of involuntary infertility. Indeed, some doctors claimed to be able to read a woman's life history from the disposition of her genitalia.[9] Her cervix could be too short or too long, too big or too small, too high or too low down, rigid, malformed, long, conical, pendulous, pointing in the wrong direction – downwards, upwards, backwards or forwards – and of an unhealthy texture. Her vagina could be too long or too short, its capacity too roomy or too small, the surface harsh, congested or inflamed. Her uterus might be retroverted, retroflexed (believed to be a common cause of inability to conceive), anteflexed (more likely to produce a miscarriage), small or enlarged, infantile, inverted, atrophic, crescent-shaped and ovaries prolapsed.[10]

Anomalies of the structure of the genitalia could be either of local origin or a localization of a more general pathology, a symptom of a disordered sexual instinct which had unbalanced the woman's physical, mental and moral health. In isolation, these signs were easy to read. However, their interpretation was complicated by the frequency with which women in a childless union tended to mental ill-health. Because, as medical texts claimed, motherhood was the source of women's greatest happiness and their highest aspiration, inevitably its denial told against both mind and spirit. The doctors' task was to decide which came first: a local derange-ment of a woman's reproductive organs which compromised her fertility and hence unsettled her mental state; or a nervous system weakened by a disordered sexual system – considered a much graver condition – which had caused and then concealed itself behind an insignificant local change.[11] Their task necessitated a judgement of a woman's moral worth: a doctor's diagnosis indicated whether a woman's sterility was a tragic accident of fate or had been self-imposed; in the latter case, childless-ness was a deserved punishment of indiscipline. Therefore doctors had perforce to travel far outside the narrow field of the generative organs to get their bearings on the cause of a woman's childlessness. Every aspect of her life had to be scrutinized in order to reveal the source of structural anomalies.

Sterility was considered the price paid by women for slack moral habits. Women who led a worthless life, filled with idleness, sensuality and rich food, were less fertile than hard-working women who ate simple fare. Sexualized and sexually active women – epitomized by prostitutes – who took a great many hot baths, rose at ten or eleven in the morning, and generally led an 'animal life', rarely had children.[12] A similar fate awaited depressed or melancholy women, those who drank too much alcohol or abused drugs. A medical commonplace was that women who consulted doctors about neurasthenia and similar nervous conditions were usually sterile.[13] While these women were often held to blame for their inability to conceive, others were considered innocent victims of sins committed by their forebears. Heiresses were notoriously sterile, especially those who had inherited their wealth by dint of being an only child; furthermore, the inability to produce a son indicated degenerate stock and that the line was dying out. Both civilization and its converse, degeneration, had this effect on the well-born. Francis Galton (1822–1911), the founder of eugenics and husband in an involuntarily childless union, had calculated that just

under one in seven of the marriages of British peers which had lasted
five years or more, and in which the husband was under 57 years of age,
was childless.[14] By the Edwardian era, Galton's ideas had become well
entrenched within medicine. In 1906, for example, the eminent obstetric
physician Francis Champneys (1848–1930) instructed his colleagues to
include in a typical consultation of a woman who was experiencing
difficulty in conceiving an enquiry as to 'the number of her relations, for
her sterility may be merely the sign of a failing race'.[15]

Sterility – the only medical term used by the Victorians and Edwardians
to describe involuntarily childlessness in a woman – denoted a barren
mind and body. A woman's sexual system was said to interact with other
parts of her body, most notably the brain, therefore a consideration of
mental health was central in the diagnosis of sterility. Some doctors saw a
mechanical connection between women's sexual organs and their minds;
frequently the one put the other out of kilter. Hence Victorian psychiatry
justified the deployment of gynaecological procedures – notoriously
ovariotomy and clitoridectomy – as treatments for women's mental disorders.[16] The reflex theory of nervous organization was also used to
explain the relationship between women's minds and bodies. According
to this theory, the body was organized on hierarchical lines; the higher
brain levels controlled the lower levels – bodily functions, including
reproduction – by means of an inhibitory mechanism. Repression or
excitation of organ activity, such as childbirth, masturbation, dysmenor-
rhoea and uterine fibroids, made women vulnerable to insanity. Hence
mental ill-health led to gynaecological pathology and gynaecological
pathology made women mad.[17]

An economic model of nervous organization was also used to explain
the way in which women's minds interacted with their bodies. According
to this theory, 'the body was a closed system in which organs and mental
faculties competed for a finite supply of physical or mental energy; thus
stimulation or depletion in one organ resulted in exhaustion or excitation
in another part of the body.[18] Excessive mental application used up energy
stores and made women barren. Some doctors blamed the decline in the
marital fertility of the middle classes on the fashion among women for
bicycling, golf and gymnastics; physical exertion both used up fecund
energy and made women less buxom, tending in figure towards the male
model. A depletion of fecund energies after childbirth was also used to
explain the relatively common condition of 'one-child' or relative sterility,
which might take one of two forms: 'as an exhaustion of the fecund
energies leaving the general bodily health vigorous, or as an exhaustion of
both sexual power and general constitutional strength'.[19]

Any imbalance of energy, however caused, was said to have a deleterious influence on ovarian function. The ovaries were afforded a pivotal

role in the female reproductive system by Victorian gynaecology, a role they have not yet ceded. Ovaries were held responsible for women's less developed and more instinctive state of mind, and were used to explain why they lacked the rationality and reasonableness purported to characterize men. Ovaries were also said to make women eager to procreate and to make them desire the male. Healthy ovaries guaranteed the continuation of the species and the cohesion of the marital relationship, for it was mutual sexual attraction which bound man and wife into an exclusive society of interests and affections.[20]

Healthy ovaries created 'sexually ripe' women who produced ova capable of fertilization; women with disordered ovaries produced immature or dead ones. As no one had seen a human ovum, this theory could not be proven or disproven; an analogy with sperm led plausibility to the claim that ova might be as lifeless as some sperm seemed to be when looked at under a microscope. And because it was believed then that, like oestrus in animals, ovulation in women was accompanied by a show of blood, menstruation was taken as proof of the 'parturition of an unimpregnated ovum'.[21] Menstruation, the visible concurrence of ovulation, acted as an external barometer of ovarian health. Hence the warning to doctors: 'amenorrhoea is not a disease; it is the smoke coming out of the chimney . . . you can only remove that symptom by treating the disease which has been the origin of it'.[22]

Doctors applied similar diagnostic techniques to men in order to judge their fertility. They 'read' the external, visible signs of virile masculinity for evidence of procreative power: the male voice, the growth of the beard and moustache, the male chest, breasts, waist, limbs and muscular development – dubbed 'secondary sexual characteristics' by evolutionary biologists – were considered, as well as the disposition of the penis. The extent to which these signs approximated to the norm of virile masculinity was taken as an important indication of testicular health. As a doctor put it in 1910, 'the secondary sexual characters are a far more exact measure of the value of the testicular tissues than are the presence of spermatozoa in the external secretion. It may almost be said that a man's male plumage is in direct proportion to the weight or amount of testicular tissue present.'[23]

Testicular health was also evaluated by assessing a man's assertiveness, the energy he devoted to participating in public life and his capacity for productive work. Vigour was considered a crucial sign of male fertility; indeed, unlike women, whose moral conduct had a direct bearing on their ovarian health, in men it was the extent to which they pressed their advantage that influenced their testes. As long as a man worked hard, it mattered little whether he applied himself to good or evil; for, as one doctor put it:

> There is some truth in the statement that there is something in common
> between the judge on the bench and the criminal in the dock . . . Both are
> men of energy and accomplishment; one for good, which has raised him as
> a judge above his fellows; the other for evil, which has raised him as a
> criminal above his more colourless fellows who have neither the energy nor
> capacity for deeds of good or evil.[24]

(During the nineteenth century, anatomists investigating the human testes
were dependent largely on the executioner for 'fresh research material'.[25])
The 'economic' model of nervous organization also worked differently for
men and women: for men, achievements in the public world stood as
proof of sexual and reproductive potency. Men succeeded in both spheres
through appropriate investment of their capital: financial, intellectual and
sexual.

Excessive masturbation and too frequent sexual intercourse were said
to have a deleterious effect on male fertility: men who drew heavily on the
'bank of their sexual capital', unless that capital was very large, were
prone to become sexual 'paupers' at an early age.[26] Yet with the exception
of these 'bad habits', doctors failed to conjure up anything which might
put in jeopardy the procreative power of an energetic man. In keeping
with the contemporary association of sexual potency (*potentia coeundi*)
with the ability to effect fertilization (*potentia generandi*), almost the only
treatment offered the husband in an involuntarily childless union was
advice on how to perform his conjugal duties. In his analysis of the causes
of sterility in men, the author of *The sexual disabilities of man and their
treatment*, first published in 1906, gave equal weight to defects of the
seminal fluid and sexual impotence.[27]

The male norm was infused with health, whereas women's bodies were
defined by their susceptibility to radical instability.[28] It is not suprising that
doctors found it difficult to think of British men as having deviant behaviour, for they represented the gold standard of the human species. British
man stood at the pinnacle of evolution, and was the envy of all women
and men of other races. In the Edwardian period, the inability to think in
terms of norms, distributions and deviations of masculinity defeated the
ambitions of a few general surgeons who hoped to develop a new science
of 'andrology', the equivalent to gynaecology in women; they had no
evidence of pathology on which to work.[29] Paradoxically, Edwardian
Britain was exercised by an apparent epidemic of male sterility said to
be sweeping the country (discussed in chapter 1), which makes more
remarkable the failure on the part of doctors to consider diminished
procreative power in the husband of an involuntarily childless marriage.

A number of related tendencies contributed to doctors' stubborn adher-
ence to an image of men as robust, and women as inherently unstable and

in constant need of medical attention. To some extent, the intensity of reproductive medicine's scrutiny of women was sustained by an older suspicion and distrust derived from men's uncertainty about whether or not they were indeed their children's biological fathers or had been cuckolded by their wives. Indeed, before 1949, a husband was deemed the legal father of all of his wife's children, however conceived. Marriage, and not biology, mediated the relationship between men and children; paternity was not dependent on proof of fatherhood, only on proof of marriage.[30] From this viewpoint, doctors may have considered it prudent to leave well alone the examination of the procreative power of men. Yet Victorian and Edwardian doctors are also notorious for turning a blind eye on men's promiscuity while encouraging the seeking out and punishment of female 'indiscretion'.[31] The double standard of sexual behaviour also condoned doctors' reducing women's bodies to objects of specialized interests, yet treating their own sex conservatively and gently. In relation to the investigation of involuntary childlessness, it encouraged doctors to collude with errant husbands who had contracted a venereal disease and hide from their innocent wives the cause of their ill-health and sterility. Yet in public, it was acknowledged that venereal infection was a major cause of sterility: some doctors said one in two childless marriages was caused by infection by the gonococcus; others put the rate at one in three.[32] Gonorrhoeal infection can render both man and woman incapable of becoming parents.[33] It was believed then to be the 'most fruitful source of azoospermia'; in women it causes salpingitis, which occludes the fallopian tubes.

In practice, few doctors carried out the pathological investigations that detected the presence of either gonorrhoea or syphilis because, as the report of the Royal Commission on Venereal Diseases published in 1914 claimed, either they did not understand their importance or they found them too expensive.[34] Indeed, in 1914, a commercial pathology organization charged seven shillings and sixpence (37.5 pence) for a bacteriological investigation of the gonococcus.[35] Doctors seemed to have relied on other, non-technical strategies to reach a diagnosis of venereal infection. Hospital medical records are suggestive of some of the devices used. Women – mostly working-class – admitted for treatment for salpingitis or sterility were questioned about their husbands' health. 'Husband is a healthy man – his work is packing in a warehouse', or 'husband is a strong and healthy man', were taken to mean that the woman did not have a venereal disease. 'Husband has sore places on his arms and treats them with sulphur ointment' was sufficient to confirm a diagnosis of syphilis.

Towards the end of the Edwardian period, the moral panic around the epidemic of venereal diseases, and concern about its contribution to the declining birth rate, were deployed with dramatic effect in the suffragettes'

campaign; they brought to the public's attention the extent and implications of this gross injustice to women and the nation.[36] Doctors began to
question the medical commonplace that sexual potency in men proved
they were fertile; indeed, the obverse was likely to obtain as sexually
active men frequently contracted a venereal infection. In 1910, in an article
in *The Lancet*, a physician *accoucheur* commented:

> Although until comparatively recently it was always assumed that the
> woman was at fault if the man seemed physically fit for the sexual act, we
> now know that *potentia coeundi* does not necessarily mean *potentia
> generandi*. It is only in comparatively recent years that we have come to
> learn how much men are to blame for sterile marriages.[37]

A popular turn-of-the-century representation of the reproductive relationship of the gametes was that they complement each other: zealous,
hungry sperm, with the power of spontaneous locomotion, seek out a
passive egg, incapable of independent movement. Sperms' largely de-
structive metabolic processes are replenished by the nurturant egg, which
is wholly constructive.[38] This model of 'gamete copulation' conveyed an
idyll of sexual, conjugal and domestic harmony; it was favoured largely by
natural scientists, sociologists and political economists. Medical texts on
sterility preferred to represent the relationship between the gametes in
terms more suggestive of rape; spermatozoa had been endowed with
remarkable vitality in order to enable them to overcome the obstructions
and morbid secretions that littered women's genitalia and lurked in their
reproductive tracts. Medical journals and textbooks on sterility are replete
with reports by doctors who had been called to attend a woman in labour
because she had an unruptured hymen or a malformed vagina. As
Champneys remarked: 'I have myself seen pregnancy repeatedly under
such circumstances, and at the time of labour the orifice through which
impregnation occurred is sometimes closed so absolutely as to admit no
escape of fluid.'[39] When doctors marvelled at the number of women who
had conceived despite the deposition of sperm outside of the vagina on
the vulva, it was in order to deliver a paean on sperms' vigour and
prowess. Indeed, any suggestion of blame for infertility is confined largely
to women, even where the subject under discussion is men's contribution
to involuntarily childless marriages.[40] If sperm failed in their mission, it
was because the woman's generative tract was inhospitable or rejected
them. Doctors claimed that the diseased surfaces of the vagina of some
women emitted toxic spermicidal discharges. And some women suffered
from *profluvium seminis* – a condition with an unknown cause which was
said to be very common among involuntarily childless women – where
the seminal fluid escapes from the vagina immediately after intercourse.

According to the surgeon Victor Bonney (1872–1953), a leading light of Edwardian gynaecology, 'the phenomenon of *profluvium seminis* must be due to the sperms retreating en masse from an environment hostile to them'.[41]

Some medical texts on sterility instructed doctors to subject semen to chemical and microscopical analysis. In the 1860s and 1870s, the eminent American gynaecologist James Marion Sims is reputed to have been the first to examine semen under a microscope in the course of investigations of sterile marriages.[42] Yet although doctors might recognize that both egg and sperm had the potential to be 'seeds which are incapable of germinating in any soil', it seems as though a husband's semen was rarely scrutinized. Champneys described what this might mean for women:

> It is not very uncommon to find that the patient has wandered from doctor to doctor, that one operation after another has been performed, and that the patient's pelvis is matted with inflammatory remains, making conception hopeless in any case, while the idea of the husband's sterility has never been entertained.[43]

Perhaps the prohibition against male masturbation, which had intensified during the Victorian period, had made many doctors loath to ask patients to produce a semen sample in case its production corrupted them. Rather than evaluate semen, doctors investigated a man's capacity for hard work and his ability to perform sexual intercourse, and read the appearance of his secondary sexual characteristics. On the rare occasions that the procreative power of sperm was considered, it was assessed according to the same criteria used to judge external signs of virile masculinity. Vigour was considered the most important characteristic of a fertile sperm; sperm that lacked it were said to be 'one-half shorter, more slender, and although under the microscope they can be seen to oscillate, they do not move across the field'.[44] Should the microscope reveal dead sperm, the subsequent investigation would take on the trappings of a murder enquiry; doctors played detective and searched for forensic evidence that would enable them to prosecute a guilty party – wife or husband – who was responsible for spermicide. The corpse was examined for clues; the tail of a sperm that died 'naturally' before ejaculation was said to be coiled or bent at an angle wheras those that had been slain after emission by toxic vaginal secretions had a straight or only slightly curved tail.[45] In part, the refusal to develop more complex measures of sperm fertility stemmed from patriotism; the indicators published in Edwardian medical books and journals were derived from research carried out by German and Austrian doctors. The vigour of British men could not be gauged according to foreign standards.

The medical gaze was fashioned by considerations of class and race as well as gender. The nation had been divided into socio-economic classes by the nineteenth-century industrial economy and justifications of the cleavage were expressed in biological terms. Middle-class women were figured as domesticated angels, divorced from the material realm of the marketplace, their lives devoted to homemaking and their bodies to the uncontrollable processes of reproduction.[46] Their husbands were defined by their desire to achieve; their capacity for action and aggressiveness operated both materially and sexually, the one articulated with the other. The large family of a successful wealthy man demonstrated both that his quiver was full, and that his arrows hit their target. These representations of the sexes were interdependent: a middle-class woman's idealized passivity and asexuality both contained and provided a necessary antidote to the base, lustful nature of her husband. Since control over one's body was associated with the claim to authority over others – and middle-class men were born masters – the interdependent conjugal relationship was established as the key to a well-ordered society.

Unfortunately, situated as they were in the vanguard of progress, middle-class British women and men were both exposed to its deleterious influences. The association of progress with diminished reproductive vigour was supported by evidence collected by Victorian anthropologists of the strong sexual and maternal instincts of women of savage races. It became clear that the action of civilization might not always be wholly beneficial; it divorced some British women from basic maternal and sexual cravings by encouraging egoism and shallowness and by making them regard the sexual act as abhorrent, a degradation demanded of women by men for their own gratification.[47] Little wonder, then, that India and South Africa, the native homes of more primitive and fertile peoples, seemed to have a beneficial effect on the ovarian health of some involuntarily childless British women, especially those whose natures flourished in a hot climate. As one doctor put it: 'Plants put in hot-houses will frequently bloom and fructify, whilst exposed to the ordinary atmosphere they are barely alive and quite or near barren.'[48]

Perhaps because doctors recognized the greater vulnerability of the middle classes to the deleterious influences of civilization, those rare semen samples that were examined were more likely to be requested from private patients than from the husbands of women who had sought free treatment at a voluntary hospital.[49] It was considered unnecessary to evaluate the semen of men of the lower orders, who were less refined and hence more fertile (this is discussed further in chapter 3). According to the organic model of society predominant during this period, middle-class men did the brain work and their wives were the 'heart', the seat of morality and tenderness, while the lower orders were the 'hands' who did the menial tasks. (The 'nether' regions were inhabited by 'stagnant pools of moral filth': criminals, paupers, the work-shy and prostitutes.[50]) The working classes were locked into their subservient positions for life by their brutish biological origins. Being closer to animals, because they were less highly evolved, their fertility was assumed to be more robust than that of their betters. Indeed, belief in the physical strength of working-class women facilitated the cult of middle-class domesticity because it allayed any anxieties that the shift of heavy, manual tasks on to the shoulders of female domestic servants, might have a deleterious effect on their health or fertility. In any case, according to the economic model of bodily organization, there was little cause for concern; a majority of these women were unmarried, had no reproductive role to fulfil, and hence could devote their energies safely to domestic duties.

In a society attuned to the biological basis of class differentials, it is not suprising that the type of treatment offered for sterility – and no doubt, other ailments – was tailored according to a patient's social position. Middle-class women were often advised to change their habits and environment, to remove themselves to a quiet country village, a coastal resort or, preferably, a foreign spa town, apart from their husbands, where a different climate and mineral waters would promote a healthier state of mind and body and thereby make them fertile. And the following advice was almost certainly confined to the servant-keeping classes: 'Connexion reserved for the morning after breakfast; the wife breakfasts in bed and keeps warm; the husband must also have breakfasted and be warm. Probably night is the worst of all possible times for those women who conceive with difficulty.'[51] Medicine practised as an art tailored to suit an individual's personality and social status was more appropriate to private general practice, where a system of patronage by patients of doctors prevailed.[52] As doctors to families, they saw their role as that of friend and confidante to their social peers or betters, a guide to successive generations, providing 'domicilary-based whole person medicine' to patients – mostly women – in their homes.[53]

In contrast, local treatment and surgery were advocated for less refined women, partly because a 'holistic' approach was inappropriate; they were hardly in a position to alter their lifestyle. There can be little doubt, though, that, from the doctor's point of view, one advantage of local treatment and surgery was that it enabled him to avoid a lengthy or intimate social encounter with a female patient who was his social inferior. Working-class woman who sought free medical treatment from a dispensary or voluntary hospital – like the women whose medical histories open this chapter – would have the structure of their reproductive organs and genitalia realigned by the insertion of a ring pessary, which supports the uterus, or surgery.[54] Sometimes surgery was performed in order to rearrange the disposition of a woman's uterus. However, the impression conveyed by Edwardian voluntary hospital records is that the most common surgical procedure performed in order to treat sterility was dilation of the cervix and sometimes cutting it through to prevent its closure. Many women were diagnosed as victims of stenosis, a condition in which the opening of the cervix is too narrow to permit either the ingress of seminal fluid or the issue of menstrual blood (hence the apparent coincidence of sterility and dysmenorrhea and dyspareunia [pain on intercourse]). Between January 1895 and August 1910, at the Middlesex and Chelsea Hospitals for Women, London, surgeons Comyns Berkeley (1865–1946) and Victor Bonney (1872–1953), both leading Edwardian gynaecologists, operated in this way on 498 women suffering from dysmenorrhea and sterility.[55]

In the early twentieth century, competition was particularly fierce among doctors who specialized in diseases of women. Gynaecologists were seen as parvenus and faced an uphill struggle to wrest control of women's bodies from both physician *accoucheurs* and abdominal surgeons. At the turn of the century, very few British hospitals had a gynaecological ward or a surgeon who specialized in gynaecology.[56] In fact, gynaecology was considered one of the most controversial fields in medicine. Ovariotomy, the operation on which gynaecological surgeons advanced their special skills, had been met with fierce opposition both within and outside the medical profession. While the high death rates associated with the procedure were the ostensible cause of outrage, the most vociferous criticism of ovariotomists was symbolic: they stood accused of unsexing women.[57] Gynaecologists began to represent themselves as champions of fertility: they claimed that a sterile woman stood a better chance of becoming a mother in their skilled hands than if treated by a general surgeon. The difference was that a general surgeon was more likely to remove organs from the pelvis, wheras a gynaecologist would seek to conserve them. Intra-professional competition for patients made gynaecologists conscious of the need to establish a good reputation. They were advised that in dealing with a sterile woman, the gynaecologist should

> be perfectly open with the patient and tell her that he cannot guarantee a successful issue, but that in a large number of cases the operation is successful whilst on the other hand there is no serious danger in it if it is properly performed. The patient will fully appreciate this, and will practically in all cases consent to an operation. The disappointment of a patient who, having been told by her surgeon that some operation will cure her, discovers that she is little or no better, is naturally great, and she will very likely lose faith in that surgeon and turn for relief to someone else.[58]

Middle-class women were more likely to seek treatment from a physician than a surgeon. Gynaecological interventions were deemed potentially degrading of both patient and doctor and hence were avoided. The vaginal speculum represented women's concerns about gynaecological practice. When it was introduced into medical practice during the second half of the nineteenth century, it was dubbed the 'steel penis', and a 'corrupting instrument', because it broke down women's modesty and was said to have the potential of exciting them sexually. The instrument also met with hostility and even moral outrage in both medical and lay communities because it exposed those parts of women's bodies defined as 'private'.[59] However, middle-class male doctors could use it with relative impunity to examine the reproductive organs of their working-class patients. Indeed, enforced internal examination of women – usually working-class – by a naval or military surgeon using a vaginal speculum was enshrined in legislation in the Contagious Diseases (CD) Acts of 1864, 1866 and 1869. The CD Acts provided for the compulsory examination of a woman believed by a special police superintendent sworn before a magistrate to be a 'common prostitute' in certain 'protected districts', which covered up to ten miles beyond the limits of major garrison stations.[60] In effect, the employment of the vaginal speculum was governed by the same conventions that tacitly sanctioned illicit sexual relations between women and men across the social divide. Leonore Davidoff describes vividly how, in the Victorian era, young working-class women were deemed sexually available, both symbolically and physically, to middle-class men.[61] Doctors rarely questioned their right of direct access to these women's bodies. A working-class woman who sought medical help for sterility at a voluntary hospital was quite likely to have a speculum inserted into her vagina, perhaps by a young male medical student using her as material on which to learn. Indeed, in the late nineteenth century doctors who practised at hospitals, especially teaching hospitals, stood accused by antivivisectors of substituting laboratory animals with working-class women, who were preferred because they allowed investigators to avoid making the species error: assuming that an effect exhibited by a non-human animal could be elicited in a human.[62] In contrast, consultations with middle-class women were governed by the etiquette rituals of middle-class life. A married woman who saw a doctor in his private practice might escape examination of her private parts. London voluntary hospital case notes of this period include the records of women inpatients who had been referred by their family doctors, sometimes from places many miles distant from London, in order to have a speculum inserted in the vagina when they were unconscious, under a general anaesthetic.

Paradoxically, although medical investigations and treatments focused on the wife in an involuntarily childless marriage, a relatively small proportion of women came within their purview. According to a survey carried out on behalf of the Royal Commission on Population in the mid-1940s, only thirty-four of the 176 childless women respondents of completed fertility – that is, assumed to be past their child-bearing years – married between 1900 and 1924 had consulted a doctor; indeed, four out of five had no idea why they had failed to conceive.[63]

Why had so few women sought medical help? Unfortunately, little is known about how, in the past, women experienced childlessness: whether or not they saw it as a medical problem or a predicament to be dealt with by different means. For reasons discussed in chapter 1, contemporary oral historians have tended to focus on women as mothers; the childless have been excluded from their samples, and so we know very little about them.[64] The only published information is the testimony of working-class women interviewed by the oral historian Elizabeth Roberts. She observed that while childless women expressed regret, they displayed none of the passionate sorrow of the women whose children had died.[65] Many explained how they had found fulfilment as substitute parents of members of an extended family.

Nowadays the idea is commonplace that only recently have involuntarily childless women come to rely on medicine to provide a solution to their predicament: the argument is that informal adoption of children was far easier in the past than it is now – the legislation and regulations are of recent origin – and furthermore was considered by women to be an appropriate solution to involuntary childlessness. To some extent, adoption has been confused with fostering of related children, which was a common practice; many more women died in childbirth or at a young age, leaving children to be cared for by relatives or neighbours. Sometimes, children of large families too poor to care for them were 'farmed out'; and many children were orphaned or made fatherless by the First World War, and were looked after by relatives or in institutions.[66]

There is some evidence that unrelated children were adopted by childless couples; for example, in 1920 Miss Clara Andrew, of the National Children Adoption Association, told a Home Office Committee set up to consider the need for legislation on adoption that a majority of her clients had been married for anything from ten to fifteen years, most of them without a child, and wanted to start domestic life.[67] Yet the debates of the 1920s about the evils of the so-called traffic in older children suggest that some people took unrelated children into their homes for reasons other than childlessness: children were often exploited as a cheap source of labour or forced into prostitution. In fact, before The Adoption of Children Act 1926 the law discouraged adoption of unrelated children as a solution to childlessness: the rights and duties of parents were inalienable by any act of the parents themselves.[68] As a result, biological parents could reclaim their child whenever they wanted to. If anything, the evidence suggests a developing tendency throughout this century to consider adoption of unrelated children a solution to sterility: in 1927, 2,943 adoption orders – registrations of adopted children in the Adopted Children Register at the General Register Office – were made, this figure rose to 6,826 in 1939; 16,357 in 1945; and 21,280 in 1946.[69]

Roberts's working-class respondents lived in central and north Lancashire, particularly the towns of Barrow, Lancaster and Preston. A different picture emerges from the medical records of women treated for sterility at London voluntary and teaching hospitals: the impression they convey is of involuntarily childless women eager for medical help and assiduously seeking it out. However, these women lived near major voluntary hospitals – such as Guys and St Bartholomew's – where free or cheap treatment was available. Women living in smaller towns and rural areas had that avenue closed to them; they may have had little idea where to seek medical help, and lacked the resources necessary so to do.

There is no doubt that inability to pay the fee prevented many women from consulting a general practitioner for any sort of illness, including sterility. The same constraint did not necessarily apply to their husbands. Many working-class men in employment were attached to a doctor's practice by some form of contract, and the cost of consultation was low. A British Medical Association inquiry into contract practice published in 1905 revealed that about half the working population – mostly men – were covered by contracts between doctors and friendly societies or industrial works, whereby in return for a small fee the doctor provided specified medical treatment.[70] The view of sterility as a 'woman's problem' doubly disadvantaged women: not only were they made the focus of any medical interventions, they were denied access to them when wanted by virtue of their supposed dependency on their husbands (more of this in chapter 4). Furthermore, general practitioners were loath to treat problems of male fertility and sexuality, perhaps because both conditions were associated with quacks. A thriving industry produced remedies and appliances which promised to cure 'lost manhood', impaired vigour, varicocele (a varicose vein in the testicle, which was said to develop through constant draining of the seminal fluid – meaning excessive masturbation), and spermatorrhoea, the unconscious loss of seminal fluid.[71] Only doctors practising on the fringes of medical respectability, usually in a smart private practice, treated problems related to sexuality and fertility in men. One of the two textbooks on sexual disabilities and sterility in men cited in this chapter was written by a doctor (Corner) with a private practice in Harley Street,

London; the other was written by a surgeon (Cooper) attached to a 'lock' (veneral diseases) hospital.

Although some women had a contractual relationship with a general practitioner – through a medical club, slate club, or a doctor's own sub-scription scheme – a majority were not tied to any one practice. Poorer women depended on voluntary hospitals and dispensaries and the Poor Law medical service; indeed, more women than men sought help from the Poor Law medical services.[72] Women could buy one of the many quack remedies and nostrums said to cure disorders of the female sexual instinct, including sterility; for example, Mrs Arons' women's remedies, 'made by a woman for women', promised to remove the irregularities and barriers that troubled young, unmarried women, and also to strengthen and invigorate the sexual organs of females of mature years in the change of life and those of barren women.[73] They might also consult an un-licensed practitioner, perhaps someone who assisted women during their labour and helped them terminate unwanted pregnancies. Women may have preferred such help to that of a licensed practitioner as it allowed them to avoid the embarrassment of consulting a male doctor about their childlessness, especially as that often meant having a speculum inserted in the vagina.

No doubt the association of sterility with venereal infection, which was widely advertised during the First World War, had some influence on women's response to their predicament, and made them reluctant to seek help. Men appeared to have suffered fewer qualms – and less severe symptoms – in consulting doctors about venereal infection; figures for patients attending clinics for the treatment of venereal diseases in the 1920s disclosed that men made up around three-quarters of the total.[74] Furthermore, in theory, many voluntary and teaching hospitals would not admit patients suffering from a venereal infection which was said to be self-inflicted; victims were not deemed worthy of the charitable assistance on which the hospitals depended. In practice, women suffering from gonorrheal infection were admitted; some doctors estimated that as many as one in four of the major operations performed at gynaecological clinics and hospitals for diseases of women were for gonorrheal complications.

The Edwardian market for medicine was very competitive, with doctors fighting each other in order to earn a decent living. The profession had become increasingly overcrowded; the ratio of population to medical men had fallen from 1,700 per doctor in 1881 to 1,407 in 1908, while over the same period the number of doctors had increased from 15,308 to 25,092.[75] The *British Medical Journal* is replete with articles advising doctors how to attract patients; it compared, for example, the merits of a horse-drawn carriage and a motorized vehicle.

Doctors' preferred solution to the overcrowded medical market was to find ways of defeating competitors operating outside the profession: manufacturers of proprietary medicines and 'secret remedies' – nostrums and patent medicines of unknown ingredients – and unlicensed practitioners. People from every walk of life were purported to consume vast quantities of secret remedies. Twice – in 1909 and 1912 – the British Medical Association collected and published evidence which it hoped would discredit them and persuade the government to legislate against them.[76] However, the government was dissuaded from introducing legislation to control their sale by powerful newspaper publishers whose own survival depended on income from advertisements placed by their manufacturers.

In 1909, the Local Government Board wrote to every Medical Officer of Health in England and Wales asking them for a report on the extent of unlicensed medical and surgical practice in their patch. The report of the investigation concluded that in some parts of the country unlicensed practitioners enjoyed a larger practice than licensed general medical practitioners; their clients were usually poor, unable to afford a doctor's fee.[77] However, no official action was taken against them.

In many respects, The National Insurance Act 1911, which came into effect in 1913, was designed to overcome the difficulties experienced by general practitioners in the competitive Edwardian medical market. The Select Committee on Patent Medicines, for example, which had asked 14,000 questions on every aspect of their production and consumption, concluded that legislation was unnecessary as sales would decrease through the introduction of the Insurance Scheme.[78] The Scheme brought the services of general practitioners to a larger population, guaranteed them a secure income, and at the same time made few demands on them in terms of the type of treatment or service they had to provide to contracted patients.[79]

The Act perpetuated the discrimination in favour of working men; very few women were employed in the insurable occupations that it covered. None the less, the Insurance Scheme seems to have increased the take-up of medical care by everyone, not just insurance patients, by enhancing the authority of the medical practitioner.[80] Women and children were increasingly turning to sources of help other than a general practitioner: to the free services offered by outpatient clinics in hospitals and to the maternity and infant welfare clinics, ill-suited to the treatment of sterility. Hence, despite the fact that reproductive medicine considered the wife in an involuntarily childless marriage the appropriate focus of its work, in the early part of the twentieth century, financial considerations prevented many women from consulting a doctor.

3

Images of Sterility

When the thyroid tablets he had prescribed failed to cure her steril-
ity, in 1930, Peggy Watson's doctor referred her to Mr Gilliatt at
King's College Hospital, London. On examination, her cervix ap-
peared rather big and the os looked very small. Under a general
anaesthetic, her cervix was dilated, her uterus curetted and her
fallopian tubes insufflated. Both tubes proved patent. A pathologist
examined a specimen of her husband's semen and his report stated
that it contained large numbers of normally active spermatozoa.[1]

In 1938, Gerald Williams wrote to Marie Stopes asking her if she
could recommend a specialist whose fees were very moderate. Both
he and his wife had been examined by their respective doctors,
neither of whom had found any reason why they should not have
children, although his sperm were said to be a little sluggish. Mr
Williams's doctor had prescribed a course of pluriglandular tablets;
his wife had taken another pluriglandular preparation, called
Hormotone. On their doctor's advice, they were having coitus on the
tenth day after the cessation of menstruation after observing a week
of abstinence.[2]

In the interwar period, a revolution took place in scientific and medical
ideas and practice around fertility and sterility in both women and men.
None the less, in Britain, the tendency of doctors to focus on the wife and
avoid investigating the procreative power of the husband in an involuntarily childless marriage was maintained, even exacerbated. Although on
several occasions it was proposed that men are susceptible to sterility,
invariably the idea failed to arouse enthusiasm in doctors, albeit for different reasons.

Shortly before the First World War began, it had looked as if the belief
that the wife was almost always responsible for an involuntarily childless

marriage was about to be undermined, when uncontrolled male lust stood accused by suffragettes and social hygienists as the cause of both an apparent epidemic of venereal infection and the declining birth rate. The association of venereal infection and sterility was deployed during the war in propaganda posters which displayed the evocative symbol of an empty cradle. The campaign sought to bring home to recruits – a large section of the young male population – the shocking fact that sexual potency is not proof of fertility; indeed, where it resulted in venereal infection, the former might put the latter in jeopardy. It looked as if many men might have lost the potential of fathering children; in the course of the First World War, 400,000 troops were treated for some form of venereal disease.[3] However, wartime conditions made it hard to add insult to injury and lay the blame entirely on 'our lads'. The campaign against venereal diseases subverted the image of women as innocent victims of men's lust: the high rate of venereal infection among the troops was traced to 'amateurs', young, working-class women who were free with sexual favours not necessarily for financial reward but in repayment for being taken out and given presents, or simply for fun.[4] In order to safeguard respectable family life from their fecklessness, middle-class ladies took to the streets; they patrolled public spaces – parks, fields and alleyways – near military camps to watch out for and challenge any behaviour in young women which might tempt men to succumb to 'irregular intercourse'.[5] Indeed, the regulations for the control of venereal diseases introduced during the war, which in theory applied to both sexes, in practice fell more heavily on women. The policing of 'harpies' reached an apotheosis in March 1918 with the addition to the Defence of the Realm Act of Clause 40D which made it an offence for any woman with a communicable venereal disease to have sexual intercourse with a soldier.[6]

As a result of the recommendations contained in the Report of the Royal Commission on Venereal Diseases (1913), in 1916 'special' clinics for their investigation and treatment began to be set up at general hospitals throughout the country. Facilities for diagnosis of the diseases in pathological laboratories were also extended and improved. The gift of a microscope seems to have encouraged some venereologists to diversify their skills into developing and carrying out tests of the procreative power of semen. Indeed, in 1924, one doctor claimed that a venereologist was the most competent of medical professionals to examine microscopically seminal discharge.[7] The measures of sperm potency advanced by venereologists crystallized the belief that venereal infection was the only suspect in a case of spermicide. As Kenneth Walker (1882–1966), a genito-urinary surgeon and leading British specialist in men's sexual dysfunction and problems of male fertility, put it in 1920: 'Whereas with the female it is Nature that plays the chief role in producing sterility, with the male the condition is more often the legacy of the disease.'[8] By disease, Walker meant gonorrhea; at that time there were no other suspects.[9]

Venereologists were confident that they could diagnose a gonorrheal infection from the appearance of sperm. According to them, men were made sterile through pollution: sperm were poisoned by pus. They cited as sinister evidence pyospermia (pus in semen); necrospermia (dead sperm); asthenospermia (sluggish sperm); and oligospermia (few sperm). Treatment of male sterility was usually the same as that recommended for a gonorrheal infection.

Venereologists' attempt to monopolize the examination of semen made almost no headway. Venereology was held in low esteem both inside and outside the medical profession; few medical practitioners were willing to be associated with 'pox doctors' for fear of being infected by the stigma they carried.[10] The success of public health measures undermined venereologists' claim to special authority in relation to sterility. During the 1920s, notifications of venereal diseases began to fall as the use of condoms increased and fewer people put themselves at risk of infection. Anxieties about an epidemic of venereal disease were also assuaged when effective free treatment became available at the 'special' clinics.[11] Around this time, venereal infection ceased to dominate discussions of the etiology of male sterility. There is no doubt, though, that the stigma associated with involuntary childlessness as a result of the connection between sterility and venereal infection lingered on.

In an article on tests of sterility in the male commissioned by and published in *The Lancet* in 1929, Walker made the revolutionary claim that constitutional factors had a depressing influence on the fertility of men more often than in women.[12] Like several of his colleagues, Walker had been drawn to this conclusion, albeit reluctantly, by the diminishing significance of venereal infection in the etiology of male sterility and the increasing use of the microscope in the diagnostic process. Among their patients, doctors were encountering healthy, vigorous young Englishmen, free from any history of venereal disease, who nevertheless failed to produce spermatozoa.[13] They began to consider the possibility that the process of spermatogenesis itself might be vulnerable.

In their early struggles with the radical new idea that an apparently healthy man might be sterile, doctors looked to well-established deleterious influences of habits, lifestyle and 'civilization' on the constitution. Walker, for example, argued:

> The fact that conception frequently occurs at the end of a long summer holiday is an indication of the close relationship that exists between general physical efficiency and fertility. Veterinary surgeons deal with sterility in

stalled non-human animals by letting them run wild in fields. If bank clerks
and other followers of sedentary occupations could be treated similarly their
fertility would undoubtedly be increased.[14]

During the latter half of the 1920s, it looked as though study of the
newly discovered sex hormones might throw some light on causes of
idiopathic male sterility. Unfortunately, scientists investigating the nature
of the male sex hormone focused on its contribution to the development
of splendid male secondary sexual characteristics – the features that were
said to attract the female of the species – and did not explore its relationship to male procreative power. The test they used in order to establish
whether a substance was indeed a male sex hormone was the capon (a
castrated cock) comb's growth test.[15] If a substance isolated from, for
example, a bull's testes or men's urine succeeded in making a capon's
comb grow, it was assumed to be a male hormone.[16] Almost no consideration was given to the relationship of the male sex hormone and
spermatogenesis.[17]

British scientists were reluctant to work on the male sex hormone.[18]
Indeed, during the 1930s, most of the research into the action of the
male sex hormone carried out in Britain was conducted by Vladimir
Korenchevsky, a Russian emigré doctor. Like many continental scientists,
Korenchevsky was interested in the influence of the male sex hormone
on senescence.[19] The idea that testes produce a 'dynamogenic' substance which can rejuvenate ageing men had first been ventured by
Brown-Sequard (1817–94), an eminent French physiologist. In 1889,
the thrice-married 72-year-old doctor tested his hypothesis by injecting
a preparation made of dogs' testes into his own body. The effect of
'spermatic fluid' lived up to his expectations; Brown-Sequard reported
experiencing a reinvigoration of his waning mental and physical powers.

Brown-Sequard's experiments were widely reported in the medical and
popular press, and stirred up the age-old search for the secret of eternal
youth. Rejuvenation therapy became fashionable among the rich, titled
and famous. Over the next fifty or so years, different ways of using glands
were heralded as treatments for senescence. The best-known surgical
rejuvenatators are the 'gland doctors', Steinach and Voronoff, who trans-
planted glands from monkeys and other animals into men.[20] Preparations
of dried testes or active male sex hormones were also marketed as treatments of the male climacteric; 'Viriligen' was advertised as an endocrine
tonic that compensated for the penalties of a tumultuous life; and in an
advertisement which displayed a drawing of a heavily wrinkled man, Ciba
claimed that 'Perandren', a potent androgenic therapy, corrected the dis-
turbing symptoms that accompanied ageing in men. Rejuvenation therapy
succeeded in making research into the male hormone disreputable; in

the mid-1930s, as an eminent scientist put it, 'male reproductive endo-crinology lapsed in a diapause that lasted for nearly 30 years'.[21]

Voronoff claimed that a majority of his patients were English; in 1932, he said that at least 800 English septuagenarians were looking forward to thriving for a further fifty years. However, it looks as though British scientists and doctors felt more at ease working with another approach to boosting male procreative power: one derived by analogy to a factory organized and administered according to modern principles of scientific management, sometimes called 'Taylorism' or 'Fordism'. During the 1920s and 1930s, this method of factory organization, designed to facilitate mass production, represented the apotheosis of modernity. When applied to spermatogenesis, it proved a productive model, perhaps because in both factory and testes the rate of production is typically high, and obsoles-cence of their products is inbuilt (vast numbers of sperm are 'wasted'). The factory model seems to have inspired investigations into 'working condi-tions' within the testes, for example in experiments on the relationship in different species between the temperature of the scrotum and that of the iliac fossa from where the testes descend.[22] When the former was found to be, on average, lower than the latter, it was concluded that testes work best at below body temperature. Doctors began to advise husbands in involuntarily childless marriages to take frequent cold baths, in order to create a cool environment inside the testes that was said to be favourable to spermatogenesis.

The factory analogy had another advantage: it accomodated the older representation of sperm as sexual capital, although increasingly expendi-ture of sperm was seen as a technical rather than a moral issue, a way of maximizing productivity. Gradually inefficiency replaced profligacy in the etiology of male sterility. The theme of sperm as sexual capital was played out in terms of the numbers of days' continence stipulated before the collection of semen for analysis; it also began to crop up in advice on spacing intercourse in order to 'concentrate' sperm numbers at ejacula-tion, on the basis that ejaculating a vast number of sperm might increase the chance of conception.

Medical texts began to advise doctors to take a sample of testicular tissue – a testicular biopsy – in order to differentiate between male sterility caused by obstructive azoospermia, which was suggestive of damage caused by a venereal infection, and aspermatogenesis, indicative of idiopathic sterility, that is, a problem within the testes.[23] A biopsy was considered necessary because doctors could ascertain almost nothing about the condition of a man's testes by examining a sample of his semen.

In the late 1920s, a small coterie of doctors from the American east coast set out to develop systematic ways of analysing semen.[24] The interwar

period in the USA saw an effloresence of research into different aspects of human sexuality and reproduction. The Committee of Maternal
Health (CMH), a New York-based organization set up in 1923 by the
gynaecologist Robert Latou Dickinson (1861–1950), sponsored much of
this work.[25] Dickinson, an ally of the famous American proponent of birth
control Margaret Sanger, hero of the sexologist Alfred Kinsey and one of
the first doctors to provide artificial insemination using donor semen in
the USA, believed that a systematic, scientific approach to the management of gynaecological, marital and sexual dysfunction and to problems
of fertility – which he took to include both unwanted pregnancies and
involuntary childlessness – would solve many modern social evils con-
sequent on uncontrolled parentage: poverty, overcrowding, delinquency,
infant mortality, child labour and war.[26] Dickinson's liberal ideas had
much in common with those of the international campaign for sex reform.
Ostensibly an apolitical movement, its followers promoted the application
of science and rationality to the management of personal relationships.
They advocated the decriminalization of homosexuality; the reform of
abortion laws; the provision of birth control; widespread sex education;
and sexual equality between women and men.[27] This last goal embodied
a new sensibility in sexual matters in which the right to sexual pleasure
was divorced from concerns about reproduction.

Uniquely placed because it could draw on the financial support of
American foundations – especially those in the Rockefeller stable –
the research programme of the CMH effectively transformed the sex reformers' radical agenda into a programme of 'applied' empirical research
into the regulation of human sex and reproduction which embraced
sexology, the development of scientific contraception and investigations
into reproductive physiology.

The CMH sponsored a unique investigation into the significance of
sperm morphology. Unlike those of almost all non-human animals,
human sperm show a remarkable variation in shape and size; in contrast,
sperm of all other animals are notably uniform. Doctors had attempted to
explain this conundrum in terms of a causal relationship between the
appearance of a sperm and the offspring to which it contributes, on the
grounds that non-human animals of the same species are often very
similar. In a short note published in *The Lancet* in 1919, for example, a
doctor described his search for evidence of twins in the family of a 25-
year-old man who suffered from spermatorrhoea, and who had large
numbers of two-headed and two-tailed spermatozoa in his semen.[28]

Gerald Moench, a gynaecologist working in the New York Post-
Graduate Medical School, painstakingly documented in elegant drawings
the many different shapes and sizes of sperm found in the semen of men
undergoing investigations for sterility. The premise underlying Moench's

scheme was that all the necessary information as to a man's fitness for reproduction could be read from the appearance of the heads of sperm in his semen. Each anomaly was weighted – sperm with long, tapering and narrow heads were said to be of especially sinister import – and the numbers of sperm in each category were totalled. Over 20 per cent abnormal sperm heads indicated sterility. Moench reasoned that

> the relative number of abnormal sperm heads affords an index to the reproductive fitness of the individual. This must mean that a disturbance of spermatogenesis is present which affects all the sperm cells, but that only the more grossly deformed ones are visible because our microscope is too crude an instrument to detect slighter changes.[29]

Although his systematic approach to sperm morphology was much appreciated, Moench's belief that an evaluation of the appearance of sperm heads reveals everything there is to know about a man's procreative power provoked little enthusiasm: the fertility of complex creatures like men could not be inferred from just one measure. Morphology left unexplained the significance of the vast number of sperms that might be contained in a single ejaculate. In 1929 Donald Macomber, also sponsored by the CMH, published a reliable method of counting sperm.[30] Given the popularity of the factory model of spermatogenesis, it is not surprising that a sperm count became a popular measure of procreative power. However, unlike evaluations of sperm morphology, in which the shape and appearance of each sperm is compared favourably or unfavourably with those of its siblings, a baseline sperm count has to be established in order to determine deviations; doctors began to ask how many sperm a 'normal' man produces, and how many demarcate the lower limit of fertility. The first authoritative pronouncement was made in the early 1930s: a man was incapable of fathering a child if his sperm count was less than 60 million sperm per ml. Later, in 1951, John MacLeod, working in the Department of Anatomy and Obstetrics and Gynaecology, Cornell Medical College, New York, published in *Fertility and Sterility*, the new journal of the American Society for the Study of Sterility, 'the most complete study of semen to date'. From his comparison of the semen of fertile and infertile men, MacLeod confidently drew the line at under 20 million sperm per ml.[31]

Almost everyone agreed that it was not just the number of sperm but their motility which was significant. However, there was no consensus on how many sperm had to look lively in order for a man to be pronounced 'normal'. Rather than one test being singled out for preferential treatment, tests were combined in a new 'multi-factorial' approach to the evaluation of seminal quality. In 1938, American doctors declared that the fertilizing potential of semen depended on a combination of four factors: the total volume of ejaculate; sperm numbers; sperm motility; and the percentage of abnormal forms present.[32]

In 1943, an editorial published in *The Lancet* admonished its readers as follows: 'It is not sufficient to glance down a microscope and report no sperms, sperms in pus, or sperms dead.'[33] On other occasions, doctors judged a semen sample simply as 'all right'. Yet reports of the American investigations into systematic tests of the procreative power of semen were published regularly in reputable British medical journals. However, as the history of the post-coital test in Britain confirms, new approaches to evaluating male fertility were fated to meet a hostile reception in British establishment medical circles.

In order to undergo a post-coital test, also known as a procreation or insemination test, husband and wife have sexual intercourse; a doctor then takes a sample of fluid from around the wife's cervix which is scrutinized under a microscope. The post-coital test is reputed to have been described first by the nineteenth-century American gynaecologist James Marion Sims; hence, for many years, it was often called the Sims test. According to Sims, the cervix assumes an active role in encouraging or preventing the ingress of spermatozoa into the uterus; in many women, he claimed, the uterus and cervix emit toxic secretions that poison or kill sperm, and the post-coital test enabled him to ascertain whether these were preventing conception from taking place.[34] Sims contributed to the etiology of sterility the idea that a woman's reproductive organs can be hostile to her husband's semen (although nowadays, the language he used seems more suggestive of nineteenth-century ideas about the relationship between spouses than descriptive of reproductive physiology).

Max Huhner (1873–1948) was the first medical researcher to suggest the post-coital test as a means of evaluating the husband's contribution to an involuntarily childless marriage. His *Sterility in the male and female* (1913) contains the results of numerous post-coital tests which he had carried out on his patients nearly twenty years before the hormonal control of the menstrual cycle had been delineated. Huhner, a German-born urologist who had graduated from Columbia University in 1893, served on the staff of Bellevue Hospital College, New York, one of the first American hospitals equipped with a laboratory and microscopes.[35]

The practice at the time was to ask a man to collect a sample of semen for examination by having sexual intercourse wearing a condom. However, Huhner had found that the dusting powder used by manufacturers to ensure the easy application of condoms was a powerful spermicide. As a result, condom specimens frequently demonstrated a high rate of necrospermia, then considered a sign of venereal infection. It became Huhner's mission in life to persuade his colleagues all over the world to

stop asking men to collect semen for examination in a condom and to
send it instead in their wife's body. Like the condom method, the post-
coital test had the advantage of allowing men to avoid the evils incumbent
on masturbation, an important consideration as the Catholic Church
perenially declared masturbation a moral issue; the Holy Office stubbornly denied men permission for 'voluntary pollution' in order to obtain
semen for examination.[36]

Over more than two decades, Huhner published paper after paper in
international medical journals spelling out clearly the reasons why his
colleagues should cease using the condom test and replace it with the
post-coital test, which he called the Huhner test.[37] Yet his arguments
seem to have fallen on deaf ears in Britain: the practice of asking men
to collect semen in a condom persisted. In 1936, for example, Vivian
Green-Armytage (1882–1961), founder of the famous Sterility Clinic at the
Hammersmith Hospital, London, and renowned for his dexterity and skill
as a gynaecological surgeon, recommended to general practitioners the
following method of collecting semen:

> Request husband to wear a condom and have intercourse with his wife in
> the early morning. After removal, the condom is securely ligated at the tip
> and placed in a thermos of water which has been prepared overnight at a
> temperature of 99°F. This is then sent within four hours to a pathologist for
> full biochemical and microscopical report.[38]

Indeed, as late as 1949 there is evidence of some laboratories accepting
condom samples.[39]

Walker believed that Huhner's warnings fell on deaf ears in Britain
because doctors, especially those working in hospitals, found tedious and
even distasteful the post-coital test which necessitated searching female
passages for the presence of active sperm.[40] The proposal by a urologist
that gynaecologists are reluctant to examine women's genitalia is un-
convincing, and perhaps reflects his own feelings. A more likely explanation is that in a post-coital test a doctor is responsible for the evaluation of
the procreative power of a man, whereas a pathologist judges only a
condom sample. Some doctors were prepared to accept this responsibility
only where paid to do so.

During the early part of the century, American doctors had begun to
make great use (some claimed abuse) of the increasingly available technologies, in part because their private patients demanded it but also out of
fear of the developing threat of malpractice suits.[41] The political economy
of medicine in the USA differed from that in Britain, where doctors did not
experience the same pressure to use available technologies in order to
ward off malpractice suits. None the less, like their counterparts in the

USA, British doctors treated differently fee-paying patients and those receiving free or cheap medical care in a voluntary hospital or under the National Insurance Scheme.

Gynaecologists who possessed their own microscopes seem to have confined its use to private patients.[42] Victor Bonney believed the only time when semen could be examined in the expectation of reliable results was immediately after ejaculation, and advised doctors to take a microscope to the patient's home.[43] According to doctors whose opinions were published in medical journals, private patients nearly always agreed to have their semen examined despite the cost to their mental health. Indeed, the anxiety the test engendered was said to have made some men attempt suicide.[44] One doctor argued that the risks of asking a sensitive man to undergo a semen test far outweighed those of unwarranted surgery on his wife.[45]

In contrast, some (but not all) doctors claimed that men of the 'hospital class' – a euphemism for poor people who could not afford the cost of a private consultation – would rarely submit to examination, their reluctance arising from ignorance, embarrassment, religious scruples and/or fear of loss of male prestige.[46] As one doctor put it in 1922: 'It seems to be a law amongst the artisan class that it is always the woman who is at fault, and much unhappiness and even persecution is endured by the wife from her female relations-in-law in consequence.'[47] Sometimes it was the wife who objected to the test, 'either because she is afraid of the effect that knowledge of his infertility may have on their relationship, or because she believes that male infertility cannot be treated succesfully and she prefers to live in hope rather than know the truth'.[48] Vartan, a gynaecologist at St Bartholomew's Hospital in London, exploited the reluctance of women and men of the 'hospital class' to agree to a semen test in order to cut down the number of people on his waiting list. He wrote to the patient's doctor saying that he would only investigate the wife if given an assurance that the husband had an adequate number of motile spermatozoa. As he expected, many patients failed to keep their appointments.[49] Yet other doctors had found that if approached with tact, men of the 'hospital class' would agree to be tested if it was explained to them that it might save their wives from unnecessary surgery. Just over two out of three husbands of women who attended Margaret Moore White's clinic consented to examination.[50]

In the 1930s, most voluntary hospitals tried to discourage the poorer sections of society from using them as open institutions offering free or cheap health care, and encouraged them instead to seek help from a general practitioner. They sought to transform the outpatient clinic into a centre for specialist practice, to which patients of all classes would come bearing a doctor's letter.[51] However, despite the increasing tendency

towards specialization, facilities for tests of male fertility were not available in every hospital. In 1944, only fifteen out of twenty-seven London
hospitals and forty-nine out of ninety-four outside the capital said they
had facilities for investigating male fertility.[52] Not all voluntary hospitals would permit the pathological laboratory to analyse samples of
semen; this applied particularly to those with religious affiliations, whose
trustees refused to grant permission to the conduct of investigations
that necessitated male masturbation. Even where access to facilities was
allowed, attempts on the part of the doctor or pathologist to systematize
the method of semen collection were often sabotaged on moral grounds;
it was not uncommon for Catholic nurses to enlist the support of a local
priest in a protest against the issuing of written instructions.[53] In such
cases, the doctor was advised to have 'a quiet word' with his patients; the
impression he was forced to convey to patients was that a semen test was
somehow disreputable.

Very few general practitioners had the facilities necessary for the
evaluation of semen. A survey carried out in 1949 revealed that many
general practitioners' surgeries were not furnished with a couch or a
sterilizer for instruments used in routine examinations, let alone a microscope. The National Insurance Scheme discouraged investment in equipment. It also made doctors pay out of their own pocket a fee for tests
carried out by commercial pathological laboratories.[54] Moreover, pathologists prepared to analyse semen were few and far between. Sometimes
specimens of semen were despatched by post. Indeed, in Ireland, they
were sent to England for examination, although doctors there knew that
the sperm would be dead on arrival.[55] Little wonder, then, that commercial
laboratories focused on sperm morphology; little significance could be
attached to an absence of motility.[56]

In 1943, the Family Planning Association (FPA), a voluntary organization of birth control clinics, set out to 'open up the "andrological" side
of this work from its present dark corner, where it is acting as a bottle
neck to all other sterility work'.[57] Its decision coincided with the establishment in the USA of the American Society for the Study of Fertility, set
up in order to develop a consensus on good practice and encourage
the standardization of procedures used in the investigation and treatment
of sterility.[58] However, unlike its American counterpart, which grew in
prestige and influence, the FPA remained on the fringes of the British
medical establishment (I shall examine this situation in more detail in
chapter 4). To add to its problems, the tiny world of British seminology
was a disharmonious one. As a result of these tensions, the FPA's attempts
at standardizing measures of male fertility succeeded only in exacerbating
the confusion.

During the 1930s, leading figures within the FPA had established links with the CMH which, through the British Birth Control Investigation Committee, had sponsored research into the spermicidal powers of chemical contraceptives, carried out by John Baker at Oxford University.[59] Baker trained the biologist Clare Harvey in the elements of handling and examining sperm; for many years, Harvey worked with Margaret Hadley Jackson at her famous family planning clinic in Exeter, where they established an international reputation in seminology.[60] Harvey's research was sponsored first by the FPA and then by the Medical Research Council (MRC).[61]

In the late 1930s, the FPA had decided to add investigation and treatment of sterility to the services offered in its clinics (discussed in chapter 4). In 1945, the FPA opened in London a seminological centre which offered semen and post-coital tests and testicular biopsies to clinic, hospital and private patients. The FPA hoped that the centre would become a model of good practice and thereby encourage standardization of methods of collecting and measuring the quality of semen in England. The centre trained other pathologists in its techniques.[62] Uncompromising standards were set; semen had to be tested within two hours of ejaculation; postal samples were not accepted; men who lived too far away produced a specimen in the clinic.

At that time, in addition to the fifteen voluntary hospitals that had facilities for evaluating semen, there was in London only one laboratory where patients referred by private practitioners and general practitioners could be tested: that of Berthold Wiesner, a biologist of Austrian extraction, whose second wife Mary Barton ran an infertility clinic.[63] Wiesner and Barton worked as a team with Walker and together appear to have monopolized the investigation and treatment of problems of male sterility in and around the private consulting rooms of Harley Street.[64] Wiesner, Barton and Walker all belonged to the British Social Hygiene Council, a competitor of the FPA, which in the late 1930s had tried (albeit unsuccesfully) to establish in London a clinic for the treatment of sterility and an independent laboratory for fertility tests.

Wiesner evaluated the procreative power of sperm by considering uniformity of size and 'viability', an approach considered idiosyncratic and highly subjective by the FPA.[65] Aleck Bourne, obstetric gynaecologist at St Mary's Hospital, London, who also had a large private practice, described his methods as 'unsound and really not far distinguished from those of charlatanism'.[66] Yet Walker praised Wiesner's ingenuity and enterprise: 'I have no hesitation in saying that he has done better work on this subject during the last few years than anybody else in this country.'[67] None the less Hans Davidson, the pathologist who in 1945 had been appointed to run the FPA's seminological centre, was sent for training to the agriculturalists

Drs John Hammond and Arthur Walton at Cambridge University.[68] As their contribution to the war effort, Hammond and Walton had pioneered artificial insemination in animal husbandry in order to overcome sterility in cows and thereby increase production of beef and milk.[69] Although their expertise had been developed in relation to bulls, the FPA considered their guidance appropriate to seminal analysis in men. At the FPA's seminological centre, Davidson used eight tests to evaluate the procreative power of semen: volume; number of sperm per ml; degree of motility; degree of viability; pH value; buffering power; differential count of stained film to establish percentage and types of abnormally shaped sperm; number of pus cells per ml.[70]

In 1944, the FPA organized the first in a series of annual conferences where it was intended that a consensus on tests of fertility, with an emphasis on men, would be reached. These proved very popular and out of them grew the Society for the Study of Fertility.[71] Yet despite the best efforts of the participants, no agreement on the measurement of semen emerged. In some respects, the issue was no longer considered important: separate consideration of the fertility of the husband in an involuntarily childless marriage had been sidestepped when the term 'sterility' in relation to men fell into disrepute. It was replaced by a new conceptual scheme which focused on 'relative infertility' and 'incompatibility'.

In theory, 'incompatibility' and 'relative infertility' absolve individual husband and wife of blame for an involuntarily childless marriage: it is their union and not the individuals who are sterile. The term 'incompatibility' is derived from an old idea that sexual pleasure is essential for conception. In the interwar period, a diagnosis of incompatibility seems to have been arrived at when no cause of involuntary childlessness had been discovered. As Eardley Holland put it:

> For reasons as yet unknown, certain individuals are infertile inter se, but when mated with other individuals beget offspring. Amongst non-human animal breeders this has been known from time immemorial, and is easily adjusted. There is every reason to believe that the same phenomenon exists in human beings.[72]

Incompatibility was unsexed, codified, systematized and transformed into 'relative infertility' by Samuel Meaker, an eminent professor of gynaecology at the Boston School of Medicine, one of the CMH coterie. Meaker organized the causes of sterility under nine major headings.[73] He went on to argue:

> While Nature unaided often overcomes one or two obstacles to conception, four or five such obstacles commonly oppose a barrier which she is unable

to surmount . . . absolute causes occur in about 30 per cent of clinical cases of sterility. Even then there are nearly always other causative factors in the background, which would become operative if the absolute cause were removed. In the remaining 70 per cent of cases the sterility is due, not primarily to a single abnormality, but to a summation or totality of multiple causative factors, of which any one alone might be of small importance.[74]

It is not suprising that Meaker, a sex reformer, should have exploited the older idea of incompatibility and elaborated it into a scientific theory of 'relative infertility'. Sex reformers believed that a happy marriage provided society with a stable foundation. In order to make a successful marriage, they proposed that husband and wife suppress their individuality in order to strive for mutual sexual satisfaction and an intimacy in social interests and inner thoughts. Husband and wife should each be the other's best friend and lover, and should share family and communal interests. Marriage guidance, sexual counselling, advice on contraception and treatment of infertility were linked together in a scheme which enabled couples to achieve both happy marriages and planned families.

Both incompatibility and relative infertility readily found a niche in the British medical establishment, as they relieved doctors of the responsibility to consider men's procreative power: in 1946 for example, the author of a review in the *British Medical Journal* of two textbooks on sterility – one written on women, the other on men – argued that they should have been combined and published together in a single volume: 'it is unreasonable to consider the fertility of the man except in relation to that of his mate, and vice versa.'[75] However, medical practice continued to focus almost exclusively on women. Indeed, even sex reformers encouraged separate spheres: women were not expected to participate in the public world of men and men were excluded from the personal intimacies of female kin and friends.[76] The double standard of medical practice in relation to sterility was still tenable.

Although in theory the new concept of 'infertile marriage' gave equal weight to women and men, in practice few English doctors paid the same amount of attention to the investigation of male and female fertility. In 1949, for example, the FPA's seminological centre tested the husband of a childless woman who had undergone two 'D & C' (dilation and curettage) operations, a tubal insufflation, a salpingogram, an endometrial biopsy and a host of injections, tablets and douches, extending over a period of two years and costing a considerable sum, before someone suggested that her husband's fertility should be tested. According to Dr Davidson, the man's semen contained no spermatozoa on repeated examination.[77]

British gynaecologists were highly selective consumers of new ideas exported from the USA; they may have taken little notice of American sperm pictures but they found highly attractive the new techniques of representing women's fallopian tubes: tubal insufflation and (hystero) salpingogram, both American innovations, which were developed in tandem as tests of patency (openness) of a woman's fallopian tubes. From women's point of view, both tests were welcome innovations as in theory they reduced the chance of undergoing unnecessary surgery. Before their introduction, patency of fallopian tubes was either determined by inspection at laparotomy – a major operation – or it was ignored. The new techniques opened up new vistas of women's reproductive organs. By demonstrating that a suprising number of women who, according to older methods of diagnosis, appeared normal had tubes that were not freely patent, they undermined surgeons' faith in older techniques of evaluating women's fertility.

Isidor Rubin (1883–1958), a German-born gynaecologist who worked at both the Beth Israel and Mount Sinai hospitals in New York, is credited with being the first to develop a non-surgical technique of testing the patency of fallopian tubes. In 1914, while working in the laboratory of Professor Wertheim in Vienna, Rubin began a series of experiments on non-human laboratory animals. Using different test media, Rubin obtained X-ray pictures of the female reproductive organs. If the medium escaped into the animal's pelvic cavity, then he concluded that its fallopian tubes were patent; if not, then the tubes were closed and it was sterile because the obstruction would prevent sperm from meeting egg. The first tubal insufflation test on a woman was carried out in New York in 1919. The medium used was gas, which Rubin introduced under pressure through the woman's cervix into her uterus until her stomach was visibly distended, when X-rays were taken. Three days later, the woman returned for a further X-ray which showed a pneumoperitoneum (residual gas beneath her diaphragm), thereby providing further confirmation of the patency of her tubes. In 1920, after the publication of a preliminary report of the results of tests on a further fifty-four infertile women, Rubin's test was enthusastically adopted by his colleagues; indeed, by 1940 356 gynaecologists contacted by Rubin claimed to have carried it out on 80,376 American women.[78]

Invited to the UK in 1925, Rubin described the insufflation test at a gathering of the Section of Obstetrics and Gynaecology, Royal Society of Medicine, where it was hailed as the most important gynaecological discovery of recent years.[79] Gynaecologists unanimously agreed that a test of tubal patency was essential in the investigation of an involuntarily childless marriage. British doctors, like their American counterparts, used Rubin's test enthusiastically and extensively: one hospital estimated that it had performed it on 6,500 occasions over twenty-five years.[80] Various gynaecologists sought to make their mark by adapting Rubin's test. In the 1920s, for example, Bonney, Forsdike and Green-Armytage, all London-based gynaecological surgeons, each designed modifications of Rubin's tubal insufflation apparatus which were then made and marketed together with a handbook of instructions by Allen & Hanbury Limited, a manufacturer of surgical instruments.[81] Modified equipment was demonstrated to colleagues at professional gatherings such as the British Medical Association's annual meetings and described in articles published in medical journals.[82]

Ways of performing and interpreting tests of tubal patency also proliferated. Blair Bell, a Liverpool gynaecologist and first president of the British College of Obstetricians and Gynaecologists, called radiographic observation of the gas in order to detect a pneunoperitoneum an unnecessary refinement; the equipment was cumbersome and also expensive, as it involved the services of a radiologist. An experienced gynaecologist should be able to judge tubal patency through the movements of a manometric needle. Bell claimed to be able to detect the seat and extent of any damage by using a stethoscope to listen for air whistling through the abdomen.[83] Some doctors claimed to be able to gauge gas pressure without the aid of any technology, simply by placing their ear on a woman's abdomen; others – blessed perhaps with less sensitive hearing – found a manometer essential.

Rubin maintained that by monitoring gas pressure, the site of an obstruction in the fallopian tubes could be located. In 1925, the first salpingogram (X-ray of the pelvis) using lipiodol, an oil containing 10 per cent iodine and opaque to X-rays, was taken by a British gynaecologist: Sidney Forsdike, surgeon to the Soho Hospital for Women, London. Forsdike believed in combining the two tests; where a Rubin's test indicated that a woman's fallopian tubes were blocked, he followed it by a salpingogram in order to locate the site of the obstruction and enable him to decide whether or not to operate.[84] Eardley Holland, gynaecological surgeon at the London Hospital, relied solely on salpingograms because he had found Rubin's test unreliable, producing a high rate of both false negatives and false positives. Green-Armytage agreed, declaring all gas – oxygen, carbon dioxide and air – useless; in his experience, gas suggested that tubes were patent when in fact, they were clubbed or constricted.[85] In the 1940s, kymograph tracing (a graph of air pressure) was introduced by Albert Sharman (1904–70), a gynaecologist at the Royal Samaritan Hospital, Glasgow, as a means of distinguishing false from true findings of the Rubin test.[86] The kymogragh, however, found few enthusiasts, and considerations of safety displaced the pursuit of validity in discussions of preferred technique. Yet doctors were unable to agree on which procedure was safer. Some supported salpingograms because insufflation

had caused a fatal embolism in a number of women; other doctors advocated insufflation, fearing that the oil used in salpingograms could
transfer infective material from the genital tract to the pelvic cavity and
might thereby give rise to the condition it set out to detect.[87]

In America, Rubin's test was performed routinely either in a gynaecologist's consulting rooms or in the patient's home. Women were not anaes-
thetized. They were asked to tolerate this painful procedure on technical
grounds: they could report pain in one or both shoulders, a sensation
caused by the gas and believed by American doctors to be an important
sign of tubal patency. Rubin, however, had little faith in women as reliable
witnesses; he advocated X-raying them in order to confirm whether or not
they were telling the truth. Bonney claimed that few Englishwomen would
submit to such a painful procedure and carried it out under general
anaesthesia; reports from his patients were not used in the diagnostic
process. In some British hospitals, both insufflation and the lipiodol test
were carried out as surgical procedures, under anaesthetic, in an operating theatre, often at the same time as a D & C. But by the mid-1930s this
practice had to be abandoned because it was too expensive and was
putting pressure on hospital beds. Some British doctors claimed that their
patients could tolerate the pain of a salpingogram and hence that it was an
appropriate outpatient procedure. But during the 1930s, as hospital X-ray
departments became more overcrowded and money tighter, they had little
choice but to use insufflation because it was cheaper.

By the 1940s, indications of tubal patency included: a pain in the
shoulder; the sound of air whistling in the abdomen; the wavering of
the needle of a manometer; a kymographic tracing; an X-ray picture;
and a radiogram. Why had approaches to establishing tubal patency
proliferated? Surgery is an applied art, a craft activity that demands a
high degree of technical competence. Surgeons with flair can achieve
immortality by devising new ways of performing operations, and design-
ing new instruments; both operations and instruments are then named
after their surgeon-inventors. Eponymy, the naming after a person of a
bodily part, technique, operation, instrument, syndrome, sign, symptom
or rule, is common in medicine and rife in surgery.[88] Surgeons honour
innovators in their craft; the insufflation test is synonymous with Rubin,
and in 1958 his seventy-fifth birthday was celebrated in a commemorative
edition of the prestigious American journal *Fertility and Sterility*.

Another reason why the test inspired enthusiam in gynaecologists is
that it was purported to cure sterility. Ninety-five out of 1,000 of Rubin's
private patients had conceived after undergoing the procedure.[89] Rubin
said that women became pregnant after the insufflation test for mechanical reasons, because tortuous tubes had been straightened or a blockage
shifted, or through curing a psychic difficulty and correcting tubal spasm.

Gynaecologists announced their 'scores' in British medical journals. Forsdike claimed a success rate of 31 per cent with insufflation and 20 per cent following a salpingogram.[90] Vartan succeeded in making 38.9 per cent of his patients pregnant by administering the lipiodol test.[91] Moore White was the winner: 47.8 per cent of her patients who underwent one test or the other became mothers.[92]

In the 1930s it was impossible to talk about patency of fallopian tubes without conscious or unconscious reference to controversies relating to anxieties about the health of the body politic. There were suggestions at this time that a nation's well-being depended on tubal patency. Campaigners eager to rid society of that segment which constituted a 'social problem' group agitated for legislation which would permit and encourage 'voluntary' sterilization by the destruction of the fallopian tubes of women considered unfit to have babies. Another related battle was being waged with the aim of preserving tubal patency in order to safeguard the childbearing potential of 'normal' women. Politically motivated interventions into tubal patency reached brutal extremes in National Socialist Germany. One of the first experiments on women performed in Nazi concentration camps was carried out in order to test the effectiveness of non-surgical methods of destroying fallopian tubes. In both Ravensbruck and Auschwitz concentration camps, Professor Clauberg, an internationally renowned gynaecologist and head physician in the Hospital for Women, Königshütte, Upper Silesia, tested the 'effectiveness' of injections of caustic material as sterilizing agents. Clauberg had also been recruited by the Nazis to investigate ways of curing sterility in German women. In both experiments, Clauberg exploited Rubin's test.[93]

Similar tendencies, albeit expressed in less coercive terms, were evident in Britain. In June 1932 the Eugenics Society succeeded in persuading the Minister of Health to set up a Departmental Committee on Voluntary Sterilization under Sir Lawrence Brock. The Committee sought medical opinion on the after-effects of different methods of sterilization and sent a questionnaire to gynaecologists attached to twenty-nine London and provincial teaching hospitals asking them for their views. A majority stated that occlusion of the fallopian tubes did not ordinarily have any prejudicial effect on the mental or physical health of women; a few warned of a slight risk to life, but they assured the Committee that only neurotic young women regretted the loss of their fertility. Clearly, a double standard was in operation; 'neurotic' is almost a euphemism for an involuntarily childless woman seeking medical attention in her desire to become a mother.[94] Yet gynaecology as a collective medical specialty thought better of lending support to the campaign. The British College of Obstetricians and

Gynaecologists, established in 1929 (it received a Royal Charter in 1938), joined with sections of the medical community who began to oppose legislation on the grounds that it would put too much power over medical practice into the hands of officials in Whitehall. The campaign for voluntary sterilization failed for a number of related reasons; probably the most important was growing horror at developments in Nazi Germany, where compulsory sterilization was introduced.[95]

To some extent, the British College of Obstetricians and Gynaecologists owes its existence to the concern over the health of mothers expressed during the interwar period. Britain's high rates of maternal mortality and disabling sequelae of child-bearing – one in ten women in England and Wales was said to be crippled as a result of child-bearing – meant that the procreative potential of large numbers of women was being damaged.[96] Official reports repeatedly testified to the vulnerability of women in labour to their medical attendants. Both government and public began to demand improvements in standards of clinical practice.

The expertise claimed by gynaecological surgeons in order to justify the creation of a separate surgical specialty was experience of obstetrics. As surgeons who attended women in labour, they were more conscious of the need to preserve women's ability to become mothers (a similar argument had been used to discredit unqualified midwives and handy-women).[97] Perhaps that is why, during the 1930s, gynaecologists would approach surgery on a woman's pelvis with caution. Although they possessed the technology necessary to diagnose cases of blocked fallopian tubes, few were prepared to operate in order to try to repair the damage. Salpingostomy, a surgical operation with the purpose of reopening closed fallopian tubes, is said to have been first attempted in 1889; in 1912, an English surgeon described it as 'one of the triumphs of modern abdominal surgery . . . the risk in the hands of those accustomed to such operations is a small one, amounting, indeed, only to that of the anaesthetic, and for this reason it is not more dangerous than the too frequently performed operation of curetting'.[98] Yet in 1936, at the sixth British Congress of Obstetricians and Gynaecologists, a poll was taken to see how many of the surgeons present were in favour of opening up the abdomen directly for the purpose of operating on the fallopian tubes; a majority were against the procedure.[99]

The chance a woman had of becoming pregnant following surgery was low, particularly when the fallopian tube was blocked at the isthmus (the narrow end). The outcome of operations on the fimbriated end (nearest the ovary) were marginally less disappointing. According to a survey of fifty-three gynaecologists of international repute, the incidence of pregnancy after salpingostomy averaged from 8 to 10 per cent.[100] Yet few gynaecological procedures have been rejected on the grounds that they rarely work; D & C, for example, has not been subjected to similar critical evaluation. Indeed, during the 1930s gynaecologists were encouraged to curette vigorously on the grounds that 'new wallpaper would attract a new tenant'. Gynaecologists' uneasy relationship with the body politic during the 1930s made them adopt a cautious attitude towards surgery on women's fallopian tubes, but their eager attitude towards women's other reproductive organs, notably the cervix and uterus, was undiminished.

Tests of tubal patency introduced a new way of representing women's fertility. Descriptions of the topography of women's reproductive organs were replaced by X-ray pictures of the uterus with the dye spilling out of fallopian tubes or held back and distorted by an obstruction in the tube. These powerful images of fertility and sterility were reproduced in another, related context. During the 1930s, advertisements for the recently discovered female sex hormones displayed in their copy photographs of the splayed reproductive organs of immature castrated female laboratory non-human animals. Before they reached sexual maturity, these creatures – mice, rats and rabbits – had their ovaries removed; they were then given either injections of female sex hormones or no treatment at all. The difference between treated and untreated non-human animals was dramatic. The untreated animals displayed castrate atrophy (a small, immature uterus and thin fallopian tubes); those which had received female sex hormones had ripened and rounded organs. The message the advertisements conveyed was easy to read: these new drugs could transform a barren woman into a fecund mother.

The 1920s and 1930s have been described as the heroic age of reproductive physiology, during which scientists competed in an 'endocrinological gold rush'.[101] In 1934, reproductive physiology was described as 'probably the most active growing-point of physiology'.[102] A huge number of papers bearing directly or indirectly on reproduction was published (indeed, this section offers only the briefest sketch of this programme).[103]

The idea that a substance derived from animal tissues – called a 'biological' – influenced the growth and action of reproductive organs emerged towards the end of the nineteenth century, when ovariotomy – the surgical removal of the ovaries – became a relatively more common treatment of ovarian disease. Gynaecological surgeons observed an association between cessation of menstruation, an 'infantile' uterus, weight gain, sterility and an absence of ovaries, a condition called 'castrate atrophy'.[104] This observation was confirmed experimentally by extirpating the ovaries of rabbits, which were later killed and their reproductive organs dissected.[105] At the same time as the role of the ovary was being reviewed, in other branches of medicine other organs were being studied.

One by one, they were scrutinized in health, in disease and *post mortem* in order to discover their hitherto secret purposes.

It was one thing to show that the absence of an organ was responsible for a specific effect, that (for example) castrate atrophy followed removal of the ovaries; it was another to explain why that happened. How did one organ influence the development and activities of another? Some doctors argued that castrate atrophy followed ovariotomy because in the course of surgery nerve centres that govern the growth and nutrition of the reproductive organs are severed. By the turn of the century, another account of the relationship of one organ with another began to gain ascendancy: they were managed by 'internal secretions'. According to this theory, organs produce secretions which are transported around the body by the bloodstream and influence the growth and function of others that they meet; when an organ is removed or diseased, the secretion it produces is eliminated and the functions it controls are perverted or lost altogether.

Internal secretions were said to work in one of two ways: some confine their influence to the organ of origin; others are responsible for the development and action of other organs. This second kind of secretion became known as a 'hormone'.[106] Hormones were defined as chemical messengers that co-ordinate the activities of different parts of the body. Their action – principally by excitation but also by inhibition – may lead either to the increase or diminution of function, or the alteration of nutrition or rate of growth. While doubt remained about the role and function of some parts of the body, by the turn of the century both ovaries and testes had been admitted as hormone-producing organs that influence the development and functioning of other organs of reproduction and encourage the emergence of secondary sexual characteristics.[107]

The idea that an organ is nourished, develops and functions on arousal by means of a substance produced in another part of the body was first exploited clinically by the now infamous physiologist Brown-Sequard, whose experiment with a 'dynamogenic' substance extracted from dogs' testes was described earlier in this chapter. Fired by the success of his experiment, Brown-Sequard claimed that all internal secretions had a therapeutic potential and advocated the use of preparations of other organs in medicine. The dramatic discovery in 1890 that eating fresh thyroid preparations reversed the symptoms of myxoedematous patients convinced many doctors that Brown-Sequard was right: disease in or absence of an organ could be compensated for by ingesting, injecting and even grafting preparations made from the organs of non-human animals. 'Organotherapy', a new branch of medicine, was launched.

As no one was certain which organs produced internal secretions and which organs they influenced, no organ or tissue in the body was denied a therapeutic value. The ovary, mammary, lymph, adrenal, thyroid and pituitary glands, testis, spinal cord, brain, intestine and blood of non-human animals were crushed, mixed with water, saline or alcohol, boiled, filtered, precipitated, subjected to reagents and finally dried. Manufacturers searched medical and scientific literature in order to justify the different applications.

A science of organotherapy was fashioned, with signs and symptoms of perversions matched by appropriate therapeutic preparations.[108] Individual organs of non-human animals were prescribed as treatments for conditions ranging from asthma and pancreatic insufficiency to indigestion; this approach was called 'substitution' or 'supplemental' therapy, namely, the making up for a deficiency by supplying the needed amount of hormone which a patient requires, but which her own gland fails to elaborate in adequate quantities. In its crudest form, 'substitution therapy' meant advising patients to consume non-human animal offal in the belief that it would cure them of their ill-health. Sceptics ridiculed this idea, comparing it to the belief of the savage that the courage of the lion may be acquired by eating its heart. Manufacturers also used abattoir waste to make creams, pills and injections of single gland preparations.

More often though, non-human organs were combined in 'pluriglandular' tonics for indefinite affections arising from the effects of general glandular insufficiency; neurasthenia, certain mental conditions and malnutrition fell into this latter category. The administration of pluriglandular preparations was supported by a systemic theory of organic functions in which glands influenced each other; a mixture of organs was warranted in order to correct a systemic imbalance.

Manufacturers of organotherapies claimed that sterility was caused by a systemic imbalance, sometimes described as an insufficiency of the endocrine complex, and recommended pluriglandular products as the treatment of choice. The pre-eminence in determining female characteristics and reproductive functions assigned to the ovary by Victorian medicine was unsettled by the proposition that the organs of reproduction act as a team. Although the ovary remained the pivot of women's sexual metabolism, it was allowed that it might be influenced by other glands, in particular the thyroid and pituitary.

Pluriglandular preparations for the treatment of functional sterility could be bought in chemists' shops without a doctor's prescription. Nu-Organic Remedies Limited, manufacturer of Dr Richard Weiss's preparations, 'best seller in 70 countries', offered 'Fertilinets' for use in female disorders, menstrual and climacteric disturbances and frigidity, and 'Pregnantol' to combat barrenness and miscarriage, influence the natural events of fertilization, regulate the course of pregnancy and ensure healthy offspring.[109] Under the brand name 'Juvigold', the Middlesex Laboratory of Glandular Research sold hormone beauty baths, bust development glands, slimming glands, gland tablets for male and female impotence and sterility gland tablets for barrenness.[110] 'Vit-alexin', 'a unique extract of embryonic tissue mixed with the specifically active hormones of placenta, ovary, testes, pancreas, etc.', offered a unique combination of internal secretions that stimulated metabolism and restored hormonic balance; 'Hormotone' tablets, recommended in the treatment of amenorrhea, dysmenorrhea and the menopause, consisted of extracts of ovary, thyroid, pituitary and testes. Bioglan Laboratories, which produced a wide range of organotherapies including 'Bioglan L', said to be useful in amenorrhea, infantile uterus, sexual frigidity, sterility and menopausal syndrome, assured its customers that its raw materials were extracted by the most scientific methods on a strictly seasonal basis and came from the organs of special breeds of non-human animals, farmed in selected localities throughout the world.[111]

Organotherapies were also marketed by post; between 1932 and 1939 the Institute of Endocrinology, Baker Street, London, sent out over 200,000 copies of a booklet entitled *Hormone Therapy*; readers were warned that 'glands seldom work correctly' but reassured that they could be restored to balance by taking the Institute's fresh glandular preparations. Its turnover was reported to be enormous.[112]

Gynaecologists eschewed pluriglandular preparations because they resembled too closely patent medicines, yet many were enthusiasts of single-gland preparartions.[113] They prescribed extracts of ovaries as stimulants to rectify menstrual irregularities, amenorrhea, asexualism, a loss of or lessened sexual capacity and sterility. Thyroid extract was said to have a stimulating action on women's ovaries, which worked well in cases of ovarian insufficiency with its various manifestations: infantilism, amenorrhea, scanty menstruation and sterility. A malfunctioning thyroid would cause a poorly developed maternal instinct, which is why, as Green-Armytage explained, the adoption of an infant, with its release of maternal feelings, is often sufficient to stimulate normal function in the thyroid, and thereby permit conception.[114] Extracts of the anterior lobe of the pituitary of non-human animals were said to correct disordered sexual development in both women and men: sexual infantilism and underdevelopment of secondary sexual characteristics.

There was no consensus on where or how to administer organotheraputic preparations. In a sterile woman with an undersized uterus and frequent, scant menstruation, Arthur Giles, consulting surgeon to the Chelsea Hospital for Women, prescribed thyroid and ovarian products.[115] In 1931 Eardley Holland told medical students that he had obtained almost miraculous results in sterile women with genital hypoplasia by prescribing half a grain of dessicated thyroid every night for one month and then raising the dose by half a grain until the patient was taking two grains each night. All his patients took an active pituitary extract every night and morning.[116] Cedric Lane-Roberts (1888–1960) believed that thyroid extract might be employed to great advantage. In some cases of primary ovarian failure, he prescribed 10 units of insulin before breakfast and dinner to improve genital function.[117]

The National Insurance Scheme allowed general practitioners to prescribe organotherapeutic preparations for their panel patients. The commercial potential of organotherapy was quickly recognized by manufacturing chemists and companies associated with the meat trade, who saw in it a profitable use of abbatoir waste. In 1918, the *Chemists' and Druggists' Diary* listed five manufacturers of organotherapies: Armour & Company, British Organo-Therapy Company, May & Baker, Parke-Davis, and Squire & Sons. The market was clearly an attractive one: these companies were soon joined by Evans, Sons & Lescher, and Duncan and Flockhart. And because merchants were responsible for a large section of the British pharmaceutical market, organotherapies of foreign origin were marketed alongside British-made products.[118] Imported products were often cheaper than their British equivalents, especially those that had been manufactured in countries with a vast livestock industry, for example the USA and Argentina.[119] In the 1930s several British manufacturers lobbied the Minister of Health – unsuccessfully – with the aim of persuading him to increase the duty levied on imported organotherapies.[120]

Throughout the 1920s a small coterie of British physiologists waged a rather ineffectual war against organotherapies, repeatedly declaring them to be worthless products. Yet the evidence they cited in support of their claims failed to convince enthusiasts. Each camp used different criteria to judge activity and efficacy of medicines. Enthusiasts relied on empirical proof, and were satisfied when patients reported relief of symptoms. But as Swale Vincent, Professor of Physiology at the University of London and arch-enemy of organotherapy, warned members of the Royal College of Surgeons in 1922, patients' reported relief of subjective sensation by gonadal hormones was not proof of their value.[121]

Physiologists claimed that a bioassay was the only scientific method of judging whether or not a preparation had had any effect.[122] To the uninitiated, coming to grips with the bioassay involves a conceptual leap. Yet it is fundamental to modern pharmacy. A typical bioassay involves a stimulus applied to a subject – a manipulated non-human or human animal, a piece of animal tissue, or a plant – in order to see if it elicits a predicted response.[123] The capon's comb growth test mentioned earlier, for example, was the bioassay of the male sex hormone. A physiologist would consider that an organotherapeutic preparation of testes had a potential therapeutic value if it could demonstrate the capacity to make a capon's comb grow. Most organotherapies failed to pass the bioassay test.

At first, manufacturers of organotherapies were undismayed by physiologists' attacks on their products. As a writer in the *Journal of Organotherapy* put it: 'when he [Swale Vincent] tells us that "it had never been shown that treatment by pituitary extracts had the slightest effect in remedying the symptoms thought to be due to pituitary insufficiencies" . . . How does he know?'[124] They had numerous satisfied customers. When it suited them, manufacturers misquoted physiologists in their promotional literature, sporting headlines such as: 'An English physiologist's proof that Endocrine Substances supplement each other.'[125] In 1924, at the Annual Meeting of the British Medical Association, Swale Vincent conceded that 'the enemy's line is not yet broken and the sale of worthless preparations goes on apace.'[126]

Physiologists enlisted in their campaign against organotherapies powerful allies: the Medical Research Council (MRC) and modern, science-based pharmaceutical companies intent on exploiting the commercial potential of 'biologicals' – medicines extracted from the 'body's own chemistry laboratory' – in a different way. The enormous commercial potential of insulin, discovered in the early 1920s, had excited pharmaceutical companies and encouraged them to invest heavily in the search for other hormones, including sex hormones.[127] The bioassay was central to their ambitions. In 1922, Allen and Doisy, two American scientists, used it to test the action of a substance extracted from sows' ovaries collected at an abattoir; when it provoked the typical signs of oestrus in ovariectomized non-human laboratory animals, they called it an 'oestrus-producing' hormone.[128]

Abbatoir waste was an impoverished and inconvenient source of active hormone.[129] Investigators had to look elsewhere for raw material; human and non-human animal urine provided a larger quantity of oestrus-producing substance, although gallons were needed in order to extract a tiny amount of it. The search for richer raw materials containing the hormone proceeded alongside investigations into the role and potential clinical application of the active substances extracted from them. Once the chemical structure of the oestrus-producing substance had been ascertained, it became possible to use other raw materials in the manufacture of oestrogen, the name given to the synthetic hormone capable of producing the same effect as the natural oestrus-producing hormone.[130]

Other hormones passed through the same developmental process, albeit at different rates. The first corpus luteum extracts with a demonstrable predictable activity were obtained in 1929 by George Corner, who used as a bioassay the proliferation of the lining of the uterus of a young rabbit that, immediately following ovulation, had had its ovaries removed. Corner also established that the corpus luteum hormone exerts its action only on a uterus previously sensitized by an oestrogenic substance. The techniques involved in extracting the corpus luteum hormone from non-human animals were long and tedious; the ovaries of many cows were required to produce corpus luteum hormone sufficient to cause uterine proliferation in one rabbit. Alternative sources were sought. In 1934, the chemical structure of the corpus luteum hormone was ascertained. The following year, progesterone, the name given to the analogue of corpus luteum hormone, was synthesized from soya bean oil.[131]

Investigations into the anterior pituitary gland were encouraged in 1927 when an injection of macerated pituitary tissue into immature female rats was followed by a dramatic increase in the weight of their ovaries. By placing small pieces of pituitary gland under the skin of hypophysectomized rats – rats that had had their pituitary gland extirpated – scientists established that the anterior pituitary body is responsible for follicular maturation, ovulation and corpus luteum formation in the ovary. Substances prepared from pregnant mare's serum and the urine of pregnant women demonstrated an action on non-human laboratory animals similar to that of macerated pituitary gland. However, these hormones were reluctant to reveal their biochemistry; only naturally occuring substances were available and they were – and still are – very expensive (I shall return to pituitary hormones in chapter 6).

The bioassays used in the isolation of female sex hormones are associated with the processes of procreation, and are suggestive of an intention to develop treatments for problems of fertility. However, they were fashioned according to the dictates of physiologists, pharmacologists and commercial and even political interests, who shared the aim of encouraging the development of a modern science-based pharmaceutical industry in Britain, an ambition which paradoxically and for complex reasons was at odds with everyday medical practice.

The interwar period witnessed a transformation of the British pharmaceutical industry from numerous small-scale manufacturers, wholesalers and pharmacists into a few large-scale producers who distributed a growing proportion of mass-produced medicines through growing chains of chemists' shops.[132] For strategic reasons, the British government backed the development of modern pharmacy. Before the First World War, Germany had developed science-based industries which succeeded in overpowering their British competitors. During the war, British manufacturers had disregarded patents on German products such as aspirin, lysol and saccharine, and had made considerable profits out of them. In the 1920s, in order to stem the rise of unemployment, the British government decided to protect certain key industries, including the chemical and pharmaceutical industries, by means of the Safeguarding of Industries Act 1921.

According to the principles of modern pharmacy, doctors prescribe uniform treatment regimes of mass-produced, standardized medicines, whose potency and therapeutic value are established by means of experiments on non-human and human animals. Standardization extends to both medicines and patients: everyone presenting a similar cluster of signs and symptoms receives the same treatment regime, regardless of sex, age, weight, constitution, etc. Standardization is anathema in the older system of therapeutics, where difference is valued. According to this scheme, a doctor's art lies in his ability to tailor medicine according to the needs of individual patients; both ingredients and dose are adjusted by him according to a patient's constitution and reports of symptoms.

Biologicals are standardized by means of a bioassay: every standardized preparation of oestrus-producing hormone, for example, was said to be capable of exerting the same effect on a specially prepared non-human laboratory animal (although it was admitted at first that its effect on a human animal was unpredictable). The technique of biological standardization gained official recognition when it began to be used in tests of the toxicity of medicines where an ill-effect is sought.[133] In Britain, the MRC was made responsible for regulating tests of the toxicity of medicines during the First World War.[134] After the war, country after country began to refuse entry to imported medicines which had not been subjected to a nationally recognized test of toxicity, and trade suffered as a result.[135] It became imperative to agree international standards of biological tests of toxicity.[136] The MRC represented Britain at a series of conferences organized by the Permanent Commission on the Biological Standardization of the Health Organization of the League of Nations which convened scientists of international repute from both academic and commercial laboratories in order to reach agreement on standard bioassays.[137]

In the early 1930s the demands for internationally agreed standardized bioassays of sex hormones became urgent, although this time it was the need for proof of potency – proof that, unlike organotherapeutic preparations, the substance was capable of eliciting a physiological effect – and not of toxicity, that was the motivating force. Similar programmes of research into the isolation, synthesis and clinical application of sex hormones were being developed in academic and commercial laboratories in the USA, Germany, the Netherlands, France and Italy. The MRC was also heavily committed to this work. Unfortunately, bioassays of sex hormones had proliferated, with every scientist favouring a particular animal: the oestrus-producing hormone, for example, was tested on rats, rabbits and mice.[138] In the absence of an agreed single standard bioassay, scientists were unable to compare notes and pharmaceutical manufacturers unable to develop export markets in sex hormones.

A standard bioassay of each sex hormone was finally agreed at a series of conferences organized by the League of Nations between 1932 and 1938. Britain was represented by members of the MRC's Sex Hormones Committee, which had been set up in 1930 in order to develop national standard methods of assay.[139] Once an international biological standard of potency had been established, the activity of both old and new naturally occurring and synthetic sex hormones could be compared against it. Substances were now marketed as equivalent to so many times the potency of the international standard; diethylstilboestrol (DES), a synthetic oestrogen, for example, was said to be five times as active as a standard preparation of oestrone, a naturally occurring ovarian hormone.

The concepts and language associated with biologically standardized sex hormones were alien to a majority of British doctors and pharmacists; indeed, in 1935 the British Medical Association and the Pharmaceutical Society collaborated on an investigation into new medicines, in order to develop guidelines for the perplexed.[140] Oestrone tablets, for example, were dispensed in international animal units (guinea pigs, rats and rabbits). The rationale behind this system of measurement was that sex hormones act qualitatively in relation to body weight, and so it followed that a woman required many more hundreds or thousands of units of them than a small mammal, although a method of comparison was not provided.[141] The confusion was exacerbated when it was realized that synthetic analogues were not strictly comparable to their naturally occurring equivalents, so that, for example, each type of oestrus-producing hormone required its own method of administration. A proliferation of brand names compounded doctors' difficulties. By 1939, twenty-one companies either made or imported limited quantities of expensive natural and synthetic sex hormones and marketed them under their own brand names alongside a plethora of cheaper organotherapies.[142] Manufacturers were promoting organotherapeutic preparations of ovaries, naturally occurring oestrone and synthetic oestrogens in the same trade catalogue, and incorporating each of them into creams, tonics, tablets of different weights and ampoules for injection.

Sex hormone preparations were far more expensive than organotherapies. Bought on the open market, an individual's treatment might cost hundreds of pounds. In the depressed economic conditions of the 1930s, few hospitals could afford to prescribe them. Even though it was provided with drugs at a cheap rate, a 'hormone clinic' attached to St Mary's Hospital, Manchester, spent about £1,000 a year on sex hormones which the hospital could ill afford; the clinic attracted so many patients that it was forced to close after two years.[143] And one in three patients attending an endocrine clinic attached to the Elizabeth Garrett Anderson

Hospital, London, failed to attend regularly because they could not pay for treatment.[144]

Most hospital patients who received sex hormone treatment in the 1930s were participating in one of various experiments organized by the MRC. During the 1920s, the MRC had been approached repeatedly by the Association of British Chemical Manufacturers, the organization representing the interests of British pharmaceutical manufacturers, with the request that it arrange scientific tests of new medicines which had demonstrated activity on non-human laboratory animals.[145] In 1931, the MRC set up the Therapeutic Trials Committee (TTC).[146] Its remit was to liaise between doctors and pharmaceutical manufacturers and to develop clinical trials of the efficacy of new medicines.[147] By 1939, the Committee had arranged clinical trials of sixty-five new medicines including eight sex hormones, eight treatments of syphilis, seven of broncho/vascular dilators and four sulphonamides.

The model of reproductive physiology which informed the design of the MRC's clinical trials of gonadal sex hormones was a radically new one, wholly different from the ideas of most doctors. During the late nineteenth and early twentieth centuries, ideas about human reproduction had been developed in two ways: by descriptive anatomy, and by a comparative anthropological approach that located human sexuality and reproduction within an evolutionary framework. In the interwar period, in their laboratories and animal houses, biologists, physiologists, biochemists and pharmacologists built on these insights and pieced together descriptions of the physiology of reproduction in non-human and human animals. Widely held preconceptions were challenged. A major milestone was the refutation of the long-held belief that the menstrual flow in women is comparable to the oestrus phase of the animal cycle. By the early 1930s the occurrence of ovulation in women at mid-cycle had been recognized, thereby disproving the idea that ovulation in women coincides with menstruation. This discovery permitted the delineation of the chronology of the menstrual cycle.[148] Medical texts began to include the now familiar diagrammatic representation of typical behavioural changes of ovary and uterus during the menstrual cycle.

Although they agreed on some of the features of a normal menstrual cycle and the signs of castrate atrophy, doctors had no idea how to investigate perverted physiology in women. How did absence, excess or diminished production of a gonadal hormone or generative ferment influence fertility? During the 1930s a few research-minded gynaecologists struggled to discover and systematize signs and symptoms of perverted physiology in their sterile patients and to relate them to the new diagrammatic representations of the menstrual cycle and thereby map out an etiology of functional sterility. What were the links among the menstrual

cycle, ovulation and sex hormones? Some doctors believed that conception could take place during a period of amenorrhea; others claimed
that the uterine cycle was an index of ovarian activity; yet other doctors diagnosed ovarian dysfunction in women who experienced normal
cyclical loss from the uterus.[149]

Scientifically minded doctors developed tests of reproductive physiology. Endometrial biopsies were performed in order to investigate changes
in the endometrium of patients. Unfortunately, interpretation of uterine
'scrapings' was hampered by a lack of expertise among hospital pathologists. Although this test might suggest normal or perverted physiology,
lack of agreement on the relationship between ovulation and menstruation limited its usefulness in the investigation of functional sterility.
With the exception of pregnancy – not much use in the investigation of
sterility – the only indisputable test of ovulation available then was inspection of the ovaries by abdominal incision.[150] Towards the end of
the 1930s, it became possible to measure, albeit crudely, the concentration
in the urine of progesterone; however, the tests were expensive and,
because they were conducted on non-human animals, involved the cost
and inconvenience of maintaining an animal house.[151] Only one or two
hospitals in Britain had the facilities for carrying out these assays routinely.
By 1939, scientific tests of reproductive function had failed to replace
clinical experience and patients' reports of symptoms.

The MRC's trials of gonadal sex hormones explored their value as
substitute therapies. The Council authorized the sending of supplies to
doctors who agreed to test the efficacy of preparations in alleviating the
sort of conditions that previously had been produced experimentally
by physiologists, by extirpation of organs of non-human animals; in effect,
it insisted on direct replacement of non-human research subjects by
human ones. The trial of a synthetic oestrogen, for example, was confined to women who had had their ovaries removed, but who had retained the uterus; the rationale behind this approach was the discovery
by MRC scientists that following a course of injections of the hormone,
ovariectomized monkeys experienced uterine bleeding. When almost
no suitable women could be found – doctors rarely removed the ovaries
and conserved the uterus – the MRC reluctantly extended the trial to
include menopausal women and women with primary amenorrhea
(those who had never menstruated).[152] Progesterone was tested on
women suffering from uterine haemorrhage.[153] An essential feature of
this experiment was an endometrial biopsy which, for reasons stated
above, few gynaecologists were able to carry out. By the time war was
declared, it was clear that clinical trials of gonadal hormones were inconclusive; the conditions of the laboratory proved entirely different
from those of clinical medicine. As Aleck Bourne put it in 1947: 'Our

patients are not normal animals nor have they been subjected to severe surgical mutilation, except, rarely, by removal of both ovaries.'[154]

By the end of the Second World War, the manufacture and sale of sex hormones had become a highly commercialized business. In 1951, sales of sex hormones in the United Kingdom were valued at £684,000, equivalent to 2.1 per cent of the market of drugs and pharmaceutical preparations.[155] Yet despite the enormous investment and institutional interest in the advancement of these new medicines, doctors continued to talk of the hormonal defects of one or other of their patients; they said with confidence and precision which hormone was deficient or excessive and just how the problem could be alleviated by a grain of this or a milligram of that.[156] The evolution of scientific principles of reproductive physiology had made almost no impression on the investigation and treatment of involuntary childlessness.

4
Politics, Health and Sterility

In December 1939, the County Medical Officer of the West Riding of Yorkshire inquired of the Minister of Health whether paragraph 35 of the Maternity and Child Welfare Act 1918, which encouraged local authorities to introduce schemes calculated to promote the health of mothers and children, could be extended to cover the investigation of sterility. He argued that treating sterile women as potential mothers would qualify them to receive free treatment from a local authority. The Ministry replied stating that involuntary childlessness did not fall within the competence of a maternity and child welfare scheme.[1]

In August 1943, an involuntarily childless man wrote to the Minister of Health asking him to consider setting up special clinics where people in his predicament could undergo medical investigations. Before the war, his own doctor had carried out preliminary tests on him and his wife. That doctor had been called up for military service; the other doctors he and his wife had consulted were either uninterested in sterility or too busy to give them the time and attention they sought. Special clinics might satisfy both his and his wife's personal desires; he believed they would also further the interests of the nation. A civil servant replied advising him to consult a specialist doctor.[2]

During the first half of the twentieth century in Britain a system of medical treatment provided free at the point of use was established piecemeal, to the benefit of a growing proportion of the population. Working men, followed by children, were the main beneficiaries of this tendency. Before the introduction of the National Health Service on 5 July 1948, unless they were pregnant, nursing young children, suffering from tuberculosis or a venereal infection, or seeking advice on birth control, women's decisions about whether or not to consult a doctor were influenced by considerations of money. Paradoxically, the same tendencies that encouraged doctors to focus treatment on the wife in an involuntarily childless marriage were responsible for denying these women access to medical attention free at the point of delivery.[3]

The sequence of measures that contributed to the creation of a system of medical attention free at the point of delivery and culminated in the introduction of the National Health Service were inspired less by medical need than by political considerations. Furthermore, as the early history of the National Health Service attests, doctors were often in the front line of resistance to these schemes.

Health became embroiled in politics towards the end of the eighteenth century, around the time that Malthus was expounding his famous law of population. Biology was inserted into political arithmetic. Increasingly, during the nineteenth century, biology featured in debates about national social, political and economic concerns, and, during the twentieth century, informed every new scheme offering medical care. Generally speaking, the process works as follows: first, an 'evil' is exposed, perhaps by a newsworthy event; a public 'outrage' ensues and demands are made for some form of official investigation; one of the definitions of the problem couches it in biological terms; a strong case is made for government intervention; if pressure is sufficient, the government responds by passing permissive or enabling legislation introducing a scheme offering medical care free at the point of delivery. This process was one manifestation of a tendency which extended the machinery of the state into areas hitherto defined as outside its area of competence, a development which culminated in the welfare state.

Until the end of the First World War, the biology that provoked national concern was male; British masculinity was deemed to be in crisis. Although experts and commentators were troubled by many aspects of women's lives, it was not their bodies but their behaviour, especially in relation to their husbands and children, that was considered in need of regulation. In the Edwardian period, women's bodies were considered the property of their fathers or husbands, and it was the responsibility of the male in authority to take care of them. Women's behaviour was subject to the arbitrary government of the state, and of their fathers and husbands; in addition, working-class women were supposed to respect the authority of middle-class experts and the male leaders of the labour movement. Women had no right of representation. Whole new sections of the male population had been enfranchised during the nineteenth century; by the turn of the century, sex was the principal ground for disqualification.

> Voting was a public and political and hence masculine activity, and questions of class and respectability did not come into it. Women were left out

of the process of democratisation on the grounds of their proper exclusion from public life. Their different 'natures' rendered them ineligible for 'natural rights'.[4]

Although they were disenfranchised, middle-class women with public ambitions could, and did, set up or join one of the many voluntary societies then in existence. The Victorian model of separate spheres for women and men, meant that for many middle-class women, philanthropic work and pressure-group politics were the only activities in which they could safely engage outside their front doors.[5] In contrast, working-class women had no time and little energy to devote to these organizations, and as a result were the objects rather than the architects of their programmes. Some societies were devoted to propaganda and education; nowadays, the best known is the Eugenics Education Society, set up in 1907 as a breakaway from the Moral Education League, but there were numerous others.[6] Some organizations were devoted to philanthropy; their philosophy was firmly rooted in the nineteenth-century tradition of combining good works with discipline, re-education and moral rearmament of the poor and destitute.

Eugenically minded people held the activities of philanthropists in derision; at best, they considered the philanthropists' energies wasted on people whose germ plasm destined their progeny to irremediable poverty; at worst, according to the 'better-dead school' of eugenics, any effort in this direction did positive racial harm. Social reformers with philanthropic proclivities saw eugenics as an assault on all they held dear and, up until the end of the First World War, it was the philanthropists' views that were attended to in official circles. Yet, in common with the 'better-dead' brigade of eugenists, most philanthropists regarded the poor as pathologically different from themselves: philanthropists talked about irreversible character weakness, whereas eugenists preferred to argue in terms of the immutable germ cell.[7] According to the rules of the Charity Organization Society, one of the most powerful and important of the philanthropic groups, founded in 1869, only victims of poverty of a temporary nature were eligible for help; aid was wasted on the truly destitute, whose condition was proof of a fundamental weakness of character, indicated by ignorance, fecklessness, indolence, promiscuity and alcoholism. Whichever philosophy the voluntary societies espoused – with the exception perhaps of the suffrage campaign – in Edwardian Britain class conflicts and loyalties proved a more forceful influence than sisterhood on the development of social policy.[8]

The concern over the causes and implications of the shockingly high rate of infant mortality exemplify these tendencies. Between 1900 and the First World War, infant mortality came to be defined by contemporaries as one of the major social problems facing Britain; it was discussed at length in official circles and the press. As a historian recently observed, it is not difficult to understand why this was so: at the turn of the century, with a steadily declining birth rate and a persistently high infant mortality rate (averaging around 149 deaths per 1,000 live births), fewer babies were being born, and a high proportion of those that were perished in the first twelve months of life.[9]

The high toll taken by infant mortality was added to a list of reasons why the British should be anxious that the vigour of the men of a nation that had once ruled the world was diminishing.[10] On that list were also the following: the British army's poor performance against a handful of un-organized farmers in the Boer War (1899–1902); the large number of recruits rejected for active service by the army on the grounds of physical disability and ill-health; the apparently unstoppable decline in British marital fertility since the mid-1870s; and the success of modern German and American industry in chipping away at Britain's share of world trade in manufactured goods. It was typical of the time that a biological ex-planation should represent a plausible rival of criticisms of policies and tactics in discussions of the causes of economic, social, military and political troubles.

Modern Germany provided a model on which many British reformers set their sights: according to the ideology of 'national efficiency' which many reformers espoused, the British style of muddling through was discredited; the nation's fibres had to be imbued with the spirit of science, technical expertise and planning.[11] Yet despite a plethora of experts ready with advice to offer, government application of their principles proceeded at a disappointingly slow rate. In particular, the state had little inclination to venture into spheres hitherto deemed private and the responsibility of husbands, not even in order to reverse the decline in the nation's physical, economic and political efficiency.

An impressive range of people had something to say on the subject of infant mortality; with the exception of the 'better-dead' eugenists, who were convinced that working-class babies died because they were the runts of the nation's stock, most commentators agreed that the cause was remediable, namely, the failure of their mothers to look after them properly.[12] A consensus of opinion emerged: working-class women's ir-responsible behaviour was a major factor in the diminution in efficiency of British masculinity.

Maternal neglect had two principal causes: the employment of married women and the ignorance of and incompetence in infant care of working-class mothers. Voluntary and municipal organizations developed experi-mental schemes for the protection of infant life. Although the range of projects they set up was wide – from nursing mothers' restaurants to schools for mothers to baby shows – the majority were informed by a belief that working-class mothers stood in need of an elevated standard of maternal responsibility, and instruction in infant care, in order to protect their menfolk, both child and adult.

Paradoxically, despite the emphasis on maternal adequacy as a solution to the high rate of infant mortality, in another context the traditional notion of children as the responsibility of their parents was being undermined. Measures introduced in the explosion of social legislation passed between 1906 and 1914 removed from Poor Law authorities and gave to education authorities responsibility for the care of children of the poor and needy. According to the Poor Law, enacted at a time when only men could vote, the statutory punishment for any head of family who allowed a family member to receive poor relief was disenfranchisement. Many fathers refused to allow their children to receive relief in order to avoid this penalty. By transferring responsibility for the health of children to educational authorities, the stigma attached to the father of a destitute child was reduced.

School children's welfare received attention for reasons similar to those which underlay concern about infant mortality. In response to anxieties about the nation's degenerating physical efficiency, in 1903 the government set up the Interdepartmental Committee on Physical Deterioration. It was instructed to focus on the condition of the male working population, from whom the army drew its soldiers. The attention of the Committee was drawn to the poor health of children of the lower classes. It took the view that the physical decline of the nation could be arrested by improving the diet and environmental conditions of children and by making them do physical exercise; it was unconvinced by the claims of eugenists that the cause was inherited and irremediable progressive degeneration. The Interdepartmental Committee on Medical Inspection and Feeding of Children Attending Public Elementary Schools, appointed in 1905, confirmed this viewpoint; it found evidence of acute malnutrition in school children. The Education (Provision of Meals) Act 1906 permitted, but did not require, local education authorities to provide meals for needy school children. This measure was followed by the Education (Administrative Provisions) Act 1907, which required local education authorities to establish a medical service for the regular inspection of school children. Despite the opposition of the BMA – on the grounds that treatment should be left to independent doctors – education authorities began to secure for school children free medical treatment, often at clinics set up expressly for that purpose.[13]

A contemporary banner of the National Union of Vehicle Workers (Aldgate Branch) is emblazoned: 'I was sick and ye visited me'. On it has

been sewn a picture of a man lying in bed at home, being visited by two
soberly dressed representatives of his trade union; in a corner, watching
apprehensively, are the man's wife and child.[14] They had good reason to
be anxious: the widespread belief that a working man was responsible
for the health of his wife and family meant that their welfare depended
on his ability to work. Although far from adequate, when compared to
what was on offer to their wives – and children before the introduction
of the school medical service – welfare provided to working-class men
in regular employ in the Edwardian period was lavish.

Behind the differing treatment meted out to men and women lies the
romantic partnership of 'Man the Breadwinner' and 'Woman his Dependant'. During the second half of the nineteenth century, trade unionists had
fought long and hard to establish the principle of a man's wage as a family
wage, and for 'protective' legislation which 'saved' women the degradation of work and enabled them to devote themselves to domestic duties.
Between 1847 and 1901, eleven Acts of Parliament were passed restricting
women's work in factories and workshops; yet women had had no say in
these laws, which had a dramatic effect on their ability to earn a living
wage.

In practice, a family wage was often insufficient to support a non-
working, dependent wife and children. Yet the labour movement was
obsessed with its expansion. Its success was of little benefit to women; it
was not uncommon for men to be unwilling to shoulder their domestic
responsibilities, even where they were in a position to do so. And many
women with children had no husband to depend upon, because they
were widowed, or had been abandoned by or separated from their husband. The principle of the family wage disadvantaged women in another
way: it justified paying them low wages on the grounds that women's
earnings were supplementary, 'pin' money, used to buy fripperies and
luxuries. Paradoxically, an argument which received wide support in the
male-dominated labour movement proved highly beneficial to employers
because it permitted the payment to women of wages lower than those
paid to their male counterparts. Little wonder, then, that women formed
the majority of the poorest members of the population. If they needed
medical treatment, they had to depend upon charity: the dreaded Poor
Law or, mainly in cities, voluntary hospitals, charitable dispensaries, or
those doctors who treated poor families free of charge or ran medical
clubs to which poorer patients could make small contributions. In the
Edwardian period, intense competition among doctors encouraged many
of them who had practices in working-class areas to set up medical clubs
as a way of securing income; in return for a small weekly payment, the
doctor provided rudimentary treatment for the whole family.

During the nineteenth century, increasing numbers of mutual savings organizations, friendly societies, trade unions and industrial works had established national and local schemes which, in return for regular contributions, provided working men with a rudimentary form of insurance against unemployment, sickness and old age. By 1900, friendly societies were the largest exclusively working-class organizations in Britain; in 1904 they had around six million members, drawn (because of the membership restrictions) from among skilled and 'respectable' working men; in addition, there were 1.3 million trade unionists at the same date.[15] Few societies admitted working women; even if they had done so, few labouring families, even among the better paid, could have afforded double contributions; in such families, Man the Breadwinner took priority over his wife and children. When, in the 1870s, some women had expressed a wish to join the larger societies, they had found doctors unwilling to treat them unless they paid contributions higher than those demanded of men, on the grounds that women experienced more sickness than men and would make heavier demands on their services. Some societies tried to establish separate women's branches, with higher contributions, but with little success; individual saving was difficult as women's wages were typically low.[16] Many unions barred women from joining and so excluded them from union welfare schemes. Even where they were free to do so, few women joined unions, partly because they were male-dominated but also because women's low wages made it difficult for them to pay union dues. In any case, many saw their work as temporary and peripheral to their domestic responsibilities, and were reluctant to commit time and resources to improving their wages and conditions.[17]

The organizations which had looked after the interests of working men informed the principles and provided the day-to-day administration of the National Insurance Scheme set up by Lloyd George in 1911. The Scheme extended the right to medical care free at the point of delivery to a larger proportion of the working population. From 1913 onwards, the National Insurance Act gave insured workers the right to treatment by a doctor whom they could choose from a locally selected list, or panel.[18] The scheme also made life more secure for general practitioners by providing them with a regular income. The government lacked the machinery necessary to administer the scheme – and using the offices of friendly societies, trade unions and certain commercial insurance companies was both cheaper and placated fears among these bodies that they would be destroyed by a goverment scheme.[19]

Historians have offered a number of different explanations for this landmark in social policy legislation, which established the precursor of the British welfare state.[20] No doubt one important factor was the controversy over the nation's physical efficiency which had brought into greater prominence problems concerning working men's health. And the example of Germany, to which supporters of national efficiency looked for a solution for the nation's ills, provided another stimulus; under pressure from the growth of socialism and labour dissidence, in the 1870s the German government had introduced a national scheme offering social insurance to manual workers, mainly men. Indeed, it was after a visit to Germany in August 1908 that Lloyd George gave civil servants at the Treasury the task of exploring ways of setting up a similar scheme in Britain. Another explanation of the National Insurance Scheme is that it was introduced as a result of pressure brought to bear by social activists who were exercised by the causes and consequences of destitution, which had been documented by Medical Officers of Health and amateur investigators. In this case it would seem that the plight of working men proved more affecting than that of their wives: for unless they were pregnant, a majority of women in paid employment and women working exclusively in the home as wives and mothers were unsheltered by the National Insurance Scheme.

The Act benefited the better paid man and woman working in regular employment outside the home; however, only one in ten married women worked full-time in an insurable occupation. It excluded people who were low-paid or irregularly employed and anyone engaged in domestic service, categories in which women predominated (in July 1914, 1,658,000 women were employed in domestic service, that is, seven out of every twenty of all women in employment).[21] The scheme did not cover dependants of the insured. Indeed, the only recognition of women's needs was a thirty-shilling maternity benefit which, after a campaign successfully organized by the Women's Co-operative Guild, from 1913 onwards was paid directly to the wives of men insured under the scheme.[22]

The vision of the Women's Co-operative Guild was maternalist feminist: its members agreed that a woman's place was in the home looking after her children, yet they objected to the channelling of a woman's livelihood through a man's hands, as this made her his dependant. True equality meant freeing women from economic dependence of their husbands by granting equal respect and financial support to their work in 'women's sphere'.[23] They hoped that payment of a maternity grant into the hands of mothers would act as a thin end of a much larger wedge of state provision for the independent support of married women.

The cult of maternalism exploited by the Guild had emerged during the first decade of the century; it sought to lend motherhood a new dignity. According to its advocates, 'it was the duty and destiny of women to be the "mothers of the race", but also their greatest reward'.[24] In order to fulfil their duty, women had to concentrate their energies in their 'natural' sphere of nursery and kitchen; by deploying their womanly skills on the domestic front, and imbuing it with a spirit of feminine moral purity, they would create an environment of physical and spiritual cleanliness which would safeguard the health of their children.

Different interests advanced the cult of maternalism in the corridors of power, and succeeded in getting included in the 1911 decennial Census questions asking married women – single, divorced or widowed women were excluded – how many children had they borne and how many had survived. Although it is known as the 'Fertility Census', the 1911 Census was not an investigation into reproductive capacity but a comparison of the ability of married women, classified according to their husbands' occupations, successfully to rear children. The data collected also permitted an analysis of the effect of women's work on their children's survival.[25] When John Burns, President of the Local Government Board, presented to Parliament the Bill moving the Census, he defended the inclusion of questions on a topic hitherto deemed private on the grounds that the data obtained would help prevent infant mortality.[26] It is clear that Burns' sympathies lay with the male-dominated labour movement, obsessed with the idea that a mother's wage for bearing and rearing children must be included in her husband's pay. Burns had been a militant socialist engineer, and he was the first working man to achieve Cabinet rank. Indeed, his appointment as President of the Local Government Board in 1906 was a concession to the labour movement. Burns' office put him in charge of the General Register Office, the government department responsible for the decennial Census, which was then a stronghold of environmentalism and public health medicine; its fundamental concern was to identify preventable deaths.[27]

'We want the vote to stop the white slave traffic, sweated labour and to save the children.'[28] Suffragettes also manipulated the cult of maternalism, arguing that women's enfranchisement was in men's interests because it would encourage the introduction of policies that would save the lives of their offspring. Suffragettes played on the crisis of masculinity by emphasizing men's inherent flaws and character weaknesses and drawing attention to women's virtues. A poster produced in the Suffrage Atelier around 1912 neatly crystallizes both these themes: it juxtaposes five responsible yet womanly women – a mayor, a nurse, a mother, a doctor/teacher and a factory hand – none of whom is a citizen, with five depraved, weak men – a convict, a lunatic, a proprietor of white slaves (prostitutes), a man unfit for military service and a drunkard – all of whom have the right to vote.[29]

In contrast to the image of working man as dependable husband and father promoted by both labour movement and Fabian socialists, suffragette propaganda portrayed him as an unreliable and inadequate provider. Man the Breadwinner's tendency to drunken and irresponsible behaviour was behind the high infant mortality rate. His wife was confronted by an impossible choice: seek poorly paid employment and neglect the children, or condemn herself and her children to a life of abject poverty. Middle-class men were no better. Indeed, the example they set their social inferiors was in how to enslave women through prostitution. Their innocent wives suffered too; the sexual double standard trapped them in their homes, where they languished, often involuntarily childless, or losing babies through repeated miscarriages and stillbirths, because their lascivious husbands had infected them with a venereal disease (according to the suffragettes, men's lust was a major factor in the decline in middle-class women's fertility). The message conveyed is clear: men's vested interests would always prevent them from confronting the consequences of their actions; extending citizenship to women was the only way open to the nation to achieve its demographic ambitions.

The policies introduced in the name of the cult of maternalism did not engage with woman's reproductive capacity, which was deemed the private property and responsibility of her husband. Before the First World War, this definition of women's bodies was challenged only by the suffragettes. Other people who were concerned about various aspects of women's fertility called for policies targeting their husbands. As pointed out in chapter 1, there was at this time no consensus on why marital fertility was declining. Some people claimed that the burden of taxes and cost of educating children were discouraging men of the servant-keeping classes from fathering children. Others found evidence of more women suffering from sterility. However, involuntary childlessness was deemed to be socially disruptive only in relation to a middle- or upper-class woman, married to a man with titles and estates to bestow on an heir (a context in which the size of a doctor's fee was of little import in deciding whether or not to seek a consultation). According to increasingly vocal and influential eugenically minded activists, sterility was common in the propertied classes because of a weakness in their germ plasm; they were sorely troubled by the curious phenomenon of eminent men dying without issue. Indeed, the marriage of Francis Galton, founder of the eugenics movement, was involuntarily childless.[30] In the late nineteenth century, Galton devoted much time and energy to uncovering the processes responsible for his condition. It was a face-saving exercise: he concluded that manliness, enterprise, intelligence and comparative infertility were hereditary, and linked together.[31]

According to eugenically minded people, the converse was also true: fecundity was hereditary.[32] Except for prostitutes, who were notoriously sterile, they believed that involuntary childlessness was incompatible with proletarian stock, whose germ plasm was predisposed to excess fertility. Closer to animals, women situated lower down the social scale had litters, and poor maternal instincts (hence the high rate of infant mortality associated with poverty). Eugenists found deeply troubling the correlation between fertility and income (eugenists were responsible for the development of several key modern statistical techniques, including correlations): with few exceptions, the poor, indigent, ignorant, alcoholic and criminal classes had the largest families, whereas the titled, wealthy and enterprising had the smallest. The implication of this was that in a few generations the 'quality' of the nation's stock would deteriorate, to the detriment of the Empire.

The only medical interventions into women's fertility that eugenists would condone were those aimed at preventing the birth of children who were 'unwanted' – although clearly for different reasons – by the nation and their mothers. The nation rejected them because of their 'substandard quality', whereas their mothers, ground down by the physical, financial and emotional burden of repeated child-bearing, may have dreaded the prospect of another baby to care for. A leading eugenist summed up the movement's programme as follows: 'to promote the fertility of the better types which the nation contains, whilst diminishing the birth rate amongst those which are inferior'.[33] The former element was known as 'positive eugenics', the latter as 'negative eugenics' (although clearly, it was their middle-class advocates who described the programme in those terms).[34]

A diminution of working-class fertility was also sought by neo-Malthusians, although for different reasons from those espoused by eugenists. Neo-Malthusians believed that large families sprang from a character defect which also impoverished both domestic and national economies. In accordance with the principles of a free market economy and the spirit of enterprise which they endorsed, the method of family limitation promulgated by neo-Malthusians was voluntary sexual restraint on the part of men (this idea was discussed in chapter 1 in relation to the Fabians' survey).[35] Material security was vouchsafed to men capable of exercising self-control in every form of expenditure. They also sought the application of a similar discipline to the nation's economy.

As relations between Britain and Germany deteriorated, people began to suggest that Britain's declining birth rate was putting the British Isles at risk of invasion. It has long been held that population imbalance causes war. One contemporary pundit compared population pressure to gaseous pressure: both are liable to explode on expansion. The tendency for one nation to increase rapidly in numbers while its neighbour's population remained static – as, for example, was happening between Germany and France – made war an inevitable outcome.[36]

During the First World War, the terrible slaughter of troops on both sides prompted the pronatalist camp to spread its message with even greater urgency. Recognizing the need for more soldiers to fill the depleting 'racial coffers', even eugenists toned down their propaganda about the disastrous implications of high working-class fertility. They concentrated instead on the so-called dysgenic effects of war: as long as enlistment was voluntary, it would be the fittest young men of heroic quality who would offer themselves to die for their country.[37] However, their exhortations fell on deaf ears; to many people, the soaring casualty lists made pronatalist talk seem less like patriotism and more like a thinly disguised call for the production of more 'cannon fodder.'

The war exacerbated anxieties about British masculinity. An increase in the number of boys born during the last part of 1915, for example, was seized upon as grounds for optimism; Nature – on the side of the British – was taking it upon herself to redress the nation's gender imbalance by filling its 'racial cradles' with more boys than girls.[38] The British government appointed itself Nature's handmaiden: the war occasioned massive state intervention into all aspects relating to the population. Wartime conditions provided politicians with both the incentive and the justification necessary to venture into areas hitherto considered sacrosanct. A good example of this dramatic change in attitude is the government's response to the apparent epidemic in venereal diseases. Before the war, the Local Government Board had published a report on venereal diseases which claimed that the numbers of people infected were suggestive of an epidemic and drew attention to the lack of facilities for both prevention and treatment.[39] The government's reaction was a well-established delaying tactic: it set up a further inquiry. However, by the time the Royal Commission on Venereal Diseases published its report in 1916 the rapid spread of infection among the troops had transformed venereal diseases into a threat to national security and the government was eager to act on the Commission's recommendations.

The Commission claimed that more men than women were infected by venereal diseases; it estimated that, in a typical working-class population of London, between one in twelve and one in eight men, and between three and seven out of every hundred women, had acquired syphilis. The rates for gonorrhea were higher still. The Commission also revealed strong class differences in access to treatment. The rich could easily afford treatment of syphilis with salvarsan, whereas for the poor, evidence of syphilitic infection might deny them admission to hospital, disqualify them from outdoor relief from the Poor Law authorities or mean loss of entitlement to insurance benefits.[40] The government accepted the main recommendations of the Commission. State-backed pathology laboratories were established; free supplies of salvarsan were given to doctors; and local authorities were encouraged to set up free clinics in general hospitals.

The need rapidly to refill the nation's cradles renewed the sense of importance of infant life, and schemes set up in order to preserve it underwent an enormous expansion during the war. In 1914, local authorities employed 600 health visitors; by 1918, this figure had more than quadrupled to 2,577. At the beginning of the war, 650 maternity and child welfare centres had been established; at the end, 1,278 were in operation. The scope of the activities carried on by the centres had also expanded: more attention was paid to antenatal work, medical consultations were extended from infants to include all pre-school children, milk and meals for toddlers as well as for pregnant and nursing women were more commonly offered and dental care for mothers and children began to be provided at a number of clinics. The amount of money spent rose with the proliferation of services; for example, in 1916 voluntary societies had spent £40,000 on maternal and child welfare schemes, and in 1918 their projected budget was £70,000; the corresponding figures for local authorities were £96,000 in 1916 and £279,000 in 1918.[41] The Maternity and Child Welfare Act 1918 further enabled local authorities to establish grant-aided antenatal and child welfare clinics.[42]

By the end of the war, many pregnant and nursing mothers and their infants could receive free medical attention at a maternity and child welfare clinic; doctors were employed by school health services to look after children; people infected by a venereal disease or tuberculosis could obtain free medical attention; many working men, and a few women in paid employment, were entitled to medical attention free at the point of delivery under the National Insurance Scheme. Yet most women were still constrained by considerations of money when seeking a consultation with a doctor for any other reason, including involuntary childlessness.

Marie Stopes is probably the best known of the sex reformers who, after the war, began to promulgate the idea that a great deal of unhappiness and marital disharmony is due to the failure of a husband to recognize and satisfy his wife's sexual desires. In 1918 she published *Married love*, her famous eulogy to conjugal sex; by the end of 1923, after twenty-two reprints, it had sold over 400,000 copies.[43]

According to many sex reformers, sexuality is a central organizing principle of the family, which in turn forms the bedrock of a stable society. Sex reformers acknowledged that fear of conception prevents many women from agreeing to or enjoying sexual relations, a reluctance which was to their and their husbands' detriment. Eugenists supported the separation of sexuality and procreation; it permitted people the freedom to indulge in sexual intercourse (they considered the lower orders incapable of exercising restraint and sex kept them off the streets) and also provided society with a means of exercising 'quality control' over their progeny. Before the First World War, fear of prosecution for distributing obscene literature had prevented public distribution of birth control propaganda. The war had encouraged a relaxation of official attitudes towards birth control: in order to prevent venereal infection, the government had agreed that condoms should be handed out to soldiers. After the war, sex reformers, neo-Malthusians and eugenists spread the message of birth control with impunity at public meetings, in numerous books and pamphlets, and at clinics established expressly for the purpose. In 1921, Marie Stopes opened Britain's first birth control clinic in north London and founded the Society for Constructive Birth Control. A few months later, in south London, the Malthusian League established its first clinic. The original intention, in addition to giving advice on birth control, was to undertake the full range of infant and maternity welfare services, which would create a model which local authorities might be persuaded to copy, as well as serving as a training centre for doctors.[44]

Historians of the birth control movement usually cast Marie Stopes in the role of a general, leading birth control campaigners into battle against the forces of reaction, billeted in the Ministry of Health, which was set up in 1918.[45] They have tended to diminish the extent to which relaxation of official attitudes towards interventions into areas hitherto deemed private, occasioned by the war, facilitated the fulfilment of the birth control movement's ambitions. As one historian puts it, during the war

> the state was redefined as an entity organized not only for war and the taking of life, but also for the giving of it, and the citizen as either the male soldier/producer or the female reproducer. Although the distinction between male and female spheres remained, their identification as respectively public and private disappeared.[46]

During the war, it became legitimate to define women's reproductive capacity as property, which, as some people claimed, should be exploited on behalf of the nation, even if it meant disregarding the views of their husbands.

Soon after the war, anxieties about both the quality of the population and the declining birth rate began to be overshadowed by talk about the terrible consequences of overpopulation. For although fewer babies were being born, the overall size of the population continued to grow because more people were living longer. As economic problems multiplied, labour unrest grew and unemployment increased, antinatalism became fashionable. The 1911 Census had demonstrated that the birth rate was declining most rapidly in the middle and upper classes. In order to achieve a reduction in the overall size of the population, antinatalist policy had to focus on the recalcitrant working classes.

No doubt many politicians were sympathetic to the antinatalism that prevailed during the 1920s. Yet in a liberal democracy, and in peacetime, powerful disincentives discourage politicians from pressing forward with

policies and spending public money on services that intervene in the most
intimate and private aspects of people's lives. Despite the change in
attitudes occasioned by the war, the extension of the franchise in 1918 to
all men and to women over the age of 31 had created new conditions
which made politicians think twice before venturing boldly into an area
which many new voters might consider their private affair. On the left of
the political spectrum stood the trade unions, which had emerged from
the war invigorated, their membership having doubled between 1914 and
1920.[47] They set about re-establishing the ideal of Man the Breadwinner
and opposed any attempts to channel welfare benefits directly to women;
according to them, wage levels are kept up only by the pressure of
married men for a family wage. Backed as it was by the finances and
industrial clout of the unions, it is not suprising that the Labour Party lent
its support to their definitions of masculinity and femininity.

The extension of the franchise increased the significance for politicians
of religious considerations. Until the 1930s, all the major Christian denomi-
nations were united in opposition to birth control. It was not until the
Lambeth Conference of 1930 that Anglican bishops accorded limited approval to family planning; among the nonconformists, only the Quakers
had declared in favour of birth control under certain conditions. The
Roman Catholic theology of marriage and family resisted social change.
Even if they practise a measure of birth control at home, this theology has
been a central organizing political principle for British Catholics. They
oppose materialist interventions into fertility because the Catholic family,
organized according to the ideals of separate spheres and women's dependence on men, represents a haven against a hostile, modern, urban
industrial order.[48] In response to virulent anti-papal prejudice and the
political upheavals in Ireland, the Catholic Church in Britain has been
particularly prone to ultramontanism, 'the wish for total conformity with
papal ideas and ideals in all things and not merely in those which are
essential to the unity of Christian and Catholic faith'.[49] With good reason,
the British Catholic Church saw itself as a 'fortress church', besieged on all
sides by materialists, 'progressives' and anti-papists, all giving vent to
widespread anti-Irish prejudice. Events in Ireland gave the Irish little faith
in British observance of constitutional methods towards them; this
strengthened their determination to make their presence felt in the polity.[50] Paradoxically, many Catholic men and women were enfranchised at
a time when relations between Britain and Ireland were at a nadir;
antimaterialist sentiments provided them with a way of expressing revul-
sion against the British government. Indeed, as the more rabid antinatalist
propaganda talked about the fecklessness of incorrigible Pats and Biddys,
and the importance of preventing them from both breeding and emigrat-
ing from their native Ireland, it would be suprising if they had not objected
to any suggestion of state sponsorship of birth control.

Organizations with names such as Southwark Parents' and Electors' Association were set up in order to remind Members of Parliament of the intimate relationship between policies relating to fertility and an electoral majority.[51] Catholics formed a significant minority in the electorate: in 1911, Catholics in England and Wales were estimated at 1,710,000, around 6 or 7 per cent of the total population. Although there is a dearth of demographic data on the Catholic population, it seems that from 1910 onwards the community experienced a sustained increase in numbers.[52] A majority were first- or second-generation working-class Irish immigrants; like many other immigrants, they gravitated towards the inner-city parishes of London – Westminster and Southwark – and Birmingham, Cardiff, Glasgow and Liverpool, where they exercised considerable influence in elections.

Through a combination of accident and design, British governments managed to escape being accused of responsibility for interventions into women's reproductive capacity. In retrospect, it is possible to identify three major political strategies deployed to this end by politicians: abstinence; postponement; and depoliticization.[53] Abstinence occurs where governments, parties and leaders simply refrain from taking a stand. Postponement is a delaying tactic, used in the hope that pressure groups will be unable to sustain mobilization and the issue will disappear. The most common approach to depoliticization has been to redefine the problem as a medical issue which allows politicians to pass the buck to doctors.

Up until the 1980s, abstinence worked in relation to sterility because of the absence of regulations governing what doctors could or could not do for their involuntarily childless patients. Unlike the provision of advice on birth control or helping women to terminate a pregnancy, both of which were governed by legislation introduced in the nineteenth century, doctors have been free to do whatever they liked in order to make a woman pregnant. The only restrictions on medical practice have been professional considerations – which will be discussed below – and the ability of married women to afford a doctor's fee.

Postponement and depoliticization became increasingly important strategies during the 1930s when pressure was brought to bear on the government to extend the competence of health schemes to include treatment of involuntary childlessness, a development illustrated by the accounts which head this chapter. As the remainder of this chapter demonstrates, these strategies worked in relation to sterility because of its importance to private medical practice.

Antifeminism resurfaced during the 1920s as unemployment increased and the labour movement sought to secure what jobs there were for men. Significantly, the 1921 Census investigated the number of children – including step- and foster-children – dependent on women to look after them, thereby inflating the scope of their domestic responsibilities; the dry data were published in a volume with a title that tugs at the heartstrings: *Dependency, orphanhood and fertility*. Yet poverty prevented many women from securing a home for their children. Increasingly during this period social investigators examined the extent to which an average family wage could cover the cost of reasonable housing, an adequate diet and health care for non-insurable dependents.[54] Left-leaning advocates of the 'endowment of motherhood' – later called family allowance and child benefit – proposed placing all mothers on the national payroll and channelling some of a household's income away from the man's hands.[55] Yet this proposal presented too radical a challenge to the principle of the family wage. Supporters of Man the Breadwinner succeeded in confining state protection to married women unsheltered by a male family wage: in 1925, the Old Age and Widows and Orphans Contributory Pensions Act granted pension rights to the widows and orphans of men covered by the National Insurance Scheme. The Royal Commission on National Health Insurance, appointed in 1924 to investigate the inequalities inherent in the scheme, failed to comment on the question of women's exclusion in its report published two years later. The idea that the welfare of a married woman was dependent on her husband's status remained a robust one.

The struggles working-class women faced in fulfilling their domestic responsibilities began to be associated with their physical inefficiency. The most visible indicator of the burden of ill-health borne by married women was the shockingly high and rising rate of maternal mortality: in 1918, one mother died for every 264 babies born alive; by 1932, this figure had risen to one maternal death for every 238 live births. Little wonder that this development became the focus of several competing political tendencies. Indeed, maternal mortality was made a plank in the political platform of Baldwin's second administration (1924–9).[56]

The urgent need to save mothers' lives provided the stimulus necessary for the transformation of obstetric care in Britain.[57] Medical Officers of Health, sympathetic doctors and staff of maternity and child welfare centres and birth control clinics began to claim that maternal mortality was just the tip of a vast iceberg of women's ill-health; they drew attention to the extent of untreated gynaecological problems suffered by working-class women who had had children. Of Stopes's first 10,000 patients, 1,321 had a slit cervix, 335 a serious prolapse of the uterus and 1,508 an internal deformation.[58] Yet the medical profession's disapproval and deep suspicion of birth controllers meant that for many years clinics failed to secure the constant attendance of a doctor.[59]

'Back-street' abortion followed by sepsis was another major cause of gynaecological morbidity and maternal mortality (women who died as a result of an abortion were included in statistics of maternal death). One in ten women attending the Walworth Women's Welfare Centre – set up by the Malthusian League in 1921 – admitted to an attempt to terminate a pregnancy.[60] If women had access to safe and effective contraception, it was argued, they would not need to put their lives at risk by undergoing a hazardous and illegal procedure. Pressure began to be exerted on the government to decriminalize abortion.[61] In 1934, the Women's Co-operative Guild passed a resolution to that effect; a year later, its example was followed by a committee of the BMA, which recommended the decriminalization of abortion in cases of rape or where the physical and mental health of the mother was endangered by pregnancy; and in 1936, the Abortion Law Reform Association was set up.

The birth control clinics opened by Stopes and the Malthusian League had been joined by others run by the Workers' Birth Control Group and a few local authorities who extended their maternity and child welfare schemes to include advice on birth control. In 1924 John Wheatley, the Roman Catholic Minister of Health, forbade municipal Medical Officers of Health to pass on birth control advice.[62] It was a cruel blow; birth control clinics were financed almost entirely by donations and low fees charged to clients, and they looked to local authorities for resources to enable them to expand.

In 1928, the franchise was extended to all women over the age of 21. Although the Local Government Act 1929 allowed local authorities greater freedom in arranging local health services, they had to wait until March 1931 for the Ministry of Health to permit them to offer advice on birth control. Memorandum 153/MCW empowered local authorities to set up clinics where married women who had had children could receive birth control advice and medical attention for gynaecological problems; married women whose medical condition – a venereal infection, tuberculosis, heart disease, diabetes or chronic nephritis – made a further pregnancy hazardous could also be offered advice on birth control. In effect, this landmark memorandum brought the provision of birth control advice and gynaecological attention, free at the point of delivery, within the purview of municipal authorities.

The clientele of birth control/gynaecological clinics was restricted to married women with children. Medical attention was provided for minor problems; women with a more serious condition were referred to a local doctor or hospital. This stipulation was included in order to pacify the BMA and British College of Obstetricians and Gynaecologists, who saw in municipal clinics a threat to their practice.

In the increasingly harsh economic climate of the 1930s, with unemployment rising, politicians working within the Ministry of Health could not fail either to be sympathetic to antinatalism, or to recognize the inadequacy of a family wage or unemployment benefit to cover the health care needs of the dependants of Man the Breadwinner. As the Pilgrim Trust put it: 'Beyond the man in the queue we should always be aware of those two or three at home whom he has to support.' They calculated that 250,000 long-term unemployed men were responsible for 170,000 wives and 270,000 young children.[63] The moral hedge surrounding the clinics was trimmed a fraction by Circular 1408, dated 31 May 1934, which allowed local authorities to give advice on birth control to married expectant and nursing mothers in whose cases a further pregnancy would be detrimental to health. The presence of a medical practitioner in the clinics began to be exploited by campaigners, who argued that they should be used as a basis of a much-needed postnatal medical service.

Local authorities were granted permissive powers; it was not incumbent on them to provide either a birth control or a gynaecological service. In effect, the government devolved on to the municipal rates the cost of providing services relating to women's gynaecological health and birth control; these issues were defined as the stuff of local and not national democracy. The government was able to escape direct responsibility for easier access to advice on birth control because during the interwar period municipal and national politics were not wholly assimilated into one another; indeed, in many respects, local politics had a life of their own.[64] The Ministry of Health never made it mandatory on local authorities to open a birth control/gynaecological clinic.[65] Yet any alteration in the regulations required Cabinet approval.[66] Some local authorities set to with enthusiasm, others permitted a birth control society to establish a clinic on their premises and others did nothing at all. In 1938, of 102 of the total 157 local authorities, thirty had made no definite arrangement; twenty-eight ran a gynaecological clinic; twenty-three had a special arrangement for referring patients to a hospital or other suitable clinic; eight suggested women went to their local hospital but had no special arrangement with it; eight saw women at ante- or postnatal clinics; four had arranged for periodic visits to clinics by medical specialists; one arranged consultations by appointment; and one – Essex – ran nine centres where women received attention by a gynaecologist, postnatal care and birth control advice.[67]

During the first twenty years of the twentieth century, medical services free at the point of delivery had been introduced in response to a preoccupation with men's physical robustness, epidemics of venereal infection and tuberculosis, and concern over the high rate of infant mortality. In the following fifteen years, a preoccupation with maternal mortality (caused by puerpural infection and sepsis following abortion) and the chronic ill-health of mothers (the result of mismanaged childbirth and the burden of repeated pregnancies) led to a reorganization of obstetric services and the establishment of municipal and voluntary gynaecological/ birth control clinics. Lacking the all-important qualification of motherhood, involuntarily childless married women had fallen outside the purview of these schemes. However, their moment now arrived: between the mid-1930s and the end of the Second World War, involuntarily childless women achieved the adumbration of political significance. For the first time, sterility featured in concern about the inadequacy of services available to meet women's health-care needs. In 1939, for example, still pursuing an extension of the National Insurance Scheme to 'dependent' married women, The Women's Health Enquiry Committee called on the government to establish 'centres easily accessible to every woman, to which she could go at any time for advice and treatment on any topic connected with her health, including gynaecological ailments, psychological troubles, the spacing of her family, sterility, and so on'.[68] Medical Officers of Health responsible for municipal clinics, and pressure groups, began to campaign in order to bring to involuntarily childless married women medical attention free at the point of delivery.

Why did sterility emerge as a campaigning issue? Its brief moment of fame was sparked and extinguished through a unique combination of circumstances. There is some evidence that in the 1930s women wanting medical advice on sterility began to seek help at birth control/gynaecological clinics and made people working in them conscious of the extent of their unmet need. In 1933, for example, eighteen out of ninety-three women attending a gynaecology session at the North Kensington Clinic, London, sought help for sterility.[69]

More women may have sought help because the incidence of involuntary childlessness was increasing. Of upper- and middle-class British women born during 1861–80, 16.4 per cent were childless, compared to 11.3 per cent of working-class women. The corresponding figures for women born during 1881–90, who would have been passing through their child-bearing years during the 1930s, are 20.9 per cent and 14.2 per cent.[70] Unfortunately, the data cannot tell us how many of these women were childless by choice, nor how many were married to sterile men, nor whether their numbers were increasing.

Leaving aside the imponderable question of whether or not the incidence of involuntary sterility in the population was increasing, it is possible that more involuntarily childless women sought medical attention for their condition because it had become an acceptable course of action to take. After the First World War many of the taboos had been lifted from the public discussion of sex, sexuality and the proper regulation of relationships between men and women, which may have allowed women to talk about sterility more freely.[71] Furthermore, the overall demand for doctors' attention was rising, perhaps because of the promise held out by modern scientific medicine, which may have made seeking medical help seem an appropriate course of action to an involuntarily childless woman. People covered by the National Insurance Scheme were seeing their doctors more often; and more people were being enrolled on the panel. The Royal Commission on Health Insurance estimated in 1926 that about 7.5 million people were consulting their panel doctor each year; a decade later, the BMA claimed the number had reached ten million.[72] However, although seeking medical attention was becoming more popular, for many married women it meant incurring the expense of a doctor's fee; only thirteen of the 1,250 working-class women who responded to an investigation organized by the Women's Health Enquiry in 1933 were insured under the Scheme and used a panel doctor in illness; 60 per cent said they were dependent for medical attention on a private doctor.[73] In the recessionary 1930s, a doctor's fee was beyond the pockets of many women. Expenditure surveys in 1938–9 confirmed that working-class households spent little on medical needs; under 3 per cent of expenditure went on medical care that had to be purchased outside the insurance scheme.[74] Indeed, about one-fifth of all fees owed to doctors practising in predominantly working-class districts were unpaid.[75] Lack of money may have prevented many involuntarily childless women from seeking attention from a general practitioner, who was also the gatekeeper to a hospital specialist. Thirty-four out of the 176 childless women of completed fertility married between 1900 and 1924, who were inpatients at a hospital at the time, revealed to interviewers carrying out a survey on behalf of the Royal Commission on Population, between August 1946 and June 1947, that they had not consulted a doctor about their childlessness.[76] Most of these women were working-class; better-off women were underrepresented in the sample and probably sought private medical care.

It bears repeating that, throughout this period, women were the objects rather than the architects of campaigns waged and policies introduced in their name. There is a crucial difference between speaking about the practical needs of involuntarily childless women, and invoking them in political rhetoric. Sterility gained prominence not because the needs of involuntarily childless women touched the hearts of commentators, but because it was drawn into political discourse by the depopulation scare of the mid-1930s. The brand of biological politics that provoked the resurgence of pronatalism in the mid-1930s defined the predicament of involuntarily childless women as a legitimate object of public concern.

As was pointed out in chapter 1, the depopulation scare of the 1930s was engineered largely by eugenically minded pundits who claimed that if the birth rate remained at its then low rate, the population of Britain would decline. With Germany and Italy flexing their imperialist muscles, the future looked gloomy for Britain and its Empire. In keeping with the tendency to express political and economic concerns in biological terms, anxieties about the increasingly tense international situation were articulated in terms of national reproductive pathology. Reproduction rates, a new technique for measuring fertility, demonstrated that, from the nation's point of view, working-class women were having too few girl babies. Their sterility – whether involuntary or intentional – began to be considered an urgent public health problem which the state should tackle.

Pronatalism reached pandemic proportions. Pronatalist policies were being introduced in most European countries, including Nazi Germany and Fascist Italy. They were reported in British newspapers and described in articles in learned journals. In 1935, the Population Investigation Committee, set up by the Eugenics Society, sent David Glass, its full-time research worker, on a tour with instructions to find out about and evaluate the effectiveness of pronatalist schemes recently introduced in European countries.[77] A majority offered incentives, in cash or kind, to fertile women in order to encourage them to have more children; abortion and birth control were criminalized. Both Hitler's Germany and Mussolini's Italy provided assistance to involuntarily childless women.[78] In 1936, a special committee of the Reich decided that the German health insurance scheme should recognize involuntary childlessness in a married woman as an illness, if it could be cured by medical treatment, and if its cure was in the interest of the community (meaning of course, if the woman was of 'desirable' racial stock).[79] In 1937, the Health Office of Bremen established special 'advising centers for the struggle against infertility'.[80] The German marriage law of July 1938 provided that either partner to a marriage could petition for its dissolution if the other partner had become prematurely sterile after marriage. According to the government's propaganda, the Nazi call for more babies had been attended to by patriotic German women: in 1939, there were said to be a million more German babies alive than there would have been if the birth rate had continued at the same low rate as had prevailed before Hitler rose to power.[81] At the height of the war, the Nazis continued to think of new ways of increasing German fertility. On 29 July 1943 the *Daily Mail* reported a radio broadcast in which Reich Health Minister Leonard Conti had directed every German district in the Reich to establish workshops, attached to local health offices, where childless couples could be helped to find ways of bearing children.[82] In the latter part of 1944, the infamous gynaecologist Clauberg was taken away from his experiments in techniques of sterilization carried out on women in concentration camps (mentioned in chapter 3), and appointed chief of a 'City of Mothers', a new institution for research into and treatment of sterility.[83] The Nazis were enthusiasts of research into sperm pictures and sex hormonal therapy.[84] Although he was less obsessed with promoting racial purity, none the less Mussolini was a keen pronatalist and among the many measures he ordered was establishment of centres for the treatment of sterility.[85]

Pronatalist policies were promoted by Hitler in his pursuit of barbarically racist, antisemitic and imperialist ends; Mussolini was determined to boost Italy's 'demographic power' in order to demonstrate the vigour of Italian men, compared with the effete English and French, and to fulfil his expansionist, imperialist vision.[86] In Britain, the issue of sterility – both intended and involuntary – was taken up by pressure groups mobilized around biological politics: the Eugenics Society, the British Social Hygiene Council (formerly the National Council for Combating Venereal Diseases), which in 1938 set up the Marriage Guidance Council, and the Fabian Society's creation, Political and Economic Planning (later the Policy Studies Institute).

The Eugenics Society is usually singled out as the leading advocate of biological politics, although it was certainly not the only British organization which thought in these terms.[87] During the 1930s, eugenical sentiment had a constituency far beyond the Society's membership, appealing to people of every political persuasion: conservatives, fascists, liberals, socialists and communists shared a common commitment to a belief that the salvation of mankind was to some extent bound up with the improvement of its genes.[88] The widespread currency of eugenical sentiments has made it difficult to pin down the political complexion of the Eugenics Society during the 1930s. It has even been dubbed progressive; historians have pointed to the way in which its membership was cleansed of the most rabid elements, and how it was joined by a few feminists, leading doctors and social scientists, and other professionals with leftish, pro-science sympathies.[89] In some respects, the confusion over the political orientation of the Society demonstrates the success of a deliberate policy pursued after the Second World War to disassociate campaigns around reproduction waged in Britain from the barbaric racial policies of Nazi Germany. In 1952, in a lecture on Nazi experiments on human subjects, Carlos Blacker, General Secretary of the Eugenics Society from 1931 to 1952 and its Honorary Secretary from 1952 to 1961, assured its members that Nazi policies were connected only remotely to British eugenics of the interwar period. He reminded them that Galton, the founding father of the movement, had called eugenics a merciful creed, held by men endowed with pity and kindly feelings. In contrast, the scientists and doctors who had carried out experiments on human subjects in the concentration camps in the name of eugenics, were ignorant and uneducated people, who held science in superstitious reverence.[90]

Blacker's argument proved both timely and persuasive. Nazi racial policies had demonstrated that 'dark fantasies and paranoia are not inconsistent with the most routinised and efficient "managerial" practice'.[91] They had discredited any official proposal directed at managing people's reproductive capacities. Yet the postwar fear of a global population explosion made the universal adoption of family limitation a matter of urgency. Distinguishing eugenic tendencies in Britain and other industrialized nations from those of the Nazis provided antinatalists with a neat way out of this dilemma.[92]

Another reason why the character of the British eugenics movement during the 1930s seems so slippery is that it resists analysis in terms of the dichotomous scheme that is usually applied to it. Questions about whether it was right- or left-leaning, reactionary or reformist, extremist or moderate, fascist or socialist, are the wrong ones, because the movement sought a synthesis of opposites. The appeal of British eugenics during the 1930s was its faith in the efficacy of science; its enthusiasts rejoiced in the latest techniques emerging from research in demography, reproductive physiology and genetics. They believed that science had the potential to revive the nation's past glories, save the British Empire and preserve the traditional values and culture it disseminated. In effect, British eugenics represented a weaker, less romantic version of the paradox of 'reactionary modernism', an admixture of regressive and progressive ideas that reached an apotheosis in the hands of the Nazis. No doubt for strategic reasons, the concept of reactionary modernism has been confined to an analysis of Nazism, where it clarifies their particular combination of ruthless managerial efficiency, exploitation of scientific techniques and celebration of a mythic, racially pure heritage. The blend appealed to people of radically different political tendencies and opposing attitudes towards science. In the hands of the Nazi state, it took Germany backwards into barbarism, and at the same time allowed it to rejoice in technological advances.[93] In Britain, reactionary modernism was confined to pressure groups who agitated against a state reluctant to introduce the sort of extreme, interventionist policies that would promote its vision.

Reactionary modernism celebrates the well-regulated family, where marriage, fertility and family life are managed according to scientific principles in order to satisfy both private sexual needs and public political ends. It pursued both antifeminist and maternalist ends, albeit couched in the language of liberal sexology: science could contain and domesticate, to the advantage of both family and nation, the chaos threatened by women's sexuality and reproductive capacity. As its reactionary vision of family life was based on a materialist and not a spiritual theology, it is not suprising that its most trenchant opponent in Britain was the Catholic Church. According to Catholic teaching, only God may intervene in sex and reproductive capacity in order to conserve the tradition of the family. To defend its flock against the threat of a materialist encroachment by the state, leaders of the British Catholic Church repeatedly denied the existence of involuntary sterility. The Guild of St Luke, St Cosmas and St Damian, a Catholic brotherhood of doctors and dentists, declared: 'It is beyond dispute that the commonest single cause of the fall in the birth-rate is the deliberate limitation of families by artificial means.'[94] Indeed, it claimed that concern over involuntary sterility had been invented in order deliberately to disguise the extent to which materialism was infecting British society.[95] According to the Archibishop of Liverpool, 'loss of fecundity (if it exists) is not the only widespread loss in the population. There is another – namely, an even more widely ranging loss of vital religion.'[96]

After the First World War, the nation's economic problems had fed antinatalism and facilitated the opening of clinics offering birth control advice to married women. Yet despite the deepening economic recession of the 1930s, increasingly tense international relations and the depopulation scare encouraged pronatalism. Indeed, by the late 1930s antinatalism was in danger of seeming unpatriotic. Sensitive to hostile criticism, birth controllers recognized the need to modify their platform and practice.[97] In May 1939, the National Birth Control Association (NBCA), founded in 1930 to co-ordinate the work of birth control clinics (with the exception of those established by Marie Stopes), was renamed the Family Planning Association (FPA). The NBCA's object of advocating and providing scientific birth control was enlarged to include education about and medical attention for involuntary sterility, minor gynaecological ailments and difficulties connected with the marriage relationship. The FPA's stated purpose was to promote the welfare of the family though the care of the mother's health. In many respects, the organization modelled its work on the lines of 'marriage clinics' then being set up in Scandinavian countries, the USSR and the USA.[98]

During the Second World War, British women and men were both mobilized. Yet despite the exceptional demand for their labour, women were seen as strange or temporary workers.[99] Universal pronatalism overpersonified women as potential mothers; they appeared to be constantly hovering on the edge of maternity and, as a result, production and reproduction coexisted in an uneasy relationship.[100]

During the war, the twin spectres of death and separation seem to have played havoc with people's family planning.[101] Many more babies were born to unmarried mothers: in 1938, illegitimate births made up 4.5 per cent of the total; they peaked in 1945 at 8.9 per cent. There was also a noticeable increase in the number of women seeking medical attention for sterility. In 1941, for example, fifty-seven women had sought advice at the

North Kensington birth control clinic, which responded by opening a special session for the treatment of sterility. In the following years, around one-third of the clinic's new gynaecological patients – around eighty women a year – came for advice on sterility.[102]

One reason suggested at the time for the increasing number of women seeking medical help to have a baby was that pregnancy was a convenient way of avoiding war service: the Ministry of Labour had ordered that any childless wife with no household responsibilities was liable for war work. In 1938, 393 women had sought help at the Royal Samaritan Hospital for Women in Glasgow; by 1942, the number had risen to 505. Doctors interrogated 200 patients to find out whether they genuinely wanted to have a family, or were using motherhood as a way of avoiding war work; the majority said they really wanted to become mothers.[103]

In order to achieve its new, stated aims, the FPA began to offer advice to involuntarily childless women at some of its birth control clinics. In 1942, under the rubric 'Declining population and the preservation of the race', a letter in the *British Medical Journal* described the service offered to women: a clinic doctor would ask the woman about her menstrual history, and tell her how to gauge the 'best' time to have sexual inter- course; women and their husbands who required further investigation were referred to a hospital or specialist.[104] However, in view of the patchy provision of medical services for the investigation and treatment of sterility throughout the country, the FPA considered this arrangement unsatisfac- tory. It decided to establish clinics where up-to-date methods in the investigation and treatment of sterility would be available. In April 1943, a questionnaire was circulated to all the clinics within the FPA to test the market for 'Motherhood' sessions, where a gynaecologist would carry out a thorough investigation of both wife and husband, and advise on appro- priate treatment. Twenty out of twenty-six clinics said they were keen to run a Motherhood session. Some responded to the proposal with great enthusiasm: 'I know from long clinic experience, private work, and gen- eral practice that there is a great need for such clinics.' Others were more cautious, either because they were satisfied with existing arrangements with a local hospital, or because they feared that this new venture would antagonize local medical opinion, which sometimes meant the respond- ent herself; some FPA clinic doctors saw involuntarily childless women at the local hospital or in private practice.[105]

The following month, the FPA's newly formed *ad hoc* Committee on Sub-fertility was announced in the medical press by its President, Lord Horder.[106] The Committee was made up of leading gynaecologists and medical practitioners who had a long-standing interest in problems of fertility, yet who were deemed not quite respectable by the medical establishment as represented by the Royal College of Obstetricians and

Gynaecologists.[107] Its stated purpose was to establish a medical service for the investigation and treatment of sterility which, 'by creating a demand for good thorough work, may galvanise the hospitals into more effective action, and they can act as sorting and co-ordinating centres and as sources of material for research'.[108] The plan of action included setting up a central pathology laboratory in London which, for a low or nominal fee, would carry out modern tests of fertility in men (discussed in chapter 3), and Motherhood sessions at FPA clinics. National standards of medical practice would be raised by providing training and holding annual conferences where the latest ideas on fertility and sterility could be described and a consensus on best practice agreed; in 1950, this particular aspect of the Committee's work was taken over by the newly formed Society for the Study of Fertility.

A benefactor donated sufficient money for a seminological laboratory, which opened in central London on 1 January 1945. Three weeks later, Dr Davidson, the pathologist, told the FPA's committee that his time was fully occupied. In the first year, about seventy patients attended the clinic each month for evaluation of seminal quality, a post-coital test or a testicular biopsy. In the following year, the number of patients more than doubled; some of them were referred by FPA clinics, others by hospitals or private practitioners.

Setting up the seminological laboratory proved straightforward. Competition was virtually non-existent as there was only one other private pathology laboratory in London – that of Berthold Wiesner, whose work has been described in chapter 3 – and only two hospitals had facilities for testing male fertility.[109] However, the proposal to introduce Motherhood sessions met with resistance from both general practitioners and gynaecologists, although for different stated reasons. General practitioners claimed that their role as family doctors uniquely qualified them to deal with involuntary childlessness. Most cases required little more than 'sympathetic advice about married life', which demanded their personal touch and the confidence and trust they inspired. In contrast, the FPA's clinics were cold, impersonal places; women who attended them were treated as numbers rather than individuals. And where a more thorough investigation was required, the referral system gave a general practitioner's patients access to modern gynaecological attention. Another advantage of the referral system was that it saved a gynaecologist from conveying embarrassing information to a patient he barely knew; he could pass it over to the general practitioner to deliver.[110]

This panegyric to the general practitioner – patient relationship is suprising, given how few GPs appeared to have shown any interest in sterility; indeed, many were often ignorant of how to diagnose and treat problems related to sex and fertility, as the subjects were inadequately taught in medical schools.[111] The argument is best understood as a coded defence of private general practice. For, paradoxically, despite the expansion of the National Insurance Scheme, general practitioners had become more dependent on income from private patients, a majority of whom were married women. In 1913, around 39 per cent of a general practitioner's income came from private practice; by 1936–8, it was contributing around 64 per cent.[112] With the support of the BMA, the doctors' trade union, hospitals tried to discourage the poorer sections of society, unsheltered by the Scheme, from flocking to their outpatient clinics as an alternative to consulting a general practitioner.[113] It is not suprising that the so-called problem of the inappropriate outpatient became acute during the 1930s; seeing a doctor in an outpatient clinic cost around sixpence, while a general practitioner in the late 1930s might charge between five and ten times as much for a consultation.

Examining both partners in an involuntarily childless marriage is an elaborate, time-consuming procedure, ill-suited to the National Insurance Scheme which encouraged a quick throughput of patients: a typical general practitioner consultation with a panel patient lasted perhaps five or six minutes, insufficient time for a sympathetic chat about intimate sexual matters. Sometimes a panel patient was seen by a low-paid assistant, and not by the general practitioner on whose list she or he was enrolled. The Insurance Scheme did not encourage progressive practice; as was pointed out in chapter 3, few general practitioners were equipped with a couch on which to examine a patient, and even fewer possessed a microscope. Furthermore, the Scheme stipulated that pathological tests performed at a laboratory had to be paid for out of the doctor's or patient's pocket. More often than not, treatment consisted of the ritual bottle of medicine. Looked at in this way, it is clear that the cosy relationship between a general practitioner and an involuntarily childless couple described above was confined to private practice. General practitioners went to great lengths to make life easy for private patients: they could more easily obtain a visit in their own home from the doctor; when coming to the surgery, it was common for them to be given an appointment.[114] During the interwar years, the system of referral between general practitioner and hospital specialist was established. Hospital outpatient clinics were transformed into centres of specialist practice to which patients came bearing a general practitioner's letter.[115] Yet the relationship between general practitioners and hospital consultants was not always a happy one; some general practitioners were acting as 'consultoids', refusing to refer patients to hospital, and investigating and treating them themselves. A 'consultoid', particularly in the larger northern industrial towns and in the rural areas, had an association with a local cottage hospital and private nursing home, where he could admit patients and perform minor surgery.[116]

This tendency was especially marked in obstetrics and gynaecology.

The British College of Obstetricians and Gynaecologists had been set up in 1929 in order to advance the interests of consultant obstetrician gynaecologists. One of the first tasks the College set itself was to stop 'consultoids' from stealing patients, lowering incomes and frustrating the development of proper clinical standards. It did this by developing a system of postgraduate examinations and higher medical diplomas by which obstetrician gynaecologists could prove that they had more expertise than general practitioners. The idea was to force general practitioners who lacked these qualifications to confine their practice to routine and minor conditions and send complex cases to accredited specialists. The College's ambitions proved worth fighting for; in the late 1930s, gynaecology was one of the two most lucrative fields in medicine (the other was general surgery).[117] None the less, gynaecologists had to tread carefully; they did not dare risk alienating general practitioners, upon whom they relied for referrals of patients. As a new medical institution, the College was relatively weak. It was further frustrated by legal wranglings over a large bequest left by its first President, William Blair Bell, which meant that it had to wait until 1947 before it received a Charter from the Privy Council. This meant that the College could not be given a seat on the General Medical Council or have its degrees added to the Medical Register. Indeed, that process was only completed with the passage of the Medical Act in 1950. Before then, obstetricians and gynaecologists generally had to be fellows of the Royal College of Surgeons before they could secure appointments to larger hospitals.[118]

To the College, and to GPs, the FPA's Motherhood clinics represented an unwelcome intrusion in the struggle around the referral system and competition for private patients. The FPA reassured general practitioners that it would admit to its Motherhood clinics only women whose family income was less than £5 a week, the vast majority of whom were unable to afford to consult a general practitioner.[119] However, although it promised gynaecologists that women requiring more complex interventions would be referred to them, Motherhood clinics were an embarrassment to the gynaecological establishment because they drew attention to how few hospitals had adopted a modern approach to the investigation and treatment of sterility. They threatened to undermine the strategy adopted by the College in order to clarify the referral system. As an FPA spokesperson told *Daily Mirror* readers, its decision to set up Motherhood sessions showed that 'the public are ahead of the medical profession . . . It is through public demand that this scheme is being pushed forward.'[120] Eardley Holland, then President of the College (which had received its Royal Charter in 1938), admitted that his clinic at the London Hospital was the only one in the capital dedicated to work on sterility; none the less he believed that the FPA's work was better undone than done. Holland had both political and professional ambitions: he had been involved in the investigations into maternal mortality carried out during the 1930s; he was also an active member of the Eugenics Society's Population Investigation Committee. He was aggrieved because the FPA had colonized territory he had been surveying for himself.[121] In order to appease him, the FPA said that its Motherhood clinics would serve as a stop-gap measure; they would close when sufficient hospitals were equipped with modern facilities.[122]

Childlessness was on many people's minds in 1943. In July, both Houses of Parliament debated the fall in the birth rate. The following month, the Ministry of Health convened an informal meeting on what action it should take to improve medical facilities available for the treatment of sterility.[123] At the meeting, it was agreed that the knowledge necessary to investigate and treat sterility was available in the country; the problem was that it was not properly organized. The first necessary step was to undertake a survey of hospitals to find out what skills and facilities were available, and to consider how they could be marshalled into an effective system.[124] The Ministry hoped that the survey might inspire some hospitals to set up sterility clinics. Typically loath to be associated with an intervention into women's reproductive capacity, the Ministry refused to take direct responsibility for the investigation; instead, it decided to stand by and watch developments unfold. It looked to the Royal College of Obstetricians and Gynaecologists to fund and carry out the work.[125] Holland used the occasion as an opportunity to discredit the FPA. As he put it: 'This sterility work is getting out of hand. Bodies like the FPA . . . are seeking to set up labs and clinics and to get grants in aid, and propose to make a public appeal for funds.'[126] Sterility was far too complex a medical problem to be left in the hands of non-specialists. Holland called in leading physiologists and reproductive scientists at the Medical Research Council (MRC) because, as he put it, 'allied to the MRC I feel that the hands of the College are very much strengthened as regards this work and that it is unassailable'.[127]

In December 1943 a Royal Commission on Population was set up to advise the coalition government on problems relating to the British population for consideration in planning for postwar reconstruction. It became the forum for the struggle for control over the development of sterility clinics. The College had the cards stacked in its favour. In February 1944, it had convened the first meeting of a Joint Committee on Human Fertility with the MRC.[128] The following April, this committee was appointed the Biological and Medical Sub-Committee of the Commission.[129] The influence of the FPA and the doctors active within it was limited; they were invited to submit written and oral evidence for evaluation by the 'expert' members of the Committee.[130]

The lengthy and exhaustive investigations of the Royal Commission on Population took nearly five years to complete, during which time the birth rate suffered a dramatic reversal. The 'baby boom' which began in 1944 took everyone by suprise; it undermined the credibility of depopulation Jeremiahs, some of whom were busily employed on the Commission's behalf. As pointed out in chapter 1, the victory of the Allies in war succeeded in allaying anxieties about Britain's reproductive vigour.

The Commission's deliberations on the British population coincided with the planning of and negotiations for the creation of a National Health Service. When the NHS came into existence on 5 July 1948 it made available medical care free at the point of delivery to the entire population of Britain. In many respects, women stood to gain most from this development. However, any benefit was restricted to conditions unrelated to fertility. In its report, published in June 1949, the Commission recommended that facilities for the investigation and treatment of infecundity should be a regular part of the Service. Furthermore, it proposed associating these facilities with clinics giving contraceptive advice, a duty which, in the Commission's opinion, also fell to the National Health Service. Its recommendations fell on deaf ears. Although the report received extensive coverage in the press, the only official acknowledgement it was given was on 26 July 1949 when a Member of Parliament asked the Chancellor of the Exchequer how much it would cost the taxpayer to carry out the Commission's recommendations: the answer given was between £65 million and £200 million. The Cabinet Office's file on the Royal Commission was closed in 1951.[131] Although the newly formed welfare state intervened to an unprecedented degree in people's lives, in peacetime no politician would risk sponsoring a policy relating to reproductive capacity. Postwar social reforms reinstated the belief that a married women's reproductive capacity was her husband's responsibility. Rewarded for their wartime service by free medical care, women surrendered their jobs and bodies to demobilized Man the Breadwinner, and returned to the kitchen.

5

A Crutch in the Crotch

John Williams was irremediably sterile. He and his wife had been trying to have a child for fifteen years. They had decided in favour of artificial insemination using donated semen, and against adopting a baby, because the adoption agency would tell them nothing about the child's parents, whereas with artificial insemination, Mrs Williams would be the baby's biological mother, and the doctor would satisfy them that the donor was A1. They were both overjoyed with their AID daughter, a lovely little girl, happy and healthy in every way. Writing in the late 1940s, Mr Williams felt that public expressions of disgust for AID were misguided; it should be up to individual couples to decide how to overcome their involuntary childlessness.[1]

Mr and Mrs Franklin first consulted their general practitioner about their involuntary childlessness in 1960. He referred them to an infertility clinic at a London National Health Service hospital, where both were examined by a doctor. Mrs Franklin was given several courses of tablets, and underwent a 'scrape'. When these proved ineffective, the clinic seemed unable to suggest anything else. A friend had recommended a private Harley Street doctor who turned out to be an immensely sympathetic and reassuring man. A further series of tests, tablets, discussions and an X-ray did the trick, and within two months, Mrs Franklin was pregnant. Indeed, Mr Franklin was writing to The Guardian *while his wife was in hospital awaiting the birth of their third child. The cost of her infertility treatment varied from five to 15 guineas a child.[2]*

In 1960, fifteen years after the Second World War had ended, the contraceptive pill was undergoing its first large-scale clinical trial in Britain. The introduction of 'the pill' was the first of several developments which, over the next fifteen years, transformed beyond recognition the disposition of medical services for, and technology of, birth control. Given the long-standing legal restrictions and moral prohibitions on interfering in the processes of conception and pregnancy, the transformation is a remarkable one. For by the end of the decade, in Britain, the law on abortion had been made more liberal and both married and unmarried women had legal access to, and were publicly encouraged to ask their doctors for, 'scientific' methods of contraception: the pill and the intrauterine device (IUD). In 1974, the competence of the National Health Service was extended to include the provision of advice on, and the dispensing of, contraceptive technology. Yet throughout this period the investigation and treatment of infertility remained a hole-and-corner affair, infrequently and reluctantly exposed in public, and poorly served by the National Health Service.

Why were infertile women and their husbands neglected by social policy and medicine? Several factors conspired in the development of this tendency. One was the reluctance of the British government to sponsor interventions into the reproductive capacity of its citizens. Only wartime conditions and a coalition government had made it seem safe for the state to acknowledge the predicament of involuntarily childless women and men; even then, as was pointed out in chapter 4, the government used the tactics of postponement and depoliticization in the shape of the Royal Commission on Population. By the time the Commission's report was published in 1949, one-party government had replaced the wartime coalition, and its recommendations were ignored.

No doubt exposure of the Nazis' barbaric racial and eugenic policies through the testimony of witnesses at the Nuremberg trials encouraged the government to shelve the Commission's report. National Socialists had made state-sponsored medical intervention into a population's reproductive capacity a hallmark of a totalitarian dicatatorship. Yet, as mentioned in chapter 1, shortly after the war ended, prophets of doom in the USA began to presage war, famine, epidemics and communist revolutions as a result of the high birth rate and pressure of population in both industrialized and non-industrialized nations. These warnings of a global population explosion won many influential disciples, including powerful politicians. According to the Jeremiahs of overpopulation, the future security of the world depended on women being persuaded to have fewer, or, better still, no children. As it gained ascendancy during the 1950s, antinatalism escaped association with the coercive policies around reproductive capacity pursued by the Nazis, by redeploying in its favour the progressive tendencies that had been synthesized in the paradox of reactionary modernism. As explained in chapter 4, this admixture of regressive and progressive ideas had been prevalent in all industrialized nations and had reached an apotheosis in the hands of the Nazis, who took reactionary modernism to extremes by simultaneously looking backwards into a barbaric dystopia and forwards into a technological utopia. Antinatalism captured and monopolized the utopian aspects, attaching them to medical procedures used by women to control their fertility. At the same time, pronatalist medical interventions were charged with dystopic tendencies. In effect, pro- and antinatalism became 'contrast concepts', deriving meaning and significance from their mutual difference. This relationship permitted antinatalism to feed parasitically on pronatalism; it drew off any positive associations from policies and medical procedures that assisted women to have children, and re-assembled them in representations that discouraged sympathy and support for the involuntarily childless.[3] The overriding concern was how to prevent women from having children and it became virtually impossible to recruit sympathizers of, and resources for, an assault on the problem of involuntary childlessness. Infertile women were abandoned in a mad rush to shackle the reproductive capacity of their fertile sisters.[4]

No doubt beliefs about what is wrong with the rate of increase of the population inform the way in which infertility is considered in public. However, the attachment of negative connotations to infertility was facilitated by the tendency of involuntary childlessness to become associated with other complex issues that act as a focus for wider social anxieties. The history of artificial insemination using donated semen (AID) provides several cases in point.

In the late 1930s a handful of doctors began to arrange AID as a way of overcoming involuntary childlessness caused by the irremediable sterility or sexual impotence of the husband. AID looks like another expression of the tendency in medicine to focus attention on the wife in an infertile marriage. Although in theory it exposes the vulnerablity of men's fertility, in practice it is protective of men; an obsession with secrecy has allowed men's susceptibility to sterility and sexual impotence to remain concealed.

It would be unreasonable to lay all the blame for the obsession with secrecy on doctors and patients; for each time the practice of AID has been acknowledged in public, it has been accompanied by loud expressions of disgust which must discourage any further disclosure. At the same time, it is not surprising that AID troubles so many people (including, it must be said, many involuntarily childless women, their husbands and their doctors), for it engages with the inconsistent and unsettled relationship of biological fatherhood, social fatherhood, and the legal status of marriage and paternity.[5] In many people's minds, particularly if they are prey to reactionary tendencies, the essential basis of civilization depends on a particular, fixed configuration of these elements, in which a man marries a woman and is biological, social and legal father to her children. Unfortunately for them, the configuration is far from robust; the elements are locked into a never-ending game of musical chairs, and the participants insist on bending the rules and refuse to accept the referees' decisions as binding.

The reasons why insemination using husband's (AIH) or donated (AID) semen was dubbed 'artificial' is because a syringe is used as a substitute for marital heterosexual intercourse. Marital heterosexual intercourse is not merely 'natural'; it has been endowed with the power to bind together husband, wife and children and to imbue their family home with a moral essence which is conducive to the development of clean-living and responsible young citizens. This influence cannot be counterfeited by a syringe. As one doctor put it: 'An Englishman's home is his castle, and each home forms a unit which makes up the nation; but the children thus produced would have no home in the present sense of the word, since they would never know, and feel the influence of their father.'[6] Conception through a materialist intervention like AID is a denial of the importance of spirituality in both conception and upbringing of a child. Children conceived as a result of a syringe are brought up to respect the values and ethics of a cold, inert, glass test tube.

Another advantage of marital heterosexual intercourse is that it can cushion men's anxieties about being cuckolded by their wives; it encourages them in the belief that they are the biological fathers of their wives' children. In the early days of AID, some doctors mixed donated semen with that of the husband on the grounds that introducing an element of uncertainty, however remote, would be of great psychological help to the husband during the child's upbringing.[7] This deceit is suggestive of the investment that supports the ideological sway of biological fatherhood. From the children's point of view, the legal fiction that, within marriage, their mother's husband is their biological father had been maintained for good reason: to protect them from being bastardized, and suffering the stigma of illegitmacy. However, the fiction was meant to protect only those children conceived as a result of their mothers' adultery; children conceived by AID with a husband's consent stood accused of taking unfair advantage of it. They were – and still are – registered on a birth certificate as if they were the progeny of their mothers' husbands, although both husband and wife know this not to be the case. According to the Registrar General, the purpose of birth registration is to provide evidence of descent, legitimacy and nationality.[8] For AID babies, registering the husband as biological father was illegal; both he and his wife thereby infringed the Perjury Act 1911 and were liable to a fine of £50 on summary conviction or seven years' penal servitude if convicted on indictment. Furthermore, concealment of illegitimacy operated as a fraud on the Inland Revenue; a higher duty was payable on the succession of an illegitimate than of a legitimate child.[9]

During the 1940s, a handful of enthusiasts defended AID the grounds that it is a therapeutic intervention which sustains the life of individual marriages; AID children are planned children, and their presence brings much happiness into their family home. They conceded that AID involves sinning – masturbation by the semen donor and perhaps adultery – but maintained that it is certainly not a crime. Indeed, it enables wives and husbands to be good citizens, and make a much-needed contribution to the wider society. They represented women as neither physiologically nor psychologically complete until they have borne children; according to enthusiasts of AID, frustration of maternal desire is both an individual and a racial tragedy. Opponents of AID judged too high the price of mother-hood paid by society in this instance: by countenancing the divorce of sex and reproduction, involuntarily childless women and men were permit-ting the evil of materialism to gain a foothold in the institutions of marriage and the family. For them, AID is both a sin and a crime. In many respects, this response is understandable, for as well as lending itself to overcoming the problems of male sterility and sexual impotence, AID has a tendency to keep controversial company.

During the interwar period, AID was taken up by devotees of positive eugenics who accused romantic marriage and monogamy of exercising a deleterious influence on public health. A direct consequence of Cupid's haphazard arrows was the degradation of the quality of the nation's genes; each year, thousands of mentally and physically defective babies were born. In 1935 Herbert Brewer, a fellow of the Eugenics Society, published an article in the *Eugenics Review* in which he described a scheme of evolutionary improvement called 'eutelegenesis', in which Cupid is made redundant and replaced by a scientific system through which men and women of 'superior' genetic endowment are matched in order to create superior progeny who will go on to enhance the quality of the genes of subsequent generations; insemination would be effected by a syringe.[10] Brewer was forced to concede that only a minority of the British people were sufficiently intellectually advanced to understand the advantages of disconnecting love, sex and marriage. While waiting for the population's rationality to evolve, he proposed testing his idea experimentally, recruit-ing as research subjects involuntarily childless women, on the grounds that, as Galton had argued, sterility was associated with the most civilized sections of society who possessed above-average intellectual abilities, and who could therefore appreciate the wisdom of his scheme.[11]

No doubt the doctors who arranged AID were aware of the rhetoric of positive eugenics. The criteria they used to select donors are suggestive of a belief in the inheritability of intelligence and personality traits. Mary Barton, her husband Berthold Wiesner and Kenneth Walker, for example, who in 1945 published the first account of British clinical experience with AID in the *British Medical Journal*, recruited as donors men of intellectual attainments whose family history over at least two generations demonstrated evidence of both intelligence and the capacity for social adjustment. Donors were married men who had each sired at least two legitimate children, which was taken as evidence of a genetic predisposition to a strong family desire and a healthy parental instinct. Furthermore, being married would protect donors from developing an addiction to self-abuse.[12] However, a crucial difference between enthusiasts of positive eugenics and the doctors who arranged AID is that the former advocated it as a means of divorcing reproduction from marriage, a development which was central to the realization of their utopia of genetic excellence; the latter exploited AID in order to assist in the creation of a traditional – albeit sham – patriarchal family unit. Indeed, Barton, Wiesner and Walker were firm supporters of monogamous marriage and planned families. They were active members of the British Social Hygiene Council (BSHC), which in May 1937 transformed its Marriage Committee into the Marriage Guidance Council.[13] They repeatedly assured their critics that only women married to sterile or impotent men were inseminated with donated semen.

It is possible that the opponents of AID might have felt less strongly against the technique if they had not first become aware of its use in humans towards the end of the Second World War when it looked as though the Nazis and atomic scientists had realized some of their most dreadful fantasies. AID registered as further evidence that materialism was taking advantage of men's absence from their homes; while British troops were laying down their lives on a foreign battlefield in defence of their country's values and traditions, it was taking root in cracks and crevices in their homes created by the upheavals of war. Their outrage was fuelled by a technique which looked like a cynical corruption of the family, an institution which sustained religious sentiments and which was meant to serve as a defence against materialism, not provide a site of its encouragement.

The AID scandal persisted throughout demobilization, as Man the Breadwinner sought to regain his place as head of the traditional patriarchal family. Some politicians were rumoured to be incorporating a strategic deployment of AID into postwar reconstruction plans. In October 1945, the *Sunday Despatch* announced:

> A super race of test-tube babies will become the guardians of atom-bomb secrets if a proposal presented today to President Truman [by the Military

Affairs Committee of the House of Representatives] is passed into law. Fathers will be chosen by eugenic experts of the United Nations. The mothers will be hand-picked on their health and beauty records, family background and their achievements in school and university. The idea is to get the best possible brains in the world controlling future atomic power.[14]

British politicians were said to be contemplating similar proposals: during and immediately following the war, the Eugenics Society was approached by various individuals seeking its support and lobbying expertise for wild schemes which combined reconstruction with positive eugenics, AID, and solutions to involuntary childlessness.[15]

It proved an unfortunate coincidence that in Britain, artificial insemination was introduced into farming and medicine at around the same time. In 1941, as part of the wartime effort to increase the output of food, the Ministry of Agriculture set up a scheme bringing semen from superior bulls within the reach of most farmers.[16] At the time, around one in four cows in the nation's herd was being culled because she apppeared to be sterile; wartime research demonstrated that, in a majority of cases, the cause of her failure to conceive was 'inefficiency due to the bull'.[17] People who believed that the war was being fought in defence of the home counties were offended by the introduction of AI into farming. To them, it looked as if John Bull, prototypical British farmer, gorged on beef and good beer, was being led astray by materialist reproductive science. AI was included in postwar schemes for the reconstruction of the agricultural industry in Britain and the occupied countries of Europe. To its opponents, the use of AID in involuntarily childless women represented a first step on the road to human stud farming and state registration of semen donors.

In the moral panic that surrounded AID during the 1940s, means and ends became confused with each other and formed the centre of a maelstrom which drew in other dystopic evocations. AID was declared an illegal, immoral and disgusting practice, which contravened the sanctity of marriage, made redundant heterosexual intercourse and was tantamount to adultery; it put donors at risk of developing an addiction to masturbation; and it created secret bastards who threatened the legal institutions of marriage, legitimacy and paternity.[18] The technique encouraged a pagan way of life, because it introduced the corrupting influence of materialism into matrimony, and reduced humans to the status of cattle.

What sort of people would participate in such an outrageous practice? Surely only degenerates and criminals. The disgust inspired by a technique in which a syringe replaces marital heterosexual intercourse was projected on to the participants.[19] Doctors who arranged AID were accused of being ethically rootless, neglecting their duty to attend to their patients' morality;[20] indeed, they were guilty of making medicine the servant of hedonism;[21] their arrogance was dreadfully suggestive of quackery;[22] they were little more than cattle breeders, and their veterinary approach to medicine was discrediting its humanitarian traditions;[23] clearly, they evinced no respect for the law, and were prepared to be accessories to a pseudo-adulterous practice;[24] and because the child was illegally registered as that of the husband, they were willing parties to a misdemeanour.[25] Donors were described as depraved men who happily submit to self-abuse, a moral offence whatever the objective;[26] the corrupting influence of masturbation was evident in their willingness to hawk their seminal fluid round the country, and offer it to the highest bidder;[27] a victim of perverted philoprogenitive cravings, the donor's vainglory is to father 400 children a week;[28] only an irresponsible man would in cold blood consent to take part in the procreation of children in whose up-bringing he would have no part;[29] these men were little more than stallions. Even the wives of donors had insults heaped on them; they were said to be as depraved as their husbands because they did not object to them acting as sire to an indefinite number of babies.[30] The morals and emotional stability of a woman who agreed to be impregnated with the semen of an unknown donor were impugned, for any normal woman would feel it violated something sacrosanct between her and her husband.[31] Only victims of a perversion are prepared to conceive without sexual congress;[32] no doubt, these women suffered from a neurotic child-fixation, for a healthy maternal instinct would be satisfied by adoption of a suitable child.[33] The husband was the only participant whose reputation was not disparaged, perhaps because he was deemed beneath contempt; not only was he irremediably sterile or sexually impotent, his character was further diminished by his willingness to accept the debased currency of social fatherhood as grounds for paternity.

Peers in the House of Lords were especially anxious that their un-scrupulous relatives might resort to AID in order to defeat legitimate claims to titles and estates. The government stubbornly refused to appoint a Royal Commission which might clarify the uncertain legal position of AID; instead, it referred the problem for consideration by the Royal Commission on Population.[34] Dismayed by the government's inaction, both the Public Morality Council and the Archibishop of Canterbury appointed commissions which explored the morality of AID. The evidence con-firmed AID as a damnable technique and there were loud calls for leg-islation which would make it a criminal offence (the Pope had banned it in 1897).[35] The Eugenics Society disagreed; it held that while the prac-tice should not outrun prevailing laws and sentiments, it should not be legally prohibited.[36] The Lord Chancellor was inclined to think it would be unwise to prohibit AID entirely, on the grounds that greater evils might result from it being driven underground.[37] The members of the Executive Committee of the Royal College of Obstetricians and Gynaecologists concurred, stating that 'as citizens and doctors they disapprove of this practice'; however, they refused to make a public pronouncement to that effect, on the grounds that the technique raised moral and not medical issues.[38] The College's disapproval was more than an expression of the reactionary tendencies dominant within that branch of medicine; the adverse publicity given to AID allowed the College to pursue an advantage over its intra-professional rivals.

The doctors who offered AID were general practitioner specialists who, as pointed out in the previous chapter, stood in the way of the ambitions of obstetrician gynaecologists, whose interests were pursued by the Royal College of Obstetricians and Gynaecologists. General practitioner specialists also worked in some of the FPA's clinics, including the Motherhood sessions, and AID threatened to besmirch that organization's reputation. Prominent among their number were woman doctors such as Margaret Jackson, a key figure in the FPA, one of the four authors of the textbook *Problems of fertility in general practice* and an expert on male sterility, who had begun to offer AID in 1940 (and continued to do so until 1982).[39] The FPA sought to distance itself from AID; a spokesperson told readers of the *Daily Mail* of 2 April 1945 that 'it is unfortunate that the Association should have become linked with such a controversial subject, simply bristling with legal and psychological difficulties'.[40] The politics of and rivalries within gynaecology conspired to banish to the outer fringes of the medical establishment any doctor who offered AID.

In 1948, Margaret Jackson confessed to the Commission on AID appointed by the Archbishop of Canterbury that she had assisted in the conception of seventeen babies.[41] Mary Barton admitted to having been responsible for the conception of about 300 babies.[42] In 1958, the AID Investigation Committee, which was set up under the auspices of the Eugenics Society and collected evidence from virtually all the British doctors then offering donated semen, estimated that over the past decade, about 100 AID babies had been born every year (during the 1950s, around 700,000 babies were born every year in England and Wales).[43] Two years later, the Report of the official Departmental Committee on Human Artificial Insemination chaired by Lord Feversham claimed that 1,150 children conceived through AID were living in the United Kingdom.[44] None the less, in a moral panic statistics fall victim to gross exaggeration; in an article titled, 'Fathers Anonymous', published in 1958 in the *News Chronicle and Daily Dispatch*, it was stated that there were some 10,000 couples living in Britain with AID babies.[45] An official estimate of the number of potential candidates for AID put the annual total at around 10,000 each year.[46] In 1948, four or five doctors admitted to offering AID;[47] ten years later, their ranks had swollen to just under twenty.[48] (In 1959, there were around 38,250 doctors working for the NHS in England and Wales.[49]) Yet despite the tiny number of people actually involved in the practice, the controversy over AID rumbled on, flaring up in response to other related moral panics.

It proved much easier to convince people that AID is a sin than to have it made into a crime. In 1944, the Medical Defence Union, the organization which insures doctors against malpractice suits, produced consent forms for husband and wife to sign before undergoing AID; they were asked to promise that 'the birth of such a child will not defeat the claims of any person to any titles, estates, interests or funds'.[50] However, the form contains assurances that could never be properly given or accepted.[51] There was a general reluctance in government circles to clarify the legal status of AID. In the immediate postwar years, concern focused more strongly on how to re-establish family ties than on a search for additional reasons to break them. The 1949 Law Reform (Miscellaneous Provisions) Act, for example, placed the heavy burden of proof on a man who suspected that he was not the biological father of his wife's child. It was left to case law to decide on legal questions relating to AID. Each time a judge pronounced on the uncertain relationship between biological and social fatherhood, paternity and marriage, the occasion was seized on by the opponents of AID as an opportunity to voice their disgust. Paradoxically, each time the spotlight of publicity fell on AID, practitioners reported that the field of applicants was enlarged.

Although, ostensibly, the arguments rehearsed for and against AID remained largely unchanged during the 1950s, they took on an additional gloss that reflected contemporary anxieties about male sexuality and its apparent susceptibility to sexual pathology. Women's behaviour aroused little concern. After the war, as Denise Riley has persuasively argued, women became fixed and frozen as mothers, and nothing other than mothers.[52] A woman's place was within the home, and her life's work was to keep house and care for her husband and children. Her husband was made responsible for the satisfaction of her sexual needs, and, if he acquitted himself well, she would be content and contained within the domestic sphere. Few doubted that motherhood was central to a woman's well-being, and this consensus helped to dampen fantasies about her motives in submitting to AID. In 1958, a reporter at the *Daily Sketch* described her encounter with an AID mother as follows: 'Mrs X is forty, but she looks younger. There is a kind of softness about her . . . so much so that I had to tell her. "It wasn't there before the baby", she said. "I was a different woman. Hard, selfish, a nagger. In fact, I'm sure some of the neighbours disliked me." '[53]

In contrast, modern man seemed prey to fecklessness, bad habits and psychological instability. Many men were incapable of fulfilling their duties as husband and father for reasons other than irremediable sterility and sexual impotence. Alongside the paragon husband, family man, content with house and garden, who dutifully satisfied his wife's sexual needs, coexisted several contradictory faces of masculinity. Among them, Lynne Segal has identified the old wartime hero, who puts 'freedom' before family and loved ones, and the absent father, who stands for law and order.[54] At the same time, the heroes of contemporary books and films were asserting a particularly pugnacious manliness and aggressiveness, an aspect of which was contempt for women. And to add injury to insult, it looked as though many men were too immature to sustain a heterosexual marital relationship; they were either purchasing sexual favours from prostitutes or engaging in homosexual activities (according to contemporary sexologists, 'normal' men grow out of both tendencies). Indeed, both prostitution and male homosexuality appeared to have reached alarming proportions: the annual average number of street offences rose from 2,000 in the early years of the war to over 10,000 by 1952, and to almost 12,000 by 1955; the number of indictable male homosexual offences increased five-fold in the same period.[55] Traditional prejudice against male homosexuality was exacerbated during the cold war climate of the 1950s, when a series of spy scandals seemed to suggest that homosexual men tended to commit treasonable acts; they were the 'enemy within'.[56]

The Feversham Committee, appointed in 1958 by the government in order to investigate whether any change in the law in relation to AID was necessary or desirable, articulated these contemporary anxieties about masculinity. The need for clarification of the legal status of AID had been brought sharply into focus when, contrary to the recommendations of the Royal Commission on Marriage and Divorce (1956), a Scottish judge decided that AID did not constitute adultery, and denied a husband a divorce on those grounds. The public outrage that followed his decision demonstrated that AID had won few friends; in the eyes of a majority of the population, it was still both a sin and a crime. If anything, the climate of the 1950s and the emphasis on achieving sexual satisfaction within marriage made marital heterosexual intercourse more precious and a willingness to intervene in it, on any grounds, more outrageous. The Feversham Committee noted that some doctors believed that sexual impotence in a man was a contraindication for both AIH and AID, as no doubt his marriage must be an unhappy one, and children should not be introduced into it by a syringe.[57] Once again the Archbishop of Canterbury, Dr Fisher, urged the government to introduce legislation that would make arranging AID a punishable offence. In February 1958 the

News Chronicle published two articles on AID; nine out of every ten letters written in response to them condemned the technique. That same month, the BBC acknowledged that many people found the subject deeply offensive, and before *The unknown seed,* a programme on AID, broadcast a warning advising such listeners to turn their radio sets off until the next programme was scheduled to begin.[58]

The title *The unknown seed* referred to the subject of a new moral panic which was drawn into the controversy over AID: mutant genes. The insistence on secrecy, it was claimed, put sons and daughters conceived through donated semen at risk of contracting an unwittingly incestuous marriage, and producing mutant children. A semen donor could father several thousand children whom he might never see, and who would never know the true identity of their 'real' father. No doubt the flames of moral panic in the 1950s were fanned by revelations of unsuspected genetic effects on the Japanese inhabitants of Hiroshima and Nagasaki of the explosions of atomic bombs on those cities, and of the risks of medical and other radiological procedures. Experiments on fruit flies suggested that radiation could cause widespread mutation in the human race. At the time, the controversial American scientist Herman Muller was also declaiming on the dangers of cold-blooded use of genetic manipulation in order to create a race of supermen.[59] In order to allay the public's anxieties, the statistical possibility of unwitting incest occurring as a result of AID was calculated: it worked out at around one marriage in every hundred years.[60]

The relationship between sin and crime was a topical question during the 1950s. Indeed, the Feversham Committee was one of several official investigative bodies appointed in order to reconcile tensions arising out of existing public mechanisms of regulating sex, marriage and the family, and private behaviour. The Royal Commission on Marriage and Divorce had been appointed in 1951, with instructions to investigate demands for reform of the divorce law.[61] Published in 1956, its report saw no reason for modifying the law, with few exceptions, one of which was to make AID without the husband's consent grounds for divorce (a conclusion which the Scottish judge overturned two years later). However, subsequent official investigations into the regulation of sexuality and marriage concluded that in many instances the law was outmoded. The following year saw the publication of the report of the Wolfenden Committee on prostitution and male homosexuality. Although it acknowledged and regretted the general loosening of what its members saw as men's former high moral standards, and deplored the damage men's immaturity was inflicting on the family, it recommended decriminalizing homosexual relations between adults in private on the grounds that there are areas of life that are no concern of the criminal law. Homosexuality might be a sin but it should cease to be a crime. This crucial distinction between public and private concerns, and between sin and crime, informed the deliberations of the Feversham Committee. For although a majority of its members wanted AID to be discouraged because they considered it ethically suspect, they were forced to recognize that making it illegal would deprive a married couple of a right to conceive a child in this way, and would strike at the liberty of the citizen. The Committee recommended that AID between consenting adults should not be prohibited.

The prospect of arranging AID being made into a punishable offence had been resisted by doctors, on the grounds that, as with termination of pregnancy, it would force the practice underground. Yet most doctors believed that AID was a sin. A meeting of the BMA Council convened in May 1959 to formulate the Association's submission to the Feversham Committee concluded that arranging AID did not appear to contravene any of the accepted principles of scientific medicine; none the less, it acknowledged the existence of a substantial body of opinion in the profession which regarded the practice as an undesirable one, and many doctors were absolutely opposed to it on moral and religious grounds.[62] Not one member of the Council of the Royal College of Obstetricians and Gynaecologists had arranged, or believed himself ever likely to arrange, AID. The College considered the procedure undesirable on ethical grounds, and not proper to be undertaken by a medical practitioner. This was the opposite conclusion to that reached by the Feversham Committee, which said that where AID is arranged by someone without a medical qualification, that person should be prosecuted.[63] The FPA was not prepared to pronounce on the matter officially. However, its philosophy was the promotion of married happiness, for which it considered children to be crucial. Although its doctors were told not to introduce the subject, if asked for information about AID by a patient they should give her the name of a reputable doctor.[64]

In 1948, at a meeting of the Guild of St Luke, St Cosmas and St Damian, sixty Roman Catholic doctors unanimously rejected co-operation with the National Health Service because they believed that the state would encourage and sponsor practices related to fertility and sterility that offended their consciences.[65] They had little to fear in relation to AID; ten years later, a survey carried out on behalf of the Feversham Committee revealed that the National Health Service was an AID-free institution.[66] Indeed, one of the Committee's recommendations was that AID should not be made available under the National Health Service because to do so would indicate a measure of official approval and enable it to be carried out at public expense. While the public/private distinction provided a loophole which enabled doctors to continue to arrange AID, it restricted access to women who could afford the fee, which put it out of reach of many people. In the late 1950s, the average fee charged in London by a private doctor was about fifty guineas for six months' treatment; the range was fifteen to 125 guineas.[67] In a newspaper article entitled 'My wife is having a test tube baby', an AID mother described the financial hardship she had endured: 'We managed to rake up the fifty guineas fee, goodness knows how – the scrimping and saving we did was unbelievable, but the cheque went off on the due date . . . if I can rake up the money, I'll do exactly the same thing all over again as soon as possible.'[68]

What is remarkable is that while in public doctors were claiming the moral high ground above their colleagues who arranged AID, in private they described investigation and treatment of involuntary childlessness as a 'crutch in the crotch'.[69] In 1952, Bernard Sandler, Medical Officer at the Infertility Clinic, Manchester Victoria Memorial Jewish Hospital, counselled doctors who found themselves experiencing 'mental blushes' that they were not fitted for this sort of work.[70] Indeed, looked at in relation to the procedures used routinely in the investigation and treatment of infertility in the postwar years, AIH and AID are manifestations of a medical obsession with investigating the adequacy of insemination and manipulating it in order to facilitate the passage of sperms into a woman's reproductive tract. This obsession contributed to the tendencies responsible for the relegation of services for the involuntarily childless to the outer fringes of the National Health Service.

Science had little to offer doctors obsessed with insemination. The research programme embarked upon shortly before the war by workers in several countries, spurred on no doubt by a mixture of pronatalism and new approaches to animal husbandry, and in which every aspect of semen was subjected to ingenious investigations, seems to have added to the confusion over what constitutes a fertile man. In 1954 Thaddeus Mann of Cambridge University published an exhaustive review of the research in which he cited nearly 2,400 publications (the book had to be updated a decade later in order to take account of the volume of work in the field). Yet as a paper on the diagnosis of male infertility published in *Fertility and Sterility* in 1956 revealed, clinicians were uncertain how to incorporate this research into their everyday practice.[71]

Scientific investigations seem to have exacerbated controversy over the parameters of male fertility rather than, as might be expected, promoting standardization. In part, contemporary anxieties about men were responsible for this paradox. For centuries, sperm and egg have stood for miniaturized man and woman; social sex has been projected downwards on to biological sex, even to the level of the microscope.[72] In effect, fitness of sperm is judged according to the same criteria as those used to assess manliness. In *Adam's rib*, first published in 1948, Ruth Herschberger poked fun at the way in which doctors in the interwar years doggedly perpetuated what she called the 'manly illusion' by insisting that sperm are independent, single-minded creatures, full of charm, resourcefulness and enterprise.[73] During this period, the standard of manliness, especially in Britain, was taken for granted. Although four parameters of seminal quality – volume of semen, sperm numbers, morphology and motility – had been delineated, in practice most doctors and pathologists assessed male fertility according to whether, in their eyes, sperms looked sufficiently 'manly'; test results were reported as 'satisfactory' or 'within normal limits'.[74] However, during the 1950s the emergence of several competing representations of modern man coincided with a proliferation of 'manly illusions', each one vying for the right to serve as the standard on which judgements of fitness for purpose of sperm were based.

In the mid-1950s, the minimum numbers of sperm deemed necessary for fertility had not been settled; some doctors maintained it was 60 million per ml, others 20 million per ml. A quarter of a century later, the significance of sperm numbers was still the subject of disagreement, which was exacerbated by the discovery that about one in five men undergoing a vasectomy, and hence presumably fertile, had a count of 20 million per ml or less. One response to this finding was the lowering of the threshold of male fertility to 5 million sperm per ml, which meant that very few men could be deemed infertile.[75] Test results were delivered as if fertility in men were a matter of luck; as one woman put it: 'They didn't say it's totally impossible because everybody knows of men with low fertility who get their women pregnant. They just said our chances were so remote that it wasn't worth holding out any hope.[76] Representing male fertility as a matter of luck was an attitude derived from animal husbandry, where little time was wasted on laboratory criteria of seminal adequacy. Instead, fertility was measured by the 'conception rate'. At AI centres, inseminated cows not 'returned' by the farmers for re-insemination within three months were presumed to have conceived, and the proportion of presumed pregnancies expressed as the percentage of the total of the first inseminations was referred to as the conception rate. A bull which failed to turn up trumps would be sent to the abattoir.

Whichever cut-off point they considered appropriate in their practice, doctors strove to raise a low sperm count above it. They were ineluctably drawn to the idea that numbers are crucial to fertility: more must be better. Treatment proceeded as if the testicles were refractory; sticks and carrots were used to encourage spermatogenesis. In the early 1950s the 'testosterone rebound' treatment gained popularity. Although testosterone, the male sex hormone, inhibits spermatogenesis (some sceptical doctors claimed permanently) after cessation of therapy, the process was said to experience a 'kick start' which made the sperm count rise, albeit temporarily, above its original level. Testosterone was purported to act as a stimulant which enables the husband to produce the best ejaculate of which he is capable.[77] Another tactic seems to have been based on the old idea that frequent sexual intercourse exhausts reserves of sperms. A man with a low sperm count was advised to submit to a period of prolonged sexual abstinence, and to break it at the moment during the menstrual cycle when his wife was presumed fertile. Paradoxically, some doctors recommended that during the woman's presumed fertile period husband and wife have sexual intercourse every six hours in order to concentrate numbers of sperm around the cervix. Another technique employed to increase sperm numbers was cooling the testicles. Doctors advised men to wear loose-legged cotton underpants ('boxer shorts') and to bathe their testes at least once, and preferably twice a day for five minutes with cold water.[78] This treatment was derived from the observation that the temperature of the scrotum is lower than that of the body, from which it was assumed that temperature influences spermatogenesis. This was confirmed by an investigation which found that rams which were fitted with scrotal supports which held the testes close to the body, and hence kept them warm, became subfertile within two weeks.[79]

Until the 1950s, men with large numbers of irregularly shaped sperm were discouraged from having children on the grounds that they might produce a malformed child or one deficient in some way which would put their wife at risk of miscarriage.[80] Although developments in genetics discredited this belief, sperm morphology was retained as an indicator of fertility on the grounds that a sperm with a misshapen head is unable to penetrate the cervical mucus, and therefore cannot reach its destination within the woman's reproductive tract. However, there was little agreement over which shape of head immobilizes sperm in cervical mucus; evaluations of sperm morphology are notoriously subjective, and up to seventy 'deviations' have been described.[81] Indeed, despite the diagrammatic representations of healthy and pathological sperm produced by Moench (described in chapter 3), sperm morphology seems to have been a case of beauty being in the eye of the beholder; each investigator had his or her own concept of what an 'ideal' sperm looked like and what was 'untypical'. In 1966, the Population Council funded an attempt to establish a consensus on sperm morphology. Freund, a scientist working in New York, sent microphotographs of 500 sperm to forty-seven experts in eleven countries who, he considered, represented a substantial proportion of active workers in the field; he received widely differing opinions on half of the sample.[82]

Experts began to claim that morphology is related to motility. Everyone agreed that immotile sperm are infertile; the threshold of fertility was said to be a minimum of 40 per cent of motile sperm. However, in response to the proliferation of representations of manliness, the consensus on the significance of activity began to break down around the question of what sort of movement is necessary for conception. The answer depended on which version of the story of how and when sperm arrive in the uterus a doctor believed. In the 1950s, some research workers began to reject as infertile sperm that move their tail from side to side, or swim in a circle, and to approve only those which exhibit movement which looks purposeful, an activity they called 'forward progression at a reasonable speed'. According to this narrative, sperm propel themselves into the woman's uterus. Yet not everyone was convinced. Dissenters cast women in a more active role and proposed that passive wriggling sperm are drawn into the uterus by one of the following methods: vigorous contractions of the vaginal wall; a mechanical system of negative pressure in the woman's pelvis in relation to her vagina which creates a sucking effect; or the quality and texture of the cervical mucus.[83]

Some people believed that the controversy over the criteria of male fertility would be settled if subjective, visual judgements of sperm were replaced by rigorous, scientific methods. They were encouraged by the demand for objective tests of the effectiveness of spermicidal preparations.[84] Sperm numbers were estimated using the counting chamber of a haemocytometer (an instrument used in counting blood cells), but these were found to be unreliable; considerable variation was found between the results obtained by different technicians using the same seminal sample. In the early 1960s, electronic particle-size analysers, or Coulter counters, were introduced, but even this more sophisticated technology failed to establish agreement on a cut-off point of sperm numbers necessary for fertility.[85]

In view of the medical obsession with getting sperm to their destination within a woman's reproductive tract, it is not surprising that the development of objective tests of sperm activity received a disproportionate amount of attention. Ways of distinguishing live from dead sperm were devised, which included 'live–dead' staining methods; fluoresence microscopy; and the so-called 'filtration method', based on the observation that living and dead sperm behave differently towards a glass surface, in that dead cells adhere to small glass balls, but live cells do not. Individual live sperm were subjected to exacting tests of performance: direct observation of travel across a microscopic field; cinematographic recording of sperm velocity; scanning with a television camera; counting of free-swimming sperm passing in a given time through a segment of a plane, or passing out of the seminal fluid through a tiny hole in a wire screen into a sperm-free sample of seminal plasma; a stationary photomultiplier was used to view a restricted portion of a microscopic field with the sperm rendered bright by fluorescent staining and ultraviolet illumination.[86] In addition, numerous tests of the physical, chemical and metabolic properties of sperm and seminal fluid were devised.[87]

Many of the sophisticated tests of sperm motility were developed using semen from non-human animals, especially bulls. However, as one American doctor put it: 'Clinical proof of sterility in the human male is not as easily demonstrated as it is in the bull.'[88] In practice, the low priority given to infertility by the National Health Service meant that few hospital pathology laboratories were organized to provide effective semen analysis, and few technicians were competent in the evaluation of semen according to the accepted basic parameters.[89] The FPA doggedly tried to raise standards of seminal analysis within the National Health Service, for example by introducing courses in semen analysis for technicians.[90] Steady demand at its seminological centre in London made this a consistently profitable venture. Some patients had to travel a long distance in order to undergo a semen test in which they could have confidence, and a room was set aside on the premises where men could produce a semen sample. In the 1960s, about half of the 1,200 men tested by the FPA each year were referred by a general practitioner, one in five of them by a National Health Service hospital.[91]

Unable to draw firm conclusions from routine semen analysis, some doctors turned their attention to an evaluation of 'cervical insemination' using the post-coital test. To recapitulate, the post-coital test involves husband and wife having sexual intercourse, after which the secretions around the cervix are removed for examination under a microscope by a doctor. For doctors without the necessary skill or facilities to evaluate a semen sample, the post-coital test was the only test of male fertility employed. However, textbooks and articles in medical journals repeatedly warned doctors against substituting a post-coital test for a full semen analysis.

After the war, many doctors considered the investigation of the infertile couple incomplete without a post-coital test (also known as the PCT, Sims, Huhner or procreation test). Yet paradoxically, its interpretation became increasingly ambiguous, and it repeatedly fell victim to accusations of unreliability and invalidity. The test was beset by both conceptual and technical complications which etiquette and embarrassment discouraged doctors from tackling too assiduously. The post-coital test is very distasteful; indeed, it would be ranked near the top of any list of undignified procedures performed by doctors on patients.[92] It is common for even highly motivated patients to be unable to go through with it. The fact that before the 1970s no one attempted to establish what a post-coital test result looked like in women and men of proven fertility suggests how much discomfort doctors experienced with the test. Indeed, the paper reporting the results of the first post-coital tests performed on women and

men of proven fertility – 'normal subjects' and not patients – was published in the *British Medical Journal* in 1978, the year of the birth of the
first baby conceived after in vitro fertilization.[93] Before then, doctors attempted to establish 'normality' by retrospectively comparing the results
of patients who became pregnant with those who did not.

The purpose of the post-coital test has been transformed several times
during its long history. As stated in chapter 3, the American gynaecologist
Sims had devised the procedure in the late nineteenth century in order to
evaluate the receptivity of a woman's cervix to her husband's sperm. He
attributed most cases of sterility to hostility to sperm on the part of the
vagina and cervix, caused by their spermatoxic secretions. Also working
in the USA, in 1913 Huhner had published the results of a series of post-
coital tests which he claimed demonstrated its value as a test of male
fertility. According to Huhner, an absence of sperm, or the presence of
sluggish sperm, in the cervical mucus, indicated a pathological condition
of the man's testes. By the 1950s, some doctors would give the husband
a clean bill of health if active sperm were found in the cervical mucus of
his wife; their presence was taken as a signal to begin to subject her to a
fuller gynaecological investigation. However, sceptics began to wonder
whether the presence of lots of active sperm in the cervical mucus really
was a good sign. If a healthy sperm is one which demonstrates forward progression, then several hours after sexual intercourse it should
be well on the way to its destination within a woman's reproductive tract;
only unhealthy sperm waste time and energy hanging around the cervix. Workers began to investigate how long after ejaculation it takes
sperm to pass through the cervix. In 1962, for example, doctors at the
Fertility Service of the Margaret Sanger Research Bureau, New York,
established that sperm penetrate the cervical mucus, within ninety seconds of ejaculation.[94]

Conflicting ideas about the conduct and longevity of a healthy sperm
within a woman's reproductive system informed debate about the time
interval after sexual intercourse deemed appropriate for inspection of the
cervix. Although most doctors agreed that the post-coital test should be
performed around the mid-point of a woman's menstrual cycle, some
asked patients to attend their clinic as soon as possible after intercourse,
others allowed them to wait for eight hours, and yet others delayed examination for up to sixty hours. For reasons relating to conflicting ideas about
the rate of production of sperm within the testes, there was no consensus
on the number of days' abstinence from sexual intercourse demanded
before the test, although most doctors suggested two days.[95]

During the interwar period another consideration had been introduced into the interpretation of post-coital tests: scientists had observed
changes in both the quantity and the texture of the mucus secreted by the

endocervix following fluctations in levels of oestrogen. It was established that around ovulation cervical mucus demonstrates maximum receptivity to sperm, and that at other times of the menstrual cycle, sperm are immobilized within cervical mucus. Faced with a poor post-coital test, doctors had to select the culprit from the following: weak sperm; vaginal factors; cervical factors; a technical error in the act of intercourse; the test being performed at the 'wrong' point in the woman's menstrual cycle, or after the 'wrong' number of hours had elapsed between the tests and sexual intercourse.[96] One response to this condundrum was to carry out the test again and again; indeed, infertility investigations were often repeated on the grounds that the investigation of infertility in itself has a beneficial therapeutic effect (more of this below). Many women were subjected to the post-coital test repeatedly. One woman described her experience as follows:

> I had an endless process of post-coitals which became more and more degrading. I felt nothing much at first, but lately it's become very demeaning, just going in and opening my legs and going through all that again. The more it goes on, the more undermined I feel, and the less I want to go there each month.[97]

A semen test might indicate whether the husband was responsible for a negative post-coital test, but it should be clear by now that few doctors were capable of carrying it out, and furthermore, it was often deemed inconclusive. A sperm mucus invasion test could clarify the situation, but as it required semen donated by a man of proven fertility, it was confined to AID practitioners, that is, to the private medical sector. Introduced to Britain in 1946 by Barton and Wiesner, the sperm mucus invasion test involves removing cervical mucus during the woman's presumptive ovulatory phase and depositing it on a glass slide where it is challenged by a sample of fresh semen of proven fertility. If the mucus permits the sperm to penetrate, then the couple's infertility was not likely to be a result of poor mucus and the woman was absolved of blame. Similarly, semen of doubtful invasive potency was pitted against mucus of established receptivity.[98]

Faced with an ambiguous post-coital test, and with no reliable means of clarifying the conundrum, it was tempting to shift the blame on to the woman. It was easy to do so. Doctors had few guidelines on how to detect pathology in men's reproductive organs. If a man's testicles had not atrophied, or failed to descend, or if there was no evidence of a varicocele, then unless a semen test clarified the issue, his contribution to a poor post-coital test was 'unknown'. In contrast, a host of negative terms were available to describe the way in which 'cervical factors' might prevent sperm from reaching their destination within a woman's reproductive tract.[99] The cervix might be anatomically obstructive through a maldisposition, laceration or amputation; its os (opening) might be infantile, pinhole, incompetent or restricted. Doctors were warned repeatedly that a cervix might look normal to the naked eye and still be toxic to sperm, through infection or hostile mucus. Surgery, antibiotics, sex hormones, electrocoagulation, intracervical insufflations and vaginal douches of an alkaline nature (such as bicarbonate of soda) were prescribed in order to encourage a more welcoming attitude and environment.

Another common response to an ambiguous post-coital test result was to declare husband and wife clinically 'incompatible', a verdict suggestive of an inadequate sexual relationship and encouraged by the growing literature on the sexual pathologies of marriage. Judging from the remedies suggested for incompatibility, more often than not the wife was deemed the guilty party. Yet the old idea that reserve and frigidity in women cause barrenness no longer held sway in scientific and medical circles.[100] It was recognized that women might not experience orgasm and still become pregnant. Alan Parkes, a leading eugenist and scientist, who in a lifelong career with the MRC made a significant contribution to the development of reproductive physiology,[101] was fond of quoting the following response of a mother of ten children to the observation that she must enjoy sexual intercourse: 'Oh, no, I just lie like a fish on a slab.'[102] Yet this was the attitude infertile women were warned against adopting during sexual intercourse on the grounds that it made conception unlikely. What doctors seem to have meant by a diagnosis of incompatibility was that the wife's attitude – in every sense of the word – discouraged insemination. Paradoxically, at the same time as the idea that sperm demonstrated independent, purposeful 'forward progression' was being articulated, women wanting to get pregnant were being advised to help sperm along the way. Contemporary handbooks on infertility written for lay people assured women that the 'best' position to adopt during sexual intercourse is one which ensures that sperm are shed *as near* to their destination as possible. Their husband had to reach the 'very entrance of the womb'; women were told to 'lie on your back, and draw your knees well upwards and outwards towards your shoulders'. After her husband had withdrawn his penis, the woman was told to rest for a while on her back with her knees together and drawn up towards her chin in order to ensure that the semen distributes itself all over the cervix. This posture had to be maintained for at least half an hour, in order to prevent sperm escaping from the vagina.[103] Technology came to the aid of women incapable of complying with these instructions; they were fitted with a home insemination device, a plastic cervical cap to which is attached a piece of polythene tubing long enough to protrude beyond the vulva. A jar was provided into which the husband masturbates, and, using a syringe, the woman injects the semen into the polythene tubing. The idea was to give weak sperms a 'leg up', and to contain them within the cap close to the cervix, so that they could not mistake the route they had to take.

Not every doctor was willing or able to perform a post-coital test. The eminent gynaecologist T. N. A. Jeffcoate (1907–92), for example, dismissed both the post-coital and the invasion tests as 'interesting academic pursuits'.[104] In 1973, only seventeen out of thirty-two British hospitals that responded to a questionnaire on their current methods of investigating infertility said the post-coital test was performed by their doctors.[105] However, the FPA considered it an important test, and Margaret Jackson published step-by-step instructions for general practitioners to follow.[106]

Jackson promoted the post-coital test as having another function: it was a convenient and reliable test of ovulation. By the 1950s reproductive scientists had identified twenty-five different tests of ovulation.[107] Although the purpose of these tests was to facilitate the correlation of clinical and pathological signs with measures of hormonal production and excretion, most of them were so elaborate that gynaecologists could not expect to have them carried out routinely.[108] Ten of the tests were confined to scientific research purposes because they demanded sophisticated laboratory facilities (and sometimes a colony of experimental non-human animals). Urine or serum assays of hormones, cytologic readings of vaginal smears and tests of the stretching qualities of cervical mucus were rarely used, being laborious and tedious for both patient and technician: vaginal smears have to be taken and analysed daily, and urinary assays involved the collection of every drop of urine for several days. Some gynaecologists tested ovulation by performing an endometrial biopsy, that is, removing endometrium from the uterus for examination under a microscope; but although it was judged a reliable test, it is a surgical procedure, demanding of resources, and unsuited to non-hospital practice.

The basal body temperature (BBT) was the most popular test of ovulation because, from the doctor's point of view, it was the cheapest and most convenient.[109] First observed in 1904, the BBT of a 'normal' woman is relatively low in the first half of the menstrual cycle and relatively high during the second half. The period of changeover in temperature was believed to coincide with the moment of highest fecundity, when ovulation takes place. This deduction was confirmed and extended by reproductive physiologists and doctors during the 1930s.[110] The isolation of sex hormones demonstrated that progesterone is responsible for a slightly raised BBT; its production increases following ovulation, and remains high during pregnancy.

In order to monitor her BBT, a woman takes her temperature daily, as soon as she wakes up, before getting out of bed, before drinking anything or smoking a cigarette. The result is noted on a specially prepared chart. Women were told to 'join the dots by a straight pencil line'. They were given a code with which to record significant events: a circle stood for sexual intercourse; letters were used to denote developments which might contribute to an abnormal fluctuation in temperature, such as a restless night (R), a cold (C), and a fever (F).[111] Women also noted with a cross the days on which they menstruated. The chart of a woman who fails to ovulate shows no appreciable rise or fall in temperature. If a woman ovulates, then around ovulation the line dips, and then rises as the level of progesterone in her body increases. If a woman conceives, her temperature remains relatively high; if she is unsuccessful, then a day or two before menstruation begins, her temperature falls.

For more than thirty years, BBT charts served as powerful representations of fertility and infertility; they are found in every book on the topic written for both professional and lay readers from the 1950s onwards. The BBT intruded into and controlled the tenor of life of hundreds of thousands of involuntarily childless women who perforce took their temperature daily for months, sometimes years, in the fervent hope that the line joining the dots would remain high. Women displaced their desire for a child on to a graphical representation of their menstrual cycle and sexual relationship. At each appointment, the charts were submitted for inspection by a doctor, an act which conveyed the impression that recording a BBT is a special sort of homework exercise set for involuntarily childless women. Jackson was probably typical of doctors in assuming the role of teacher and treating the patient as an ignorant pupil; she advised practitioners first to find out whether the woman knew how to shake the mercury down a thermometer correctly, and if she could, to provide her with verbal, written and practical instructions.[112] Developing the skill necessary to complete the charts was charged with therapeutic potential: a neat and tidy one would merit the prize of a baby.[113] As Jeffcoate cynically observed, 'many women, however, and suprisingly their medical attendants too, seem to think that keeping a temperature chart will help them to conceive'. He goes on to say that, 'on the contrary, it is a daily reminder of their complaint, it changes marital love into a mathematical exercise'.[114] For these reasons, many women came to loathe it.[115]

The BBT effectively placed responsibility for the success or failure of the investigation and treatment of infertility in the hands of women. In part, it can be seen as one of a growing number of techniques that facilitated self-management of fertility (the BBT can also be used to avoid pregnancy as it indicates the so-called 'safe period'). As pointed out in chapter 1, after the Second World War women were increasingly led to believe that an unplanned life, particularly in relation to motherhood, is unlivable. However, although self-management was incumbent on both fertile and infertile women, investment in the technology and infrastructure of contraception far outstripped that of infertility. A good example is the management of ovulation; at the same moment as fertile women were being invited to participate in a clinical trial of the pill, a drug which inhibits ovulation, the following method of predicting ovulation was being recommended by doctors as a way of overcoming infertility: a woman records in a diary the exact date during the month on which menstruation begins. After noting down this information for three to six months, she should be able to predict the day on which menstruation will probably occur. The 'fertility week' – five days when she is presumed fertile plus the two days when sperm remain viable – begins eighteen days (some doctors said sixteen) before the day on which the next period is expected to begin.

Around the same time as this doctrine of self-management of fertility began to be promulgated, leading British gynaecologists began to demonstrate the ineffectiveness of infertility clinics. An urgent question was raised: How many involuntarily childless women *failed* to become mothers after undergoing medical tests and treatment? In 1952 Sol Bender, of 'crutch in the crotch' fame, was the first to publish a critical evaluation of the treatment meted out to women and men in a hospital infertility clinic. Of 700 women who had attended the infertility clinic attached to a university hospital in Liverpool between 1934 and 1948, 324 or 46.3 per cent became pregnant. Bender attributed to medical intervention only those conceptions which occurred within twelve months of the completion of investigation and treatment. On this basis 154 women, or 47.5 per cent of the women who conceived, or 22 per cent of all the women who attended the clinic during this period, counted as therapeutic successes. At least half, and Bender suspected probably more, of the conceptions were unattributable to medical intervention.[116]

In the following year an even more pessimistic evaluation of an infertility clinic was published. Entitled 'The failure of therapy in the management of infertility', it reported a follow-up study of 2,800 women who attended the Infertility Clinic at the Newcastle General Hospital between April 1943 and April 1952. Nearly half of the women who responded to the investigators' enquiries said they had had a baby. Using Bender's criteria, 63 per cent of conceptions, just over 30 per cent of all the respondents, could be attributed to medical action. However, the investigators found that simple investigative techniques routinely used in the investigation of infertility, such as an internal examination of a woman's reproductive organs and a post-coital test, had had as much therapeutic success as more sophisticated procedures, if not more. Indeed, some interventions, such as tubal insufflation and hysterosalpingogram – both tests of tubal patency, described in chapter 3 – were associated with lower rates of pregnancy. Women stood a better chance of becoming mothers, it seemed, by simply attending the clinic for periodical review and avoiding all treatments, especially sex hormones, anti-tuberculosis chemotherapy, and anatomical rearrangements involving manual reposition of the uterus, the use of vaginal dilators, cauterization of the cervix, dilation of the cervix, salpingostomy (surgical repair of fallopian tubes) and myomectomy (removal of fibroids from the uterus).[117] The authors concluded that the value of an infertility clinic appears to be slight, and did not justify repeated attendance at the outpatient department, the occupation of beds and the consumption of time, both of patients and medical staff, and expensive prescribing. Patients should be discouraged from persisting with time-consuming and profitless treatments.

Jeffcoate made a notable contribution to the litany of medical impotence. According to him, the principal advantage of an infertility clinic is that it allows involuntarily childless women and men to feel that they had taken all humanly possible steps to remedy their situation. For, unlike the gynaecologists who treat them, patients do not appreciate that the remedy for their condition lies beyond the bounds of human knowledge and skill. Indeed, evidence was fast accumulating to show that, except perhaps for putting the patient in a frame of mind conducive to conception, the more usual forms of treatment of infertility have little effect. Half of his patients who conceived did so by chance, and not through any medical intervention. In his practice, patients who had undergone what he considered a reasonable number of diagnostic and therapeutic measures without success were encouraged to direct their attention to other matters. Otherwise, as he put it, a complaint is turned into an obsession.[118]

Disappointment with infertility clinics was underscored by reviews demonstrating the worthlessness of medical techniques which only a few years previously had been greeted with great enthusiasm. By the 1950s British gynaecologists had rejected sex hormonal treatments as useless (I shall return to sex hormones in chapter 6). A published claim of success in the treatment of male infertility was quickly refuted; there was no direct evidence that male infertility could be cured, and hope should not be held out to patients. If a man with a very low sperm count became a father, then it was by chance and not through medical treatments, which were administered for empirical and not rational reasons.[119] Tests of cervical insemination were similarly disparaged on the grounds that as many patients of doctors who did not pay attention to 'cervical hostility' became mothers as did those of doctors who were convinced of its central importance. The attraction of these tests was said to be the scope they offered for interpretation, which was so wide as to make it possible to find a cause for infertility in every case and to provide a 'reason' for instituting treatment with diet, local remedies, hormones or whatever is in fashion.[120]

Most astonishing is the apparent disenchantment with tubal insufflation, hysterosalpingogram and other tests of tubal patency. As pointed out in chapter 3, Rubin, the originator of tubal insufflation, had claimed that his technique worked both as a test of tubal patency and as a treatment for a constriction in the fallopian tubes. He had generated considerable enthusiasm among his professional colleagues. Women were often subjected to repeated tests of tubal patency on therapeutic grounds. Of the 1,478 women attending the infertility clinic attached to Glasgow Infirmary in the 1940s, about 400 of them underwent a test of tubal patency at least twice; one woman was insufflated twenty-three times over seven months, another daily for eighteen days. However, it was said to be worth it: results confirmed Rubin's assertion that the test had therapeutic value.[121] Tests of tubal patency were said to be followed by a pregnancy in from one in five to nearly half of women who underwent the procedures.

Jeffcoate was probably the most outspoken sceptic of the therapeutic value of tests of tubal patency. He claimed that in many cases, results were false and misleading; if a woman conceived following a negative test, it demonstrated that she had been misdiagnosed, and not that the test worked as a cure, as many doctors, including Rubin, believed. Jeffcoate performed the hysterosalpingogram in order to confirm the results of 1,023 consecutive insufflation tests performed between 1949 and 1952 on 428 private patients and 478 hospital patients (some women underwent the test twice). He found that 37 per cent of insufflation tests had given a false negative result, and just over 3 per cent a false positive. Hysterosalpingography also proved unreliable; evidence that both fallopian tubes were blocked was proved – by pregnancy or surgery – to have been fallacious in 15 per cent of cases.[122]

Few gynaecologists would operate on the pelvis of an infertile woman unless the procedure was deemed necessary for reasons of health and not fertility. The exception to this rule was Green-Armytage, of the Sterility Clinic at Hammersmith Hospital, London, who did his utmost to encourage his medical colleagues to perform surgical repair of damaged fallopian tubes. Declaring the procedure 'simplicity itself', he claimed that one in three of his patients went on to have a baby.[123] Yet almost no one seemed to share his enthusiasm. In 1963, in a lecture dedicated to Green-Armytage, the American gynaecologist Bayard Carter told a British audience that from an analysis of his patients treated between the mid-1930s and the end of the war he had concluded that the operations performed were meddlesome and actually led to a lower incidence of pregnancy.[124] Despite advances in operating techniques, the pregnancy rate following surgery failed to reach 10 per cent.

The two most effective and efficient ways of becoming pregnant were attending an infertility clinic, and undergoing an internal examination.[125] Gynaecologists began to claim that in a majority of cases where a woman became pregnant following a consultation with a doctor, it was the act of seeking medical help which had succeeded in making her fertile. A consultation with a doctor had a powerful placebo effect on the anxious patient, perhaps by relieving her of the burden of anxiety about her infertility. Medical journals began to receive and publish papers on the psychological aspects of infertility. During the 1950s, for example, *Fertility and Sterility* published articles on psychogenic aspects of infertility; sexual and marital maladjustments of infertile couples; ambivalence and conception; a psychodynamic approach to the study of infertility; and psychoanalytic evaluations of the problem of sterility.

Even where medicine was given credit for a pregnancy, it was often deemed a one-off result, a chance phenomenon. Gynaecologists despaired of their inability to transform an infertile women into a permanently fertile one, a goal they seem to have set themselves. Bender provided his colleagues with another reason for pessimism: he found that when a hitherto sterile woman becomes pregnant, her chances of spontaneous abortion are considerably greater than those of women of normal fertility, because of a higher incidence of 'defective germ-plasm'. Doctors began to observe a higher frequency of ectopic gestation and prematurity of babies in women who conceived after attending an infertility clinic than in the general population. Some – but not all – gynaecologists said there was a higher incidence of delivery by forceps and caesarean section in previously infertile women.[126]

Why were leading British gynaecologists intent on demonstrating their impotence in relation to involuntary childlessness? In print, they repeatedly referred to the wisdom of Matthews Duncan, the renowned nineteenth-century expert on sterility, whose contribution to the etiology of sterility was discussed in chapter 2. In 1866 Matthews Duncan had observed that all too often a reputation for curing sterility was spoken of as if founded on substantial claims, and that the credulity of patients and doctors alike had allowed coincidence to be regarded as consequence. By quoting Matthews Duncan, British gynaecologists conveyed their disapproval of empiricism, and their support of scientific methods. Yet these same gynaecologists were conspicuous in their absence from projects attempting to inject science into clinical practice. Few joined the Society for the Study of Fertility, set up in 1950 in order to pursue the scientific discussion of reproductive physiology and organize conferences on standardization of techniques used in the diagnosis, prevention and cure of impaired fertility, a project which had been initiated in 1944 by the FPA.[127] Doctors active in the Society were mostly enthusiasts who worked in general practice, or as clinical assistants in NHS hospitals, or in the FPA's Motherhood clinics, along with a handful of gynaecologists sympathetic to the Association's aims. The Society's membership was drawn overwhelmingly from reproductive biologists and veterinarians; indeed, the *Journal of Reproduction and Fertility*, the Society's mouthpiece, contains hardly any papers by clinicians. The Society persistently tried to encourage more gynaecologists to participate in its activities. In 1963, it approached the Blair Bell Society of the Royal College of Obstetricians and Gynaecologists, with the suggestion that they hold joint meetings on scientific and clinical aspects of fertility. In 1971, a questionnaire was sent to clinical members of the Society and members of the Blair Bell Society, asking them what action it might take to increase the participation of doctors; twenty-nine out of a possible 130 doctors replied.[128]

In the USA, the unreliability and ineffectiveness of procedures used in the investigation and treatment of infertility was also an issue; however, the response to it there suggests that special conditions were in operation in Britain. Indeed, a leading American gynaecologist publicly accused his British counterparts of misrepresenting facts and discarding accomplishments in order to discredit the efforts of doctors who specialized in treating infertility.[129] Doctors and scientists in the USA saw critical evaluation as a necessary precondition of improved clinical practice, not a reason to abandon it. In 1944, The American Society for the Study of Sterility (ASSS) had been set up as the medical establishment's alternative to the Endocrine Society, founded by the gynaecologist and sex reformer Robert Latou Dickinson, whose members were considered left-of-centre and whose activities were deemed questionable.[130] One of the first tasks the ASSS set itself was the establishment of a consensus on the best available tests and treatments, which it would encourage clinicians to use (an objective similar to that of the FPA's conferences on sterility held during the 1940s).[131] The Subcommittee on Ovulation of the Research Correlating Committee, for example, wrote to 121 members asking their opinion on the validity of the methods they used to determine ovulation, and which tests they considered reliable.[132] Other procedures were subjected to a similar evaluation by the Committee, and the results were published in *Fertility and Sterility*.

In 1953 American clinicians involved in the ASSS set up the International Fertility Society in order to promulgate internationally a more scientific approach to the care of the infertile couple. By this the Society meant determining valid procedures and encouraging clinicians to avoid misusing and distorting them in clinical practice. In 1969, thirteen national fertility societies and the International Fertility Association formed the Federation of Fertility Societies, whose task was to organize regular World Congresses on the topic.

The tendency of British gynaecologists to disparage procedures used in the investigation and treatment of infertility had emerged in response to the transformation in the political economy of their specialty which had accompanied the introduction of the National Health Service on 5 July 1948. The negotiations with government over the structure of the NHS increased the power of all consultants. Transformed from a scattered body with primarily local interests into a single group, regionally organized with a national income structure, consultants had considerable influence over national hospital policy.[133] Consultants used their new-found power to subjugate their rivals, the general practitioner specialists, who were excluded from larger hospitals, although not from cottage hospitals in rural areas. General practitioners were allowed to practise in larger hospitals only as clinical assistant to a consultant, a junior part-time appointment, usually in an outpatient department, which did not entitle the GP to admit his or her own patients to hospital beds. A clinical assistantship appealed to general practitioners with a special interest or with a desire to be more closely connected with a local general hospital, although many were not trained to use the increasingly complex hospital facilities.[134]

Although it allowed them to dominate their general practitioner rivals, the National Health Service intensified competition among consultants within hospitals. Inpatient beds, outpatient sessions and junior staff were meted out to consultants in accordance with the sophistication of their medical specialty: the more complex the body of knowledge and techniques, the more resources and assistance could be justified. Consultants developed areas of their specialty which they considered would help them defeat rival claims over resources, and neglected others which represented a handicap in this pursuit. They were free to do so, for the Ministry of Health declined to intervene in all clinical matters and refused to dictate which areas of medicine should be provided by the National Health Service.

Skill in offering a crutch in the crotch did little to advance a gynaecologist's case in the competition waged over resources with fellow consultants; the BBT, post-coital test and advice on sex technique do not add up to a sophisticated medical specialty. For similar reasons, gynaecologists were dismissive of other 'women's complaints' such as menstrual disorders and pelvic pain which, like infertility, began to be attributed to emotional causes; it was considered inappropriate for a highly trained gynaecological surgeon working in a busy hospital outpatient clinic to deal with such conditions.[135] In order to lay claim to special expertise, gynaecologists focused attention on other aspects of their specialty. No doubt the furore provoked by AID contributed to the reluctance of gynaecologists to champion the cause of the involuntarily childless. On this occasion, a syringe represented a threat to professional ambitions. In 1950, the RCOG passed a resolution that infertility should be dealt with by all gynaecological clinics and not confined to special infertility clinics.[136] The following year, the College turned down a request for support of a delegation to the Minister of Health, pressing him to set up fertility clinics throughout the country.[137]

The National Health Service gave gynaecologists no encouragement to improve services for the investigation and treatment of infertility. The 1946 National Health Service Act, the legislation which established the service, had made no mention of family planning. Indeed, it made no amendment to underlying legislation on birth control.[138] At the time, the FPA had not dissented from this omission because it believed that too few doctors knew anything about family planning, and the service was better provided by its clinics. It also felt that a voluntary organization was better able to withstand local opposition to family planning provision.[139] In any case, its President, Lord Horder, was against the proposed National Health Service and refused to negotiate on its behalf.[140] The Biological and Medical Committee of the Royal Commission on Population had found in England and Wales twenty-seven special centres concerned with the investigation and treatment of involuntary childlessness; only four of these had facilities available for examining men. The Committee stated that infertility could not satisfactorily be dealt with in a busy hospital outpatient department, and recommended that special fertility clinics should be made part of the health service of the country.[141] Yet, as has already been pointed out, the government found it politically expedient to ignore the recommendations of the Royal Commission. In 1964, the Ministry admitted that not one ministerial circular had been sent to National Health Service hospitals on the organization of infertility services.[142] Gynaecologists were free to organize services in such a way as to meet their own and not patients' needs. And, as we have already seen, it suited British gynaecologists to disparage a specialist approach to infertility. As a result, it is they who are responsible for the neglect of hospital services for the investigation and treatment of infertility.

In the early days of the National Health Service, some general practitioners attempted to stake out the field of infertility as theirs, claiming that they were better placed to offer a 'crutch in the crotch' than their hospital colleagues who lacked a sound-proof room in which intimate matters could be discussed.[143] The National Health Service gave general practitioners access to hospital diagnostic facilities (previously they had had to pay for laboratory tests out of their own or their patients' pocket). General practitioners took advantage of this facility: the proportion of hospital pathological and radiological work done at direct general practitioner request rose steadily.[144] It is impossible to tell how many of these tests related to infertility; however, what is clear is that as demands from all patients increased and the scope of their practice widened, general practitioners found too taxing on their time the lengthy interviews demanded in infertility investigations, and ceased to claim it as a condition to the treatment of which they were especially suited. Infertility was excluded from a series of articles on gynaecology in general practice published in 1971 in the *British Medical Journal*. In a majority of cases, general practitioners did little more than refer involuntarily childless patients to their local outpatient gynaecological clinic. From a survey of patients' experiences of doctors' responses to infertility carried out in the late 1970s, it seems as though the advice most often given by a general practitioner was 'keep trying', followed by encouragement to adopt.[145]

After 1945, the FPA pursued its stated aim of helping involuntarily childless women at Motherhood clinics. It concentrated its resources on those areas outside London known to be poorly served by NHS hospitals. The FPA expanded rapidly. From 1948 to 1951, it opened new clinics at an average rate of one every five weeks; from then on, it was one new clinic every week. By 1963, it had around 400 clinics. In 1951, forty-six out of fifty-five of its clinics said they gave women advice on infertility;[146] by 1960, that number had increased to 246 out of 311 clinics.[147] Most FPA clinics offered only preliminary investigations: a medical history was taken, women were examined, simple steps such as the use of a temperature chart were suggested, and advice on sex technique was offered. Only a few clinics had facilities for performing procedures such as the post-coital test. A major drawback was that doctors who worked in FPA clinics were unable to prescribe medicines on the National Health Service; women needing treatment had to be sent to a general practitioner or an NHS hospital. Nevertheless, the FPA felt duty bound to continue to advise involuntarily childless women, many of whom sought its help either because they did not know the appropriate place to seek advice, or because they felt that their general practitioner had dismissed or trivialized their plight.[148] The organization also exerted pressure on the government to expand and improve National Health Service facilities for the investigation and treatment of infertility. However, in the postwar antinatalist climate, the organization became increasingly concerned with helping women not to have babies; by the 1960s, infertile women made up just 1.6 per cent of its 102,930 patients.[149] In 1974, in response to pressure from the population lobby, the government agreed reluctantly to take over the clinics run by the FPA and incorporate them into a national family planning service within a reorganized National Health Service. Facilities for involuntarily childless women within a family planning clinic largely disappeared. A survey carried out by the FPA in 1982 found that only sixty-seven out of 192 British health authorities incorporated advice on infertility within a family planning service; two years later, that number had fallen to forty out of 145.[150]

Although the procedures dubbed 'a crutch in the crotch' were considered an obstacle to gynaecological ambitions within National Health Service hospitals, they were highly suited to private medical practice. The equipment necessary to perform a post-coital test, for example, was fairly mundane: a speculum, swab holder, bakelite spoon and holder, cannulae with lateral holes (one coarse and one fine), rubber bulb, 10 ml syringe, slides, cover-slips and normal saline. Where a patient was considered to require a procedure that demanded facilities found only in a hospital setting, then the consultant could see her at an NHS or private hospital. Indeed, in the early days of the National Health Service, consultants had been encouraged to undertake private practice within its hospitals and discouraged from sending patients to small, unsuitable private nursing homes dotted around the country.[151]

On average, in 1963, consultant obstetrician gynaecologists devoted just over three-quarters of their working week to the NHS.[152] It is impossible to ascertain how consultants spent their time. Studies of consultant work measured the responsibility they shouldered, not the work they actually did.[153] However, it looks as if treatment meted out to private patients was on the whole more sympathetic than that offered within the National Health Service. The histories that open this chapter provide a vivid picture of the differences between the two sectors. A survey of experiences of involuntarily childless couples carried out in the late 1970s found that although there was little advantage in terms of the nature and success of private tests and treatment for either women or men, 'going private' was quicker than having treatment on the National Health Service, and private doctors were thought to be more sympathetic to patients' emotional needs.[154] Yet in many cases a private doctor was one who spent most of his week working in the National Health Service.

Leaching the scientific content out of infertility investigations and treatments enabled gynaecologists to further their ambitions within both the National Health Service and private practice. However, as chapter 6 demonstrates, assisted conception techniques undermined this arrangement, and contributed to a major transformation in the political economy of gynaecology.

6

Bank Accounts and Babies

Mrs A. B. first attended the infertility clinic at University College Hospital, London, in August 1968. she was 22 years old and had been married for two years. Her periods were scanty and irregular. In May 1969, she underwent a course of injections of gonado-trophins. She conceived sextuplets. In order to protect her from publicity and harassment, other patients and staff were told that only triplets were expected. On 15 December 1969 five live and one stillborn babies were delivered by caesarean section. Although a large room had been set aside for press conferences and extra telephones had been installed, a number of journalists attempted to force entry into the hospital, and guards were posted on the doors.[1]

In 1991, 'proud mum' Jacqueline told readers of the Daily Mirror that her new 'test tube' baby daughter had been worth selling her house for: indeed, at £2,000 she considered her a fantastic bargain. Jacqueline had been told that she would never have children. She had conceived twins, but sadly one of them had died in the womb. Her baby daughter had been born ten weeks prematurely, and doctors at Liverpool's Fazakerley Hospital had fought a successful battle to save her life.[2]

The relationship between the pharmaceutical companies which develop, manufacture and market hormonal treatments of infertility, and doctors who prescribe them to patients, has not always been an easy one. Although doctors continued to prescribe them, after the Second World War scientifically minded British gynaecologists considered sex hormones – oestrogen, progesterone and testosterone – worthless preparations.[3] In 1947, for example, the gynaecologist Aleck Bourne declared himself 'greviously disappointed' by them.[4] Seven years later, the chapter on sex hormones published in a volume of papers celebrating the twenty-fifth anniversary of the establishment of the British College of Obstetrics and Gynaecology opened with the following statement:

> The study of endocrinology is still a science in the hands of a number of serious-minded research workers in various hospitals and other institutions. But the practice of endocrine therapy, at least so far as the sex hormones are concerned (and in the hands of a regrettably large number of practitioners) is no longer a scientific calling but a highly commercialized and very profitable business.[5]

Twenty years later, the difference of opinion between scientifically minded doctors and the pharmaceutical industry over the value of endocrine therapy had all but disappeared: hormones were prescribed by the former and were highly profitable to the latter. The turning point in the relationship came in 1955, when Gregory Pincus, an American research biologist, established that progestogen-type substances were active in inhibiting ovulation when taken orally. Manufacturers synthesized the chemicals, and shortly afterwards women subjects were recruited for the first clinical trial of a contraceptive pill. In 1974, the pill became available free to every woman in Britain, irrespective of age or marital status, on consultation with a doctor. In 1980, around three million British women were thought to be taking the pill every day.[6]

Profits from pharmacological treatments of infertility were less easy to accrue than those from medical contraceptives. After the war, it took gynaecologists twenty years to reach the stage where they were willing to use drugs extensively in the treatment of infertility. As pointed out in Chapter 5, after the war tests of ovulation, especially keeping a temperature chart (the BBT), became routine. However, although doctors felt able to diagnose anovulation, that is, infertility in women caused by failure to ovulate, they considered it an intractable condition and rarely treated it. If treatment was offered, it followed one of two approaches. The first took anovulation as a deficiency disease; women produced insufficient hormones to generate a full menstrual cycle. Substitute or replacement therapy sought to replenish hormones in short supply directly by administering them in a fashion which attempted to replicate a 'normal' menstrual cycle; for example, doctors prescribed a course of oestrogen for the first twenty days of the menstrual cycle, and a ten-day course of progesterone starting on the fourteenth day. This treatment induced uterine bleeding in women who failed to menstruate, which was said by doctors who prescribed it to have a therapeutic effect: women reported a sense of enormous relief from the experience of menstruation.[7]

The second approach to anovulation was derived from the school of thought which blamed a low sperm count on refractory testes; ovaries that refused to produce eggs had to be jolted into action. Devised in the 1930s, 'oestrogen shock therapy' consisted of a large dose of a potent natural or, when it became available, synthetic, oestrogen, administered on about the twelfth to the fourteenth day of a 28-day menstrual cycle. During the 1930s, thyroid extract began to be prescribed routinely to women complaining of childlessness. Thyroid extract was said to act as a tonic to the endocrine system; by adding to the effect of intrinsic thyroid activity and producing a rise in circulating thyroid hormone it was said to stimulate other glands, and provoke mild alterations in hormone production that might enhance fecundity.[8] Roentgen-ray – X-ray – therapy of the pituitary gland and/or the ovaries was sometimes used as a stimulant of menstrual function (it was also used as a treatment of heavy and irregular menstrual bleeding). There was a great latitude in the dosage of X-ray said to be necessary to produce ovulation. X-ray therapy of gynaecological problems fell into disrepute during the 1950s following the revelations of the effects of radiation from atomic bombs on the people of Hiroshima and Nagasaki.[9]

For decades, the pharmaceutical industry had little success with gonadotrophins, the chemicals produced by the anterior lobe of the pituitary gland which provoke the ovaries and testes into action. The existence of gonadotrophins had first been suggested in 1926 when, simultaneously in the USA and Germany, scientists demonstrated that ovulation is a response of the ovaries to a hormonal communication from another gland.[10] This proposition stimulated a search for the organ which released the message(s). In 1927 Bernhard Zondek, a German gynaecologist, deduced that the anterior lobe of the pituitary gland is responsible for the production of gonadotrophins when he implanted a small piece of one in an immature female mouse; five days later, her ovaries had ripened into a mature state.[11] Physiologists embarked upon an extensive and intensive investigation into the mysteries of the anterior lobe of the pituitary gland, a project which in Britain received generous support from the MRC.[12]

The first material found to have gonadotrophic activity was human chorionic gonadotrophin (HCG), which in 1927 was isolated from the urine of pregnant women by Zondek. Three years later, another gonadotrophic substance was isolated in the blood serum of pregnant mares (PMS), and for many years this was considered the best available source of gonadotrophins. Commercial preparations of gonadotrophins proliferated. In Britain just before the Second World War PMS was marketed by four companies: Boots Pure Drug Company as 'Antostab'; Roussel Laboratories as 'Gonadyl'; Gedeon Richter (Great Britain) as 'Luteonantin'; and The British Drug Houses as 'Serogan'. HCG was available from six companies: Oxo as 'Antoxylin'; Parke Davis & Company as 'Antuitrin'; Richter as 'Glanduantin'; Homburg as 'Gonan'; Boots as 'Physostab'; Organon Laboratories as 'Pregnyl'; and Bayer Products as 'Prolan'.[13] Organotherapeutic preparations of dried anterior pituitary glands made from abbatoir waste were also sold. Doctors prescribed gonadotrophins for a range of conditions said to arise out of a glandular insufficiency such as migraine, acne and obesity.

When experiments on non-human laboratory animals suggested that it was responsible for both sexual activity and reproductive function, the anterior lobe of the pituitary gland became known as the 'motor' of sexual function. Workers sought proof of their suspicion that the lobe produces a complex of hormones. Gonadotrophic substances proved capable of exerting two distinct actions: ripening of an immature ovarian follicle, and spermatozoal development in the testes; and stimulating the shedding of the ripe ovum and the formation of the corpus luteum. The former activity was known as follicle stimulation; the latter, as luteinization. Scientists struggled to separate the fractions responsible for the different activities. It was found that different materials and methods of extraction yield a substance capable of producing a preponderance of one or the other effect. HCG appeared to be predominantly a luteinizing hormone, called LH, whereas PMS was a more powerful follicle-stimulating hormone, or FSH.

The response of small non-human laboratory animals to gonadotrophic preparations was taken as justification for clinical enthusiasm. Doctors explored the effect of HCG and PMS on women suffering from conditions arising from ovarian failure, including sterility; they also administered them to men with low sperm counts. However, though timing, dose and method of administration were varied, results were disappointing. HCG and PMS began to look useless as therapeutic substances. In 1938 an explanation for their ineffectiveness emerged: it was established that animals develop immunity to gonadotrophins extracted from other species; through repeated injections they acquire the power to resist the action of a gonadotrophin. PMS ceased to be administered on its own. Doctors began to experiment with different combinations of HCG and PMS, in the hope that the human aspects of HCG might neutralize the equine elements of PMS and inhibit the production of antibodies.

Optimism about the clinical value of HCG and PMS was revived when doctors became convinced that the drugs could induce ovulation in normally menstruating women. Experiments were performed on women in order to establish the effectiveness of different treatment regimes. Some workers gave the substances to women about to undergo pelvic surgery; their ovaries were examined during the operation, and sometimes an ovary was removed in order to look at it under a microscope.[14] Work on sheep carried out in the early years of the war suggested that gonatrophins are valuable, albeit unpredictable, agents in stimulating fertility.[15] A few doctors described regimes of injections of HCG and PMS which, they claimed, had succeeded in inducing a subnormally active ovary to ovulate and had even enabled anovular women to become pregnant.[16] Yet despite these reported successes, the problem of species specificity discouraged enthusiasts. After the war, gonadotrophins prepared from non-human animals were rarely administered.

The search for a source of human FSH was pursued by a few enthusiasts, members of the Gonadotrophin Club which first met in Geneva in 1954 in order to reach agreement on a bioassay.[17] Some workers explored the potential of urine of menopausal women, others worked with pituitaries obtained from healthy women who had unfortunately died prematurely. The pituitary gland was found to yield highly potent, species-specific gonadotrophins. In 1958 Carl-Axel Gemzell, the Swedish pioneer of human pituitary gonadotrophin (HPG) research, announced that he had succeeded in inducing ovulation in anovular women, two of whom had become pregnant with twins.[18] The regime he employed was FSH extracted from the human pituitary (HPFSH), administered for several days, followed by either LH extracted from the human pituitary (HPLH) or HCG.

It took a few years for workers in different countries to organize supplies of pituitaries of dead women from which to extract gonadotrophins. In Britain, the MRC controlled the collection and distribution of human pituitaries.[19] However, few people agreed to donation of the organs of their recently deceased nearest and dearest. Human pituitaries were a rare commodity, and only a small quantity of gonadotrophins was available for clinical experiments. In 1963, a favourable report was published on a gonadotrophic preparation extracted from the urine of postmenopausal women. Called 'Pergonal', the partially pure drug had been prepared by Instituto Farmacologico Serono Rome, part of the Swiss-based pharmaceutical company Ares-Serono. Eighty thousand litres of postmenopausal urine had been processed in the course of this work.[20] Other pharmaceutical companies found it difficult to accumulate sufficient supplies of raw material. However, in return for gifts, Ares-Serono persuaded post-menopausal Italian women – nuns in convents and women living close together in small towns and villages – to save their urine for regular collection by the company's tanker. Ares-Serono has a virtual monopoly of human menopausal gonadotrophins (HMG), although it faces competition in the market for HCG (it proved far easier to organize supplies of pregnant women's urine). Pergonal compared favourably to gonadotrophic preparations made from human pituitaries, which were eventually abandoned in its favour.[21] However, Pergonal was – and still is – very expensive. Gonadotrophins are proteins and have a complex chemical structure which is difficult to describe and synthesize into a cheaper, more plentiful alternative.[22]

The thalidomide tragedy which came to light in the early 1960s made everyone apprehensive about drugs administered to would-be mothers and pregnant women.[23] Drug toxicology became of paramount importance; in 1962, for example, the MRC set up a committee to supervise the safety testing of selected new drugs. In November 1965 Shirley Summerskill, a Member of Parliament and a general practitioner, asked the Minister of Health to prohibit the general use of human gonadotrophins until their safety had been proven.[24] In 1966, with financial support from the Ford Foundation, the MRC set up a clinical trial of human pituitary gonadotrophins in order to test their safety before allowing them to be freely released in the country. The trial explored the method of administration developed by Arthur Crooke (1905–1990), a member of the Gonadotrophin Club and a British pioneer of human gonadotrophins.[25] Crooke claimed to lead the world in grading the hairsbreadth adjustment of doses of these drugs.[26] Four suitable women, aged between 25 and 35, were tested at three centres: Newcastle, Dundee and Cambridge.

Not everyone was persuaded that too large a dose caused the undesirable manifestations of gonadotrophins: multiple conceptions and ovarian hyperstimulation syndrome. Gemzell had found that a dose of FSH which produced ovarian hyperstimulation in one patient would elicit no response in another.[27] He speculated that untoward effects might be due to some phenomenon as yet not understood or recognized.[28] This was subsumed under the catch-all of women's susceptibility to FSH.[29] Professor Carey, who was responsible for the conception of the so-called New Zealand quins, said that the dosage he used had been most carefully controlled, so the woman must have been unusually sensitive to gonadotrophins.[30]

No reliable means exist of assessing before administration how susceptible a woman is to FSH.[31] The tests are rough and ready, whereas the dividing line between sufficient and safe ovarian action for ovulation and that leading to dangerous hyperstimulation is thin and difficult to gauge. Another difficulty is that ovarian hyperstimulation syndrome is poorly related to the number of eggs produced; a woman may fail to produce an egg but become dangerously ill. It is advised that women are closely monitored after FSH has been administered, and if it looks as though multiple ovulation is likely, treatment should be discontinued and the woman warned to abstain from sexual intercourse. Time-honoured retrospective clinical indicators of ovarian activity have been recruited in order to monitor the current state of ovaries undergoing stimulation; at first, the quantity and quality of cervical mucus and a bioassay of oestrogen were used, both relatively imprecise and non-specific measures. Bioassays of oestrogen are also time-consuming and expensive and require large quantities of urine; during treatment, women have to collect every drop of urine they pass. In the late 1960s, radioimmunoassays of oestrogen were introduced.[32] Radioimmunoassays give a rapid result on a relatively small amount of test material; however, they are sophisticated techniques available at only a few specialist centres. In order to make radioimmunoassays more widely available, in 1978 Ares-Serono, the manufacturer of Pergonal, introduced a free Endocrine Assay Service.[33] The company provides doctors with a complete kit: 24-hour urine containers, small postable urine collection bottles, pre-addressed Jiffy bags and all the relevant forms. Test results are available on the same day as the sample of urine is received. This service has encouraged many more doctors to prescribe Pergonal; by 1988, Ares-Serono's British laboratory was processing up to 1,000 samples of urine every week.[34] In the latter part of the 1970s, ultrasound began to be used to visualize the ovaries so that the number of follicles developing in them could be counted. However, as has already been pointed out, size and appearance of a follicle are not good indicators of ovarian stimulation; hyperstimulation may occur where only small follicles are visible.[35]

In an effort to maximize both effectiveness and safety, doctors experimented with different ways of administering human gonadotrophins. None of the methods proved reliable. When yet another specialist centre had demonstrated how difficult it was to judge the correct dose, and as a result a woman gave birth to sextuplets one of whom was stillborn, they were accused of behaving like 'sorcerers' apprentices'.[36] According to Gemzell, the risk of treatment with gonadotrophins producing a multiple pregnancy was equal to or higher than her chance of conceiving a single child; the chance of having triplets was one in five.[37] Very few women were treated with gonadotrophins, yet higher-order multiple births, once a rare phenomenon, began to seem commonplace. In July 1965, British newspapers announced the live birth of quintuplets to a New Zealand woman and the birth of five babies, only one of whom had survived, to a Swedish woman. The following month, a German doctor described the case of a woman who had delivered seven stillborn babies.[38] In May 1968, sextuplets were born in London; at the end of 1969, the 'Letts quins' were born in London; in January 1970, they were joined by the 'Hanson quins' of Rayleigh.[39]

Doctors willing to prescribe human gonadotrophins were rewarded for their industry.[40] Gemzell has admitted that gonadotrophins had made him a wealthy man; through them, he could indulge his tastes for travel and collecting modern paintings. In 1976, Crooke acknowledged that despite more than a decade of clinical experience with human gonadotrophins, he still did not know which approach was safest.[41] He received the 'Midland Man of the Year Award' of 500 guineas and a suitably engraved piece of silver as a tribute for his task of pioneering work with human gonadotrophins, which he had performed "with missionary zeal", and which had earned him few earthly rewards save for 'a place in the medical and sociological history of our time'.[42]

The doctors who conducted experiments with human gonadotrophins were reluctant to take on the mantle of pioneer: they repeatedly assured the public that they never pressed women to take them. The impression conveyed was one of involuntarily childless women clamouring to have their ovaries stimulated. One of Crooke's patients admitted that he had warned her that she was a sort of guinea pig, that she might have a multiple pregnancy or that the treatment might not work. She was undeterred: 'I was desperate and I was willing to try anything.'[43] Crooke claimed that after years of hoping and trying for a baby, most women did not mind twins or more.[44] He described a Birmingham woman who gave birth to sextuplets, of which only three had survived, as 'very, very lucky'.[45] Gemzell reported that around one in ten of his patients who became pregnant through human gonadotrophins requested a second go.[46]

Robert Edwards and Patrick Steptoe also represent involuntarily childless women as freely choosing to undergo experimental and unpredictable treatments of infertility. When they began to work on the development of the technique of fertilization in vitro and embryo transfer in 1968, they 'soon discovered that patients needed to be restrained from volunteering too much'.[47]

In the 1960s and 1970s there were few restrictions or regulations governing the conduct of medical research. It was not then incumbent on researchers to fully apprise volunteers of any risks they might run. In his study *Human guinea pigs*, published in 1967, Maurice Pappworth described controversial investigations – including several sponsored by the MRC – which had exploited and even harmed patients.[48] Some mechanism was needed to take account of the different risks and rewards of medical research for researcher and research subject.[49] Researchers risk little but have a lot to gain from research. The more sophisticated medicine becomes, the more it confirms and applauds doctors' expertise. And although it is easy to see how a researcher bene-fits from such work, defining the reward for a research subject is no easy task. Experimental medical techniques restructure the options available to volunteers; they open up new, difficult alternatives which can become compulsions, however dangerous, while old procedures are discarded.[50] However, although new treatments of infertility are often risky and unsuccessful, it is difficult to mourn the passing of most of the procedures described in this book – with the exception of a long holiday at a foreign spa resort described in chapter 2. Old and new serve as reminders of the dangers in construing involuntary childlessness as an invitation to intrude boldly, in some instances, unnecessarily, into the bodies and lives of women on the premise that they are being given a slim chance of becoming a mother.

In the 1950s three American academic investigators synthesized a substance called clomiphene citrate, an orally active synthetic non-steroidal agent distantly related to diethystilboestrol (DES), a synthetic oestrogen.[51] They passed the novel substance on to a pharmaceutical company, Merrell Corporation of Cincinnati, for elaboration in its research laboratories. Paradoxically, clomiphene citrate was found to exhibit both oestrogenic and anti-oestrogenic effects: it can both inhibit ovulation and induce it, depending on the situation in which it is administered. Its effects on non-human animals are different from those on humans. Although its mode of action has still not been confirmed, it is thought to work by tricking the hypothalamus into believing that the level of oestrogen in the body is low. A low level of oestrogen makes the hypothalamus send a signal to the pituitary gland to produce gonadotrophins; in effect, it is employed as an indirect stimulant: 'Clomiphene therapy does not directly stimulate ovulation, but it initiates a sequence of events that are the physiologic features of a normal cycle.'[52]

In the early 1960s MRL 41, an analogue of clomiphene citrate, was subjected to clinical trials in several different countries, including one in Britain under the auspices of the MRC. In 1966, the drug was given an enthusiastic write-up in the *British Medical Journal*. Of 3,500 women who had received it, about seven out of ten had ovulated, and nearly a quarter had become pregnant.[53] Taking those results together with the contraceptive pill, pharmacology appeared to have equipped doctors with several means of taming women's hitherto recalcitrant ovaries. As the MRC observed in 1964: 'Potent compounds are now available for both the inhibition and stimulation of ovarian function in human subjects and it can be confidently predicted that such compounds will become of increasing importance in human life.'[54]

The MRC restricted the clinical trial of clomiphene citrate to patients attending hospitals which had facilities for elaborate assays. Women took the drug every day for four days. Many research subjects complained of side-effects: hot flushes, blurring of vision, abdominal pain of varying severity and sometimes loss of hair. Doctors deemed most of these trivial. A study of the effect of clomiphene on healthy young men carried out in Canada had found that large doses were associated with unpleasant side-effects.[55] Yet in 1968 doctors were assured that 'at the recommended dosage [of clomiphene] side-effects are not severe, and need not neces-sarily interrupt treatment'.[56]

Under the brand name 'Clomid', clomiphene citrate became freely available on prescription in the UK at the end of 1966, and from then on, in theory, a GP could prescribe it if she or he so wished. However, in view of the unpredictability of human gonadotrophins, the use of Clomid in general practice was considered unwise.[57] Under an agreement reached with the British Dunlop Committee on Safety of Drugs, Merrell-Nation sent promotional literature on Clomid only to gynaecologists and endo-crinologists with access to facilities for hormonal assays. This arrangement threatened to restrict the drug's availability to the few centres that had facilities for and experience of human gonadotrophin therapy. Doctors began to protest that these precautions were not warranted as both the American Food and Drug Administration and the British Dunlop Com-mittee considered the drug safe. This argument was put most forcefully by Peter Bishop, then working at the Infertility Clinic attached to the Chelsea Hospital for Women. According to Bishop, the only urine test infertile women are prepared to undergo is for pregnancy.[58]

A distinction began to be drawn between exogenous human gonadotrophins, that is, those derived from donors, and endogenous human gonadotrophins, that is, those produced within a woman patient's own body, which were called the sort that 'Nature herself uses'. The im-pact of the former on ovaries was represented as unpredictable and dangerous; the effect of the latter, even where they were produced in response to a synthetic stimulus such as clomiphene citrate, was deemed at worst benign, at best, beneficial. Gonadotrophins produced as a result of internal stimulation were said to exert a weaker action on ovaries than that provoked by exogenous gonadotrophins. None the less, clomiphene citrate can lead to a multiple pregnancy, usually twins, although for infertile women such a risk may seem insignificant. Mrs Bennie, for example, who took part in the clinical trial, said that after seven years of childlessness she looked on the second baby as a bonus.[59]

Clomiphene citrate became the first line of treatment for anovular women; the use of exogenous human gonadotrophins was restricted to women with stubborn anovulation, who were sent for treatment at a specialist centre with facilities for monitoring ovarian stimulation.[60] Clomiphene citrate is considerably cheaper than human gonadotrophins; in 1968, for example, the basic cost to the National Health Service of 30 tablets each of 50 mg clomiphene citrate as Clomid – sufficient for six months' treatment – was £1 10s.[61] That same year, women attending Crooke's clinic were asked to pay £200 for a treatment cycle of human gonadotrophins.[62] Some doctors began to use clomiphene citrate as an endocrine tonic; they prescribed it for infertile women who ovulated irregularly in order to get the system working more efficiently. It was also used as substitute therapy for women who did not menstruate and who did not wish to become pregnant, in order for them to experience the psychological benefits said to be derived from menstruating.

Increasing confidence in the susceptibility of the ovaries to pharmacology encouraged other pharmaceutical companies to enter the market for both ovulation-inhibiting and ovulation-inducing preparations. The market for naturally occuring exogenous gonadotrophins is not easy to enter; the difficulties in securing supplies of raw materials were pointed out early on in this chapter. However, clomiphene citrate-type substances are comparatively simple to formulate. In 1971, for example, an announcement was made of promising preliminary trials on anovular women of ICI 46,474 – now called Tamoxifen – a close relative of clomiphene citrate and a distant cousin of diethylstilboestrol (DES).[63] It was followed by 'Buserelin' produced by Hoechst, 'Goserelin' also made by ICI, and cyclofenil, sold as 'Rehibin' by Serono. When the patent on clomiphene citrate expired, Serono began to sell it under the brand name 'Serophene'.

Paradoxically, as relatives of clomiphene citrate began to appear on the market, doubts began to creep in about its efficacy: 'double-blind' trials suggested that a placebo was as effective as clomiphene citrate in making an anovular woman ovulate.[64] Despite their initial promise, drugs for treating anovulation provided doctors with little glory. In 1975 an American review of recent developments in the investigation and treatment of infertility opened with the following comment:

> Although clomiphene and menopausal gonadotrophins have proved to be extremely effective for ovulation induction in properly selected patients, the pregnancy rate of the former is less than anticipated, and the cost, adverse side effects, intricacies of administration and high rate of multiple births associated with the latter have limited its use to the specialist in the field.[65]

None the less, both drugs allowed the pharmaceutical industry to establish a respectable foothold for its products in the treatment of infertility.

The press reported clinical trials of both human gonadotrophins and clomiphene citrate in glowing terms. Journalists dubbed them 'miracle', 'wonder' and even 'happiness' drugs, which sent barren ovaries into 'ecstatic over-excitement'.[66] The only whiff of disapproval came from people who were worried that multiple births might exacerbate the problem of overpopulation. Panic over the threat of global overpopulation was approaching its zenith around the time that both human gonadotrophins and clomiphene citrate were being tested. Gemzell defended his work as

follows: 'We doctors have to strike a human balance between the population explosion and the need for birth control pills, on the one hand, and
the supreme happiness of the mother-to-be on the other.'[67]

Both Conservative and Labour governments succumbed to pressure
from the antinatalist 'population explosion' lobby. In 1967, legislation
governing termination of pregnancy was made more liberal, and the
National Health Service began to provide an abortion service. That same
year, the NHS (Family Planning) Act, sponsored by both Labour and
Conservative parties, empowered local authorities to offer advice on family planning without regard for marital status, on social as well as medical
grounds.[68] In 1974, the National Health Service accepted responsibility for
the family planning clinics provided by both local authorities and voluntary organizations, including the FPA.

A key reason why opposition to these radical developments was muted
is that most of the vociferous opponents of materialist interventions into
reproduction were preoccupied elsewhere, albeit in a related controversy.
Many Roman Catholics had become disillusioned with the Church's teaching on fertility and sexuality, believing it to be inconsistent with a modern
world – especially one confronted with the disastrous consequences of a
rapidly growing population. In 1965, *The Tablet*, a Catholic newspaper,
was overwhelmed by the weight of letters it received on the rights and
wrongs of birth control.[69] *Humanae vitae*, the papal encyclical which
restated the Church's opposition to contraception and delivered its views
on the problem of population, was published in 1968, and was met by a
storm of protest both within and outside the Catholic community. The
encyclical exacerbated the resentment felt by many British Catholics towards papal authority over the Church in Britain. In effect, controversy
within the Church exhausted Catholic energy and weakened any protest over external developments. One consequence of the crisis was that
opposition to materialist interventions into fertility ceased to be an overwhelmingly Catholic and conservative movement; it began to be made up
of a broad church of unlikely bedfellows.[70]

Fear of global overpopulation was instrumental in persuading the
British government to make more accessible to women advice and facilities for controlling fertility. Policies were directed at women in order to
save the nation and the world from an impending Malthusian disaster, and
not in recognition of women's reproductive rights. None the less, the
government dared not openly admit to having a population policy for fear
of being associated with totalitarian regimes and of being accused of
treating the British people as if they were citizens of a poor, underdevel-
oped country instead of a nation in the vanguard of civilization.[71] It
adopted the strategy of depoliticization described in chapter 4, and placed
family planning services firmly under the rubric of health.[72] In 1971, for

example, the Conservative Minister of Health Keith Joseph told the Select Committee on Science and Technology, which was looking into the threat of overpopulation, that he regarded family size as entirely the responsibility of parents. Whether or not to provide advice on birth control should, he believed, be subject to the freedom of conscience of a doctor and not to the dictates of politicians. Furthermore, he considered the freedom of the doctor paramount, and would do all he could to preserve it.[73] Joseph neatly transformed a political problem of population into a medical concern subject only to the opinions of doctors. As an influential commentator on the National Health Service observed: 'Once an issue has been defined to belong to the health care arena (as distinct from the wider political stage) it was the doctor who represented the voice of expertise.'[74]

Doctors began to carry out procedures which hitherto they had deemed immoral.[75] They were even encouraged to do so by their august professional organizations. In 1972, for example, a working party of the RCOG made the following recommendations: the National Health Service should provide a comprehensive contraceptive service and facilities for male and female sterilization; medical students should be taught about contraception; and children should be given sex education in schools.[76] Gynaecologists were responsible for termination of pregnancy and female sterilization. General practitioners, who had been the staunchest and most persistent opponents of birth control for most of the century, became key providers of contraception. When asked to provide contraceptives to their patients in the early 1970s, many had objected on the grounds that such an activity reduced their professional status to that of a barber or retailer of rubber goods; yet when the government agreed to pay them a fee for the service, almost all declared themselves willing to provide women with contraception.[77]

Although prepared to relax legislation and regulations governing women's access to birth control and abortion, neither Conservative nor Labour governments made available sufficient resources to meet the demand their policies had revealed. One reason for their parsimony is reluctance to appear wholly committed to the measures. However, the National Health Service accepted responsibility for women's fertility at a time when politicians were exercised by the service's apparently insatiable appetite for resources. Efficiency savings were the order of the day. The impact on patient care was predictable: after the abortion law was liberalized in 1967, for example, extra hospital beds, nurses and doctors were not provided to meet the increased demand within the National Healh Service. Inevitably many women suffered; those on waiting lists for other gynaecological procedures were forced to wait much longer or seek private medical attention.[78]

The private medical sector was the major beneficiary of underfunding of gynaecological services within the National Health Service. This is especially evident in relation to abortion, where data on the number of operations performed are readily available. These show that although in theory termination of pregnancy is available on the National Health Service, in practice around half on the women seeking an abortion have to pay for it. When the Labour Party launched an attack on private medical practice within National Health Service facilities in the early 1970s, it was opposed on the grounds that the right to choose to pay for medical attention is a feature of a liberal democratic society.[79] This attack on patients' rights was challenged by the medical profession.[80] In contrast, women's right to choose contraception, abortion and sterilization was not recognized. In its Report published in 1979, the Royal Commission on the National Health Service, set up in order to deliberate on the controversy provoked by Labour's attack on private medicine, singled out two functions in respect of which the private medical sector made a significant contribution to the health care of the nation: abortions and the care of the chronically sick. In 1986, abortions accounted for 19 per cent – by far the largest single component – of the estimated total caseload of non-NHS hospitals in England and Wales.[81]

In theory, treatments of infertility benefited from the same tendencies that liberalized the law and regulations governing abortion, contraception and sterilization; in practice, the benefit was confined to women who could pay for them. This is evident in relation to AID. According to a survey carried out by the BMA in 1971, ten out of 513 leading gynaecologists, all heads of obstetrics and gynaecology units in the country, provided AID. However, a further 91 said they were willing to arrange AID for suitable patients; 115 were prepared to act as a centre for investigating suitable candidates; and 102 indicated that they referred suitable cases to other colleagues, mostly practising within the private medical sector. A panel appointed by the BMA under the chairmanship of John Peel, formerly the Queen's gynaecologist, reported in 1973 that there were grounds for making AID available within the NHS, albeit in a limited number of centres.[82] In 1976, marking a revolutionary change in its attitudes towards AID, the RCOG held a study day on the technique.[83] Three years later, the Department of Health and Social Security (DHSS) provided the College with funds to publish an information booklet for women seeking AID.[84]

When AID was introduced into a National Health Service hospital, it was in response to doctors' and not patients' perceptions of need. Arranging AID was justified as a logical development within medicine, a 'natural extension of a large infertility investigation and treatment clinic'.[85] The stubborn refusal of male infertility to submit to any of the treatments medicine devised left AID as the only effective therapy available to doctors. The right to clinical freedom, to practise medicine as she or he sees fit, means that once a doctor decides to arrange AID the only constraints on her or his practice are practical and financial. Nevertheless, doctors said it was more difficult to arrange AID in the National Health Service than in the private medical sector. Facilities available in NHS hospitals were unsuitable; AID demands secrecy and sensitivity, which were rarely found in its infertility clinics. The provision of a suitable couch and of a nurse willing to help in the outpatient clinic on a permanent basis – staff turnover was typically high – and making sure that the liquid nitrogen needed to maintain the temperature of a semen bank was delivered on the right day were considered beyond the administrative competence of most National Health Service hospitals.[86]

When in 1977 the RCOG investigated the availability of AID in the UK, lack of finance emerged as the most pressing problem confronting the twenty-two centres then arranging it. Few National Health Service clinics offering AID were funded entirely by the state; most were 'semi-private', that is, wholly or partially subsidized by research money, or a university grant, or fees charged to patients.[87] This arrangement was similar to that in force in National Health Service hospitals where human gonadotrophins were administered (described above). Yet semi-private arrangements contravene the basic principle of the National Health Service, which was introduced in order to provide medical care free at the point of delivery.

Medical and dental students studying at National Health Service teaching hospitals were the main source of semen in both private and National Health Service clinics. Yet within the National Health Service, demand for AID exceeded supply of semen; women had to wait between six and twelve months for treatment. In contrast, the waiting time within the private medical sector was a matter of weeks. The choice was stark: as one woman put it, 'it turned out there was a long waiting list for AID on the National Health Service in our area and they weren't taking on any new patients for another six months. Neither of us was very keen on the idea of going for private treatment, but it was the only answer, as we didn't feel we could wait much longer.'[88] In 1978, the British Pregnancy Advisory Service (BPAS) announced that it was setting up a network of clinics throughout Britain to provide AID (BPAS is a charitable organization set up in 1968 to provide a low-cost, safe abortion service for women unable to gain access to National Health Service facilities).[89] The following year, the AID subcommittee of the RCOG called for new facilities within the National Health Service to meet the growing demand for AID.[90]

When provided within a National Health Service hospital, albeit on a semi-private basis, fees for AID were modest; patients were usually asked to reimburse the money paid to the semen donor, which in 1977 was at most £15.[91] In the private medical sector the cost could be considerable; some private clinics were reputed to charge £1,000 for a course of AID. In 1981 Renee Short, Member of Parliament and Chair of the Commons Select Committee on Social Services, chastised the government for permitting 'cowboy clinics' to cash in on the anguish of women whose husbands are infertile. She blamed women's vulnerability to exploitation on the inadequacies of the National Health Service.[92]

It is difficult to cite a more liberal tendency as the driving force behind the increasing willingness of doctors to arrange AID. They hedged the pro-cedure with caveats and exclusions suggestive of a stubborn belief that women derive their greatest happiness through marriage, dependence on a husband and motherhood. Doctors who arranged AID insisted that they would treat only married women, although some said they would con-sider women in a so-called stable heterosexual relationship. Involuntarily childless single women were excluded from estimates of the potential demand for AID, which was measured in terms of couples whose wish for a family was denied them because of the infertility of the husband; in 1975, they were estimated to number approximately a quarter of a million.[93] Doctors' insistence that AID should be confined to women in stable heterosexual relationships looks like an attempt to turn the clock back to a mythic era when both marital and parental homes were un-broken. The 1969 Divorce Reform Act, which had made it far easier to obtain a divorce, had exposed the instability of the institutions of marriage and the family. The statistics on divorce speak for themselves: in 1958, 25,584 divorce petitions had been filed; in 1975, that number had risen to 138,048, and it continued to increase until it reached a plateau of around 160,000 divorces every year.[94]

Doctors who arranged AID went to considerable lengths to reassure themselves that the marriages of women both before and after they had undergone AID were both happy and stable. In 1976, Margaret Jackson told a meeting on AID organized by the RCOG that in her long experience, only five out of 600 marriages in which she had arranged AID had broken down.[95] Bridget Mason, who had a thriving private practice in central London, said that most of her patients were 'nice young couples'.[96] The RCOG's handbook on AID, published in 1979, described the process as being available to happily married couples.[97] An investigation into the psychological background of women and their husbands who were re-ferred for AID to the City Hospital, Nottingham, established that all of them were in a stable marriage, most lived in adequate homes, nearly all couples maintained a close relationship with their parents, and with almost no exceptions, they recalled a happy childhood which, they said, was a stimulus for their wish for their own family.[98] Bernard Sandler, who had followed up many of his AID babies, claimed that most of them turned out to be above average in both mental ability and character formation.[99] In his experience, the accepting husband adored the child and often made a better father than the average married man.[100]

In the 1940s, opponents of AID had deemed the technique immoral on the grounds that a syringe could not counterfeit the spiritual essence invested in a conceptus and its parents' home by the act of marital hetero-sexual intercourse. Yet by the 1970s a syringe had ceased to represent a threat to the institution of marriage. Instead, the ethics of the procedure were determined by the moral status of the woman in whom the syringe was inserted. Doctors began to claim that artificial was equally as effec-tive as natural insemination in terms of its ability to make married women pregnant; where it transformed an unhappy, because barren, marriage into a happy, stable family unit, they deemed it a worthwhile, moral enterprise.

During the 1970s, heterosexual intercourse posed a far greater threat to the institutions of marriage and the family than a syringe of donated semen wielded by a doctor. The former was out of control and its effects unknown, whereas certainty and morality were assured in the latter by the doctor responsible for its arrangement. A now famous study had suggested that six out of every twenty babies born to married women had been fathered by someone other than their mothers' husbands.[101] Although the investigation related to just one town in the south-east of England, its findings were exploited to suggest an epidemic of adultery and cuckolded husbands throughout Britain. Indeed, AID children took the moral high ground above children conceived 'naturally'; at least the circumstances of their conception were known and consented to by their mothers' husbands. And although AID children are technically ille-gitimate, the sharp rise in the number of children born outside of marriage, and changing social attitudes towards them, weakened objections to the procedure on these grounds.[102]

Doctors developed a classification system which described the medical and moral parameters of AID. AID was sanctioned as both ethical and medical where the patient was a happily married woman: an involuntarily childless wife is clearly ill, and in need of medical treatment. However, where a doctor is party to an arrangement with an unsuitable woman – a single heterosexual woman, a lesbian or a woman in a surrogacy arrange-ment – the procedure is still medical but ceases to be ethical, and the doctor's professional standing is called into question. From the profes-sion's point of view, AID is the wrong treatment of lesbian tendencies, and like any inappropriately prescribed medicine would have deleterious, iatrogenic effects on a resulting child and society at large. As one doctor put it, 'to use an unnatural method of conception to bolster up an un-natural relationship is unlikely to produce a satisfactory result'.[103] Ar-ranged in circumstances outside doctors' control, for example through an informal network such as a self-insemination group, AID ceases to be a medical procedure at all: in 1979 the BMA defined AID without any medical assistance as a non-medical action.[104]

Some doctors justified the rules on the grounds that attending to the moral dimension of AID offered them a way of escaping invidious com-parison with a technician working in the Milk Marketing Board's AI centre serving dairy cows. Yet an urge to pass moral judgement is evident in gynaecologists' role as gatekeepers of other medical procedures relating to women's fertility. The same set of principles governed doctors' attitudes towards abortion: many gynaecologists were loath to terminate the preg-nancy of a married woman, yet willing to do so if the patient was un-married.[105] Similarly, many doctors who frowned on abortion for social reasons sanctioned it where screening for neural tube defects indicated an abnormality in the foetus, even though most terminations on social grounds are performed at a far earlier gestational age than abortions performed for medical reasons. When asked their opinion of abortion in the early 1980s, a majority of gynaecologists supported a doctor's right to choose to prevent the birth of a child with a disability, even when the severity of the disability was unknown; a minority supported a woman's right to exercise control over her own destiny.[106]

The long-established right of clinical freedom to do what they believe is in the best interests of their patients justifies doctors' pursuit of their own interests, even at the expense of their women patients. Yet in important respects gynaecologists were working on behalf of politicians, address-ing a problem of population as if it were a medical concern. Succes-sive governments have benefited from doctors' tenacious hold on their right both to exercise clinical freedom and to make moral judgements of their women patients, as it absolves politicians of responsibility for con-troversial policies. It is doctors, and not politicians, who appear to be making the difficult decisions. The process of depoliticization is at its most visible in relation to abortion.[107] By introducing the question of a pregnant woman's mental health and her 'actual and reasonably foreseeable en-vironment', for example, the 'special clause', in the 1967 Abortion Act gave doctors greater scope in making covert moral, as opposed to technical, decisions about women's suitability as mothers. The Act also respected doctors' right to follow the dictates of their own conscience; anyone troubled by the ethics of abortion did not have to perform it.

Judgements of the moral status of women patients are used by enthusiasts to explain why the new assisted conception technologies are necessary.

These technologies include fertilization in vitro, embryo transfer and similar procedures involving the manipulation outside the body of human sperm, eggs and embryo; from here on they are referred to collectively as assisted conception technologies.[108] Broadly speaking, assisted conception technologies substitute insemination by means of heterosexual intercourse with other methods through which fertilization may take place either within the woman's body – for example, gamete intrafallopian transfer (GIFT), where sperm are injected directly into the woman's pelvic cavity – or outside of it – for example, in vitro fertilization (IVF), where eggs removed from a woman's body are fertilized in a petrie dish, and the resulting embryos placed in the uterus through the cervix. In almost all methods, women take drugs such as gonadotrophins and clomiphene citrate in order to 'superovulate', that is, produce several eggs. Some require the woman to undergo surgery under anaesthesia.

Robert Edwards, the pioneer of the embryological aspects of the research which led to the development of the techniques culminating in the fertilization in vitro of a human egg, described his primary preoccupation as 'to study human embryology and allow women, who were seemingly condemned for ever to a life of infertility, to bear their own children fathered by their husband'.[109] And Edwards' colleague, the gynaecologist Patrick Steptoe (1913–88) persisted in the face of opposition from the medical establishment and, later, ill-health: 'What kept him going was that he was determined to help his patients.'[110] According to the modern representation of infertility, infertile women are 'desperate', 'sufferers of infertility' or 'victims of childlessness'. Thankfully, assisted conception technologies can provide them with a 'miracle baby'; only the heartless and ethically rootless would ban them. As the anthropologist Sarah Franklin has pointed out, the modern myth of infertility cites 'the emotions of the couple, their "longing" and "hope" as a way into a discussion of medical achievements, thereby providing an apparently natural and obvious link between the "hope for a medical cure" and the capability of medical science to provide one'.[111] Yet, as was revealed in the chapter 5, in the 1950s despair and hope were incorporated into a different infertility myth: British gynaecologists were advised that withholding treatment which had only a small chance of working was in the patient's best interests; it would discourage the development of an unhealthy, obsessive longing for a child, and encourage women to seek and develop other sources of meaning and fulfilment in their lives.

Gynaecologists offering assisted conception technologies publicly parade their concern about the moral status of patients, although this tendency is more pronounced in doctors working within the National Health Service than in the private medical sector. A woman with a criminal conviction for running a brothel and soliciting for prostitution was refused

IVF by a National Health Service gynaecologist on the grounds that she would fail the criteria of suitable motherhood set by an adoption society.[112] Similarly, the media debated the suitability for treatment with assisted conception technology in the National Health Service of a woman who gave birth to quads; her moral status was considered ambiguous because she already had children from a first marriage, was divorced and had undergone voluntary sterilization.[113]

Enthusiasts of assisted conception are well rehearsed in the delivery of moral messages about their patients. However, they have added to their authority by spending considerable energy and resources on psychological research to demonstrate that in married women, involuntary childlessness causes high levels of anxiety and depression, and creates marital and sexual difficulties.[114] Enthusiasts of assisted conception technologies claim to seek to restore marital harmony and create nuclear families in circumstances hitherto deemed hopeless. Paradoxically, this moral enterprise sanctions procedures such as egg donation between sisters, and between mother and daughter, and surrogacy arrangements, which rewrite the rules of conception and birth and are effectively turning family relationships on their head.[115]

Despite its preoccupation with the moral status of its patients, gynaecology masquerades as a progressive profession, one that is willing to flout conventional morals in order to transform a wife into a mother. Edwards said Steptoe 'handled embryos in the laboratory – he was the first obstetrician to do so. He was streets ahead of anyone else.'[116] An article speaking in favour of human embryo research published in the *New Scientist* was given a headline which conjures up their modern image: 'New Conception Threatened by Old Morality'.[117] The choice of the name PROGRESS for an organization set up in November 1985 by fourteen voluntary bodies concerned with infertility and people suffering from a physical or mental disability of genetic origin reflects the concern of enthusiasts of assisted conception technologies to appear to be in the forefront of ideas. PROGRESS's purpose was to lobby for parliamentary support of research on human embryos, which it believes will improve the effectiveness of assisted conception and allow doctors to develop prenatal screening tests for genetic diseases.[118]

Claiming to be working in the interests of suitable women patients, and conveying the impression that opponents of the new technologies are reactionary, are two of several different strategies which have effectively obscured the real interests pursued by enthusiasts of the new reproductive medicine. Another is to accuse opponents of human embryo research of being ignorant of the facts, of muddying the waters and misleading the public. Yet clarity is not evident in the propaganda produced by supporters of assisted conception. Enthusiasts insist on declaiming who they are not; they rarely reveal what they as individuals, a profession or an industry stand to gain from the technology. The public is given only negative reassurances: enthusiasts are not the crazy sort of scientists found in science fiction; human embryo research is not being exploited in order to bring into existence a race of subhuman slaves of a mad dictator, nor as a way of conceiving a monstrous chimera.[119]

The interests served by the technology of assisted conception have also been obscured by the tendency to evaluate it in terms of abstract ethics. A Committee of Inquiry was set up by the Conservative government in 1982 'to examine the social, ethical and legal implications of recent, and potential developments in the field of human assisted reproduction'. Chaired by Mary Warnock, it is referred to as the Warnock Committee. Not only were political and economic considerations specifically excluded from the Committee's brief, but in its deliberations it gave considerable and arguably undue weight to ethics, reflecting perhaps the influence of Mary Warnock herself, a moral philosopher. Indeed, while the foreword of the Committee's report goes to the trouble of explaining the concept of ethics it adopted[120] – it refers to the word 'moral' on fifteen occasions, or once every seven lines – it makes no comment on its approach to the legal or social implications of assisted conception techniques, thereby conveying the impression that they are uninteresting and irrelevant to the issues under consideration.[121]

During the 1980s, the ethics of human embryo manipulation and research received unprecedented attention in the media, and in parliamentary, medical, ethical, and natural and social scientific circles.[122] However, in retrospect, it is clear that opponents of assisted conception technologies had the cards stacked against them. One reason for their failure to influence development is that opposition to assisted conception technologies proved a weaker mobilizing force than the other concerns exercising what was a very broad church. It was pointed out earlier in this chapter that by the 1970s opposition to materialist interventions into reproduction had ceased to be a predominantly Roman Catholic movement; instead, it was made up of a motley collection of activists including radical feminists, Catholics, neo-conservatives hostile to the liberal attitudes typified by the 1960s, and people with physical and mental disabilities – groups which had little in common save this one issue, and which were all wedded to their own campaigning strategies. Furthermore, opposition to assisted conception technologies did not necessarily top their agenda: people with physical and mental disabilities, for example, were more exercised about the implications of immediate threats to resources and diminishing opportunities than about assisted conception technologies which promise to ensure that, in the future, people like them will not be born.

The most vocal opponents of the technologies were the anti-abortion lobby, who represented the human embryo as a person endowed with a soul. In effect, the embryo was subjected to a process similar to that which had redefined the foetus as a person. 'Foetal personhood', the concept of the foetus as a child capable of independent existence waiting to be born – rather than a developing bundle of tissues and cells, wholly dependent for survival on its mother's body – was first exploited in order to mobilize a public attack on abortion.[123] The anti-abortion lobby used emotive images of a child-like foetus in order to encourage people to think of abortion as infanticide. Feminists have developed a powerful critique of the concept of foetal personhood, in particular its implications for women's civil rights. Sarah Franklin puts the argument forcefully:

> Fetal citizenship contradicts the citizenship of women; indeed, it contradicts their individuality. Endowing fetuses with full civil rights ironically confers upon them a status in relation to the patriarchal social contract *which women never had to begin with*. It is thus a double blow, extending feminine disenfranchizement from the patriarchal state, and locating within their bodies a citizen with greater rights to bodily integrity than they have.[124]

Enthusiasts of research on and manipulation of human embryos deployed a metaphysical argument in order to defeat concerted campaigns to have research on and manipulation of human embryos outlawed. The term 'pre-embryo' was developed as a way of distinguishing human embryos which had not developed a 'primitive streak' from those that had.[125] The primitive streak, which emerges when the human embryo is fourteen days old, is the earliest manifestation of a nervous system, which in turn could be said to be the first moment at which a bundle of embryonic cells takes on human aspects. The Warnock Committee chose this stage as the cut-off point after which research on human embryos was forbidden.[126] By conceding the possibility that once the primitive streak has developed an embryo may have human attributes, gynaecologists held on to a concept of foetal personhood which is crucial in their other work as obstetricians.[127] In obstetrics, an image of foetal personhood has been constructed by a range of visual techniques which provide obstetricians with a 'window on the womb' through which to survey and even treat the developing foetus. It leaves the status of abortion ambiguous, but enormously extends obstetricians' authority over women during pregnancy.

The many different participants involved in and relationships created by assisted conception technologies have made complex and unstable the development of a classification system of their medical and moral dimensions. For cash or kind, gynaecologists, patients and donors are participating in the exchange of semen, eggs, embryos and babies, in arrangements which hitherto were considered unlikely outside a science fiction fantasy. Nevertheless, using the precedent established by AID in the 1970s, enthusiasts assert that if guidelines on manipulation of human embryos are observed, and the moral status of the woman patient is policed, the procedures are medically and ethically appropriate treatments of infertility. Gynaecologists, scientists and their representatives actively encouraged the establishment of a code of practice for doctors and scientists manipulating and performing research on human embryos.[128] In 1985, the RCOG and MRC set up the Voluntary Licensing Authority for Human In Vitro Fertilization and Embryology (VLA) as a stop-gap measure until the government had formulated its response to the recommendations of the Warnock Committee. The original VLA guidelines were based on those already in use among pioneering teams, but also incorporated recommendations from the Warnock Committee, the MRC and the RCOG. The VLA had no statutory power to enforce them; it relied on a 'gentlemen's agreement', that is, on peer group pressure.[129] In 1989, the VLA was renamed the Interim Licensing Authority (ILA) in anticipation of the establishment of a Statutory Licensing Authority, which came into effect in 1991, as a result of the passage of the Human Fertilization and Embryology Act 1990. The Act acknowledges the active part played by doctors and scientists in establishing a code of practice; it stipulates that between one-third and one-half of the members of the Human Fertilization and Embryology Authority (HFEA) should be medical practitioners or otherwise involved in such activities.

Despite considerable opposition, the project of enthusiasts has succeeded in Britain, because in important respects it is in keeping with the radical spirit, purpose and ambitions of modern British Conservatives. Although they claim to be progressives, the enthusiasts' vision of womanhood endorses the Conservatives' illiberal attitude towards sexuality, promotion of sexual inequalities and traditional vision of the institutions of marriage and the family. Furthermore, many gynaecologists promoting these techniques are sympathetic to the Conservatives' plans to encourage private medicine and the reclamation of the National Health Service for private accumulation. Indeed, because previously gynaecology had established both a solid foundation in the private medical sector and the precedent of semi-private arrangements within the National Health Service, assisted conception technology was an early beneficiary of the Conservatives' political objectives.

Fertilization in vitro and embryo transfer represent the first innovations in the treatment of infertility developed by a gynaecologist since Rubin introduced the tubal insufflation test shortly after the First World War. As with AID, the formative years of these techniques were those between the wars. However, investigators were not then immediately concerned with the alleviation of infertility. In the interwar years, research into fertilization in vitro sought to uncover the processes of fertilization and embryogenesis; embryo transfer was developed both as a theoretical exercise and in order to increase the productivity and profitability of animal husbandry.[130] Although non-human laboratory animals were the principal focus of the research, at the time doctors speculated that 'conception in a watch glass' might one day prove a boon to barren women with closed fallopian tubes.[131]

Chapter 5 showed how, after the Second World War, British gynaecologists evinced little enthusiasm for research into existing or new procedures for the investigation and treatment of infertility; furthermore, some of them actively discouraged patients from seeking medical help. In relation to infertility, gynaecologists seem to have been afflicted by a general malaise. Even the laparoscope, an instrument pioneered in Britain by Patrick Steptoe which allows a gynaecologist to visualize directly a woman's pelvic organs, was regarded with scepticism; among gynaecologists it was the frequent butt of what Steptoe called 'absurd anti-laparoscopy remarks'.[132]

Steptoe failed to secure an appointment as consultant obstetrician and gynaecologist in a leading London hospital and retreated north, to Oldham General Hospital, where as well as seeing patients he pursued pet projects, like the laparoscope, which were at odds with those favoured by the gynaecological establishment.[133] Disregarding his professional colleagues' general pessimism, in 1968 Steptoe embarked on a collaboration with Robert Edwards, a scientist working at Cambridge University, on a new way of overcoming infertility caused by inoperable blocked fallopian tubes. Edwards had worked at the MRC with Alan Parkes, the reproductive physiologist who was a leading participant in what he described as 'the interwar endocrinological gold rush'. Indeed, it was Edwards who initiated the collaboration; as he put it, 'I needed a man who could get me to the ovary.[134]

The birth in 1978 of the first baby conceived in vitro demonstrates the power of clinical freedom; Edwards and Steptoe were able to persist with their research in the face of hostile criticism from both within and outside the medical profession. Because it was troubled by the ethics of what they were doing, the MRC refused Steptoe and Edwards financial support. And in the early days of their work, a paper written by Steptoe and Edwards on the use of the laparoscope for egg retrieval in women was rejected by the editors of a scientific journal on ethical grounds.[135] As was pointed out above, during the late 1960s scrutiny of medical research proposals by a research ethics committee was only just being suggested. Indeed, it is interesting to speculate what would have happened to Steptoe and

Edwards' original research proposal if it had been subjected to the procedures currently in operation. Now, if medical researchers fail to gain the approval of a research ethics committee, they are denied access to patients within the National Health Service, which means that their project is scuppered. Yet Edwards admitted that during his first meeting with Steptoe at which they discussed their collaboration, 'ethical concerns hardly entered into our conversation'.[136] Instead, the ethics of their controversial research have been subjected to extensive and intensive retrospective evaluation by, among others, the Warnock Committee.[137]

The research was successful, both in terms of leading to the birth of the first 'test tube' baby and also financially. The *Daily Mail* paid around £100,000 for the magazine and newspaper rights to the personal story of the first 'test tube family', and both Edwards and Steptoe received offers (which were not accepted) of very large sums of money for exclusive medical and scientific information about the birth.[138] Yet it is doubtful whether anyone then appreciated the enormous commercial potential of their work. It has transformed both the profit and loss account and the balance sheet of gynaecology beyond recognition. Shortly after the birth of the first 'test tube' baby, increasing numbers of gynaecologists began to treat involuntarily childless women using assisted conception techniques. In the first annual report of the VLA, published in 1986, twenty-three clinics were stated to be offering IVF in the UK, and four were planning to set up a programme in the near future.[139] The statistical analysis attached by the ILA to the first annual report of the HFEA, published in 1992, lists sixty-four centres offering IVF and sixty-seven offering GIFT.[140] Yet a large capital sum is required in order to establish a clinic offering IVF. In 1988, for example, £550,000 would buy a clinic with the facilities to offer IVF to 400 women each year.[141] In the same year, a group of enterprising gynaecologists from the St James' Hospital, Leeds, attempted to raise £1 million capital on the stock market in order to set up a private clinic for assisted conception.[142] Considerably less capital is needed for GIFT. In 1987, the equipment necessary to carry out GIFT cost a meagre £2,676.[143] Furthermore, the cost of training is often met by drug companies such as Serono.

In 1978 Steptoe retired from his National Health Service appointment and, with Edwards, set up Bourn Hall, a private IVF clinic, which was opened in 1980.[144] Seven years later, Bourn Hall was sold to Ares-Serono, a multinational pharmaceutical company and the world's major supplier of human menopausal gonadotrophins. For Ares-Serono, the purchase represented 'vertical integration', that is, expansion by buying up a major customer of many of its products. Although vertical integration is a well-established commercial strategy for increasing profitability, it is an unprecedented development in British medicine. However, from Ares-Serono's point of view, it was a logical move: it represented a good way of investing profits accrued as a result of the company's enormous expansion in sales during the 1980s, reflecting, no doubt, the increased demand for its fertility drugs stimulated by assisted conception technology. The company's total sales in 1982 were US$95.5 million and in 1988 US$420.3 million; infertility drugs contributed an estimated US$23.9 million in 1982 and US$130.0 million in 1988; overall operating profit was US$18.9 million in 1982, and US$96.0 million in 1988.[145] In 1988, Bourn Hall merged with the Hallam Centre, a Harley Street private infertility clinic run by Bridget Mason, an AID specialist, to form Bourn-Hallam.

Ares-Serono now boasts that it owns the largest IVF centre in the world, carrying out 2,500 IVF and GIFT cycles a year as well as a large number of frozen embryo replacement cycles, artificial insemination, surrogacy and other infertility treatments.[146] A stork carrying a baby in a sling hanging from its beak has been adopted as the company's logo. The stork is a migratory bird, with a strong body and easy flight. Britain is being used as a base from which to develop an export market of assisted conception technology: in 1990, for example, a dozen Bourn-Hallam specialists helped set up clinics and train staff in China, Japan, USA, India, Italy, Japan, Malaysia, Thailand, Singapore, Australia, Indonesia, Scandinavia, Korea and Austria.[147]

Although Bourn-Hallam dominates the UK market for assisted conception, other gynaecologists have been attracted into the field. At first, some gynaecologists attempted to introduce assisted conception technology into National Health Service hospitals. Their enthusiasm emerged at a time when Conservative politicians were eager to promote private medical care both outside and within the National Health Service. In 1976, the Labour government had removed the advantages of paying for treatment in NHS hospitals by giving private and NHS patients the same status on waiting lists and parity of access to diagnostic and other services. In 1980, the Conservative government which had been returned to office in 1979 under Margaret Thatcher reversed this policy. The Health Services Act 1980 reduced restrictions on private medicine in the National Health Service, legalized lotteries and permitted health authorities to engage in voluntary fund-raising. National Health Service consultants' contracts were altered so that they could undertake significantly more private practice without forfeiting their positions and privileges in the NHS.[148]

Gynaecologists took advantage of the legislation and have demonstrated considerable entrepreneurial flair in the different schemes developed for introducing assisted conception technologies into National Health Service hospitals. By attaching an IVF service on to existing National Health Service facilities, it was possible to avoid having to find the large start-up capital costs of an independent unit. In addition, the revenue costs for an IVF unit are lower if it is kept within an National

Health Service hospital because it can take advantage of operating theatre, wards, laboratory facilities, nursing and ancilliary staff, which in the private medical sector have to be fully funded. Clinics made full use of their right to raise funds within the National Health Service by encouraging patients' support groups to generate money to buy equipment. So valuable is their contribution to capital costs that one consultant advised his colleagues to set up a support group before opening a clinic.[149]

The precedent of 'semi-private' arrangements established by gynaecologists in relation to AID and human menopausal gonadotrophins was extended to IVF and GIFT. Some National Health Service clinics 'charged' patients for IVF and GIFT treatment, although they descibed the charge euphemistically as a 'voluntary' contribution. Other consultants operated a 'Robin Hood' system: 'robbing' better-off patients in order to provide free treatment for people who might otherwise go without. The most inventive scheme was that developed by the Fazakerley Hospital, Liverpool, where an incentive scheme was run in conjunction with a 'Robin Hood' system. People on the incentive scheme who raise funds for the unit get credits which count towards the cost of their treatment: £1,200 raised qualified a patient for a free treatment cycle.[150] Another semi-private arrangement led to a National Health Service centre and a nearby private clinic sharing staff.[151] Most of these innovative schemes have been developed by relatively small units where success rates, measured by chances of women becoming pregnant, are almost half those in the larger units.[152]

In the late 1980s the Conservative government launched another attack on the public sector, including the National Health Service, to encourage further reclamation of the NHS for private profit. As a result, all patients seeking medical care, including involuntarily childless women, have found it increasingly difficult to undergo investigations and receive treatment within the National Health Service. By 1991 only three IVF centres were wholly funded by the National Health Service; nineteen were semi-private, and the remainder were wholly private centres.[153] Although the HFEA looks like the official response to the recommendations of the Warnock Committee on the ethics of research on and manipulation of human embryos, in fact the Authority represents the Conservatives' commitment to a mixed economy of health care, dominated by the private medical sector, and its antipathy to the principles embodied in the welfare state. The HFEA is described as a regulatory body which licenses and inspects clinics. As Rudolf Klein, an influential commentator on the National Health Service, observed, the Conservative government is replacing the welfare state with the regulatory state: 'Every privatisation initiative led to the creation of new regulatory agencies or the strengthening of old ones. The emphasis on moving away from the public provision of services meant also increasing reliance on public authorities to regulate services provided by others'.[154] The Authority's work is enshrined in a code of practice which, although directing the Authority to respect life at all stages in its development, excludes adult women from that consideration. The HFEA is not empowered to consider the issue of unequal access to assisted conception technologies.[155] Nor has it been set up to look after patients' welfare. There is no formal mechanism whereby women who receive poor or negligent treatment at a clinic which the HFEA has licensed can bring it to the Authority's attention. Although under the terms of their licences clinics have to log all complaints by patients, and report on them annually, that information is not made available to the public, who are left in ignorance about the standards of practice at clinics (as they are about 'take-home baby rates').

The concentration of power within the private medical sector is likely to make assisted conception technologies the principal treatment for involuntary childlessness. In 1990 in the UK, 9,964 women submitted to IVF and 2,332 had GIFT.[156] A rough estimate of the number of new cases a year in Britain is around 50,000.[157] Looked at from the perspective of private clinics offering assisted conception techniques – many of which do not have the staff or facilities to carry out the other procedures described in this book – the estimated 40,000 infertile women at present not undergoing such treatment represent a marketing opportunity. Indeed, in many clinics assisted conception technologies are used irrespective of the underlying cause of infertility, on the grounds that they offer women a greater chance of becoming a mother than older treatments. Yet the effectiveness of the new technologies in comparison with the old has not been subjected to the sort of evaluation demanded of modern scientific medicine, that is, by a well-designed clinical trial. No one knows, for example, whether or not assisted conception technology is more effective in treating male infertility than established treatments such as AID, yet it is being promoted as such. Enthusiasts exploit the popular myth that most of life's ills can be cured by expensive and 'high-tech' procedures, and that most conditions will eventually succumb to scientific progress.[158]

The mixed economy of health care has also made it difficult to establish a consensus on an appropriate definition of success: should it be fertilization, a clinical pregancy (a positive pregnancy test), an established pregnancy, a live birth or a healthy baby? The answer depends on whose interest is being advanced, as the controversy about multiple pregnancy demonstrates. Although most conceptions of babies as a result of assisted conception technology are arranged in the private medical sector, a majority are born within the National Health Service. The high risk of a higher-order multiple pregnancy attendant on assisted conception technology is well known; for reasons which are unclear, sometimes they are easier to establish than a singleton conception. Doctors may be tempted to achieve them in order to boost their clinic's 'take-home baby rate', in the belief that this strategy might strengthen its competitive edge. During the 1980s, as a result of assisted conception technology, the numbers of triplets, quins and quads born increased by almost 50 per cent. However, women with a higher-order multiple pregnancy are more likely to experience complications and have a more difficult labour, and their babies have a high chance of being born prematurely and of having health problems demanding intensive medical care, as well as putting considerable pressure on special care baby units.[159] Not suprisingly, National Health Service staff resent the pressure on their resources, especially where they have no control over the circumstances which generate that demand. In 1985, for example, Ian Craft and his team, then working at the private Wellington Hospital, were warned against overloading National Health Service facilities. Craft was taken to task for placing three or more embryos in women and thereby increasing the risk of multiple pregnancy although his case was that there were good clinical grounds for doing so. In 1987, the controversy flared up again when premature sextuplets effectively closed a special care unit for three months; other preterm babies born during that period had to be turned away. As the paediatrician in charge of the unit put it, 'in order to save six babies we put 30 at risk'.[160] In order to manage this source of tension between the National Health Service and the private medical sector, the ILA restricted to a maximum of three the number of embryos a gynaecologist can place in a woman.

Robert Winston, consultant gynaecologist at the National Health Service Hammersmith Hospital, London, has been a vocal critic of what he regards as unseemly enthusiasm for assisted conception technologies amongst some of his colleagues. As he put it, 'huge resources are in danger of being squandered on IVF, while just a little more spent on the rest of infertility practice would actually be of far more benefit to our patients'.[161] Although he lacks the data necessary to support his claim, Winston and similarly minded infertility specialists argue that more women would become mothers if established tests and treatments were administered properly and appropriately. Throughout the 1980s Winston persistently and publicly criticized the poor standards of care meted out to infertile patients. The following is a typical example of his platform:

Women are given drugs to induce ovulation when they ovulate already, much tubal surgery is performed with instruments more suitable for sharpening pencils, infertile men are fobbed off with drugs which have no proven effect on sperm quality and many women are advised to adopt bizarre coital positions or employ peculiar douches which add unwelcome variety to their sex lives but do little for fertility.[162]

Winston and those who support him argue that the reason why many patients receive shoddy and inappropriate care is they are seen in general gynaecology National Health Service outpatient clinics, and not in a specialist, 'dedicated' infertility clinic.[163] They point the finger at the intra-professional rivalries, and organizational and administrative difficulties, which have a detrimental impact on standards of clinical practice within the National Health Service. The origins of this state of affairs have been discussed. For example, chapter 5 described how, after the Second World War, the RCOG resisted attempts by the British champions of dedicated clinics to establish them within National Health Service hospitals. Gynaecologists claimed that many women became pregnant just by keeping an appointment with a doctor; what medicine had to offer patients was relatively ineffective, and did not demand a specialist approach. As a result, dedicated infertility clinics were few and far between; most involuntarily childless women seeking medical attention in the National Health Service receive non-specialist attention, taking their place in gynaecological outpatient clinics and hospital wards alongside all other women seeking gynaecological treatments.

In the early 1980s, in response to difficulties within the specialty, the gynaecological establishment came out in support of a new type of specialist infertility clinic. The RCOG was troubled by the extent and complexity of obstetrics/gynaecology, which they believed had become too large a field for a gynaecologist to master. At the same time, obstetrician gynaecologists were facing competition for patients from general practitioners and specialists including paediatricians, urologists, oncologists and endocrinologists. In a report published in 1982, the RCOG set out proposals for the creation of a two-tier specialty: 'ordinary' non-specialist obstetrician gynaecologists who would continue to manage the majority of patients and presumably, fight off competition from general practitioners; and subspecialists, who would work in centres of excellence to which those patients needing more complex care would be referred. Four subspecialties were proposed: reproductive medicine; gynaecological urology; gynaecological oncology; and foetal medicine. Reproductive medicine would combine the techniques of endocrinology, surgery and assisted conception in order to treat patients suffering from disorders of menopause and menstruation and infertility; it would also develop expertise in male infertility.[164] In view of the widely recognized low standards of care received by most women with 'women's problems', and sufferers from male and female infertility, the RCOG was forced to rest its claim of the need for a subspecialty in reproductive medicine on assisted conception technology, which was changing so rapidly that it was impossible for every obstetrician gynaecologist to keep abreast of developments. The

RCOG envisaged that thirty subspecialists in reproductive medicine working in regional centres dotted around the country would satisfy demand within the National Health Service.

Three years later the Warnock Committee called for the establishment of specialist National Health Service infertility clinics, organized along lines similar to those proposed by the RCOG. Both proposals fell on deaf ears: a survey carried out in 1985 found that barely one-third of district health authorities in England and Wales had a dedicated infertility clinic, let alone a regional specialist centre.[165] And in Scotland the position is even worse.[166] The situation had not changed by 1990 when the survey was repeated.[167]

It is unlikely that more specialist clinics for infertility will be established within the National Health Service; indeed, the proposal now has an old-fashioned, outmoded ring to it. Increasingly problems of health care are being defined in managerial and financial and not clinical terms. According to the Conservatives, the National Health Service needs to make more effective and efficient use of resources; technical and professional specialization should be discouraged as they are expensive. Financial considerations have crept into decisions about resource allocation in National Health Service, to the detriment of involuntarily childless women. Health economists and health service managers are enthusiastically working out the 'trade-off' values of different procedures to the National Health Service: will they get a better return from money spent on IVF rather than on a hip replacement operation or chemotherapy for cancer.[168] And whatever their actual and relative cost, assisted conception technologies are deemed expensive procedures: no doubt, then, infertility will continue to rank low in a hierarchy of medical need.

Winston has contributed to the representation of assisted conception technology as expensive and exceptional by repeatedly calling it a 'last chance' treatment, only to be resorted to after thorough investigation of both woman and man, and when all other treatments have failed.[169] He seeks to 'cure' patients of their infertility before attempting to sidestep it by assisted conception technology. Winston holds a unique position in the gynaecological community, working at the Hammersmith Hospital, an elite National Health Service institution set up in order to provide postgraduate medical training and research and develop new techniques. Gynaecologists with interests in the private medical sector have taken a different line: more women will become mothers through developments in clinical practice than by persisting with older techniques, albeit delivered in a more efficient way. In 1988, for example, Peter Brinsden accused specialist clinics of over-investigating infertile couples; he asserted that this approach was wasteful of precious resources. He claimed that 'offering more active treatment earlier may be cost-effective both to the patient and the NHS'.[170] Trying to uncover and remedy the underlying pathology which prevents a women from becoming pregnant and having a baby may indeed be a satisfying intellectual pursuit, but it is a notoriously unsuccessful endeavour, a waste of precious time and resources. Brinsden's observations on how the National Health Service should allocate its resources were made from the vantage-point of the private medical sector; from Deputy Director of the private Humana Hospital Fertility and IVF unit, he became Medical Director of Bourn Hall.

Another similar argument sometimes advanced in favour of some assisted conception techniques is they provide a more accurate way of assessing what is wrong with the couple than the older methods described in this book. IVF is said to be able more accurately to gauge the fertilizing capacity of sperm, a consideration which is perforce ignored by the parameters used in routine semen analysis.[171] Yet this test of male fertility requires women to undergo both ovarian stimulation with gonadotrophins and a surgical intervention in order to retrieve eggs for IVF.[172]

Perhaps because they act as substitutes for heterosexual intercourse, assisted conception techniques are making men's presence seem irrelevant to the process of conception.[173] Indeed, the category 'male infertility' is in danger of disappearing. Instead, sperm may suffer from and are treated for dysfunction (by for example, 'washing'); increasingly women are diagnosed as suffering from a condition called 'male factor infertility', which is treated by assisted conception techniques.

The importance of the private medical sector is apparent in the emphasis on consumerist rather than clinical principles in the evaluation of assisted conception technology. Consumerist criteria are found in self-help literature on assisted conception technology. The *Independent* newspaper published two editions of *How to choose a test-tube baby clinic*, a guide for the perplexed consumer to the maze of clinics. Centres are rated according to cost, accessibility, convenience and 'take-home baby rates', criteria which convey the impression that assisted conception clinics are supermarkets which sell motherhood. The issue of value for money in infertility treatment has been taken up by investigative journalists, who have produced television programmes and written newspaper articles pointing out that, as some clinics rarely manage to effect a pregnancy, infertile women and men are handing over large sums of money for very little benefit.[174]

Consumerism has also invaded scientific and medical literature, a tendency which is new and unfamiliar in Britain. The 1990 report of the ILA gave a warning to clinics with the lowest 'take-home baby rates' that they were at risk of losing their licence to manipulate human embryos, a penalty which would effectively force them to shut up shop. Clinics with 'good' success rates eagerly advertise them, and are even allowed to do so by learned journals. A report published in the *British Medical Journal* in June 1990 described four years' 'experience' – the data cannot be called scientific as they do not relate to a clinical trial – of assisted conception technology in a private university service linked with a National Health Service clinic. Where the woman is under 40 and the man has normal sperm, 'after nine cycles of treatment 90% can expect to have a baby or at least 72% as indicated by the lower 95% confidence limit'. The authors concluded that where financial resources allowed, assisted conception technology was good value for money: 'There seems to be no limit to the number of cycles which couples without unfavourable indications should be encouraged to pursue.'[175]

'Bank accounts and babies', the title of this chapter, is borrowed from *Parent's revolt*, a book published in 1942 in which Richard and Kathleen Titmuss voiced the then popular explanation of the declining birth rate: young people had been encouraged to spend their money on the new, mass-produced consumer durables, instead of on children.[176] In effect, private industry stood accused of making profits out of the nation's loss of future citizens. The welfare state was intended to dismiss the question of money from considerations about whether or not to have a baby. Yet fifty years later, industry can still profit from childlessness. Assisted conception technology demands a heavy financial outlay which few patients can afford without experiencing considerable hardship.[177] A majority of treatments are privately paid for; few are free at the point of use. The medical insurance schemes are willing to reimburse the cost of routine investigations and some treatments, but refuse to cover assisted conception. In recognition of the difficulties some couples have in raising the necessary cash, one private clinic for a time offered credit facilities for patients, a marketing ploy that put IVF on a par with consumer durables such as videos and stereo equipment.[178] Little wonder that modifications to 'test tube' technology are sometimes proclaimed a boon to patients not because they offer a greater chance of parenthood, or are safer than other procedures used by clinicians, but because they are cheaper than other procedures.[179]

In a report on the management of services for in vitro fertilization, the World Health Organization (WHO) pointed out that it is against international law to discriminate against individuals on the basis of personal, racial or social characteristics. It recommended that

> countries should commit themselves, as an integral part of the provision of all infertility services, to a policy of non-discrimination by ensuring that access to these services is not based on inappropriate use of irrelevant personal characteristics, such as race, sexual preference, or social, economic, or marital status.[180]

Yet these fine words seem out of place when talking about assisted conception technologies, which, as the WHO acknowledges in the same document, have not been adequately evaluated, and which have considerable risks attached to them. In effect, the WHO report crystallizes the dilemma of whether or not to struggle to establish women's rights to access to reproductive procedures which may do them more harm than good, and if so, how to do so without encouraging further the development of a highly profitable procreation industry.

Notes

CHAPTER 1   TALKING ABOUT INFERTILITY

1 I have singled out historians' tendency to discount infertility because this book is a historical one, and not because their record is worse than that of other social scientists. A good example of the way in which modern social scientists write exclusively about fertile bodies is provided by the American anthropologist Emily Martin. She developed an interview schedule which invited women to talk about their ideas and experiences of menstruation, pregnancy, birth and menopause. The schedule did not invite women to talk about infertility. One hundred and sixty-five women were interviewed; given the claim that up to one in six couples experience infertility, then either some of her respondents had had problems having children, or she excluded from her sample women who had done so. Whichever strategy she used, the impression she conveys is that all the women who live in Baltimore, USA, from whom her sample was drawn, inhabit fertile bodies. See E. Martin (1989) *The woman in the body: A cultural analysis of reproduction*, Milton Keynes, Open University Press.

2 The historian Edward Shorter is the clearest exponent of this story. He tells how women's bodies were saved from the hazards of repeated pregnancy and childbirth by medicine, which also freed them from their inferior social position. It is not suprising to find that Shorter mentions infertility once only and then in relation to venereal diseases in the early twentieth century when women were 'almost liberated'. According to Shorter, infertility emerged then as a reminder to women of their bodies' unequal 'natural' vulnerability to sex. In common with most historians, Shorter seems ignorant of the extent to which men suffer from sexual and reproductive pathology, including infertility; his ignorance allows him to avoid considering why these conditions in men do not exclude them from the polity. I would like to use this endnote to warn him of the high incidence of prostatic hypertrophy – caused by declining levels of testosterone – and prostatic cancer, in older men. See E. Shorter (1982) A *history of women's bodies*, London, Allen Lane. For a

discussion of the modern tendency to ignore male reproductive pathology, see N. Pfeffer (1985) 'The hidden pathology of the male reproductive system', in H. Homans (ed.) *The sexual politics of reproduction*, Aldershot, Gower: 30–44.

3   O. Frank (1983) 'Infertility in sub-Saharan Africa: estimates and implications', *Population and Development Review*, 9: 137–44.

4   The French philosopher Michel Foucault offered a powerful explanation of these tendencies which informs many of the arguments advanced in this book. He located them within a new method of government which emerged during the seventeenth century, which he called 'biopower'. In place of the exercise of control through assigning death – for example, the widespread use of capital punishment and warfare – biopower rules through the administration of bodies and the calculated management of life. Biopower maps out population as a field of political practice and economic observation. Through biopower, aspects of population became legitimated as both problems and explanations of social, political and economic developments, including slums, wars, unemployment, poverty and malnourishment. According to Foucault, biopower is an indispensable element in the development of capitalism; it permits the management of bodies in relation to production and consumption. See M. Foucault (1978) *The history of sexuality*, Harmondsworth, Pelican. Jan Sawicki demonstrates the value of Foucault's biopower to a feminist analysis of reproductive politics. It indicates the importance of considering the political context of developments in reproductive medicine in order to develop an effective strategy of resistance, which, of course, is the purpose of this book. See J. Sawicki (1991) *Disciplining Foucault: feminism, power and the body*, London, Routledge: 67–94.

5   S. Hall (1984) 'The rise of the representative/interventionist state', in G. McLennan, D. Held and S. Hall (eds) *State and society in contemporary Britain*, Cambridge, Polity: 36.

6   For a discussion of *fin de siècle* fear of degeneration, see J. E. Chamberlin (1981) 'An anatomy of cultural melancholy', *Journal of the History of Ideas*, 42: 691–705; R. A. Nye (1985) 'Sociology and degeneration: the irony of progress', in J. E. Chamberlin and S. Gilman (eds) *Degeneration: the dark side of progress*, New York, Columbia University Press: 49–71.

7   G. Mosse (1991) 'Decadence and the construction of masculinity', paper delivered at Wellcome symposium, 'The history of medical attitudes to sexuality', London, Wellcome Institute.

8   J. Weeks (1983) *Sex, politics and society*, London, Longman: 91–2.

9   B. B. Gilbert (1965) 'Health and politics: the physical deterioration report of 1904', *Bulletin of the History of Medicine*, 39: 143–53; A. Summers (1987) 'Edwardian militarism', in R. Samuel (ed.) *Patriotism: the making and unmaking of British national identity*, vol. 1: *History and politics*, London, Routledge: 236–56.

10 S. Webb (1907) *The declining birth-rate*, London, Fabian Society: 17

11 The choice confronting women then was not an easy one: either accept the inferior status of 'old maid' or be a dependent wife. In a book first published

in 1909, Cicely Hamilton, an early feminist, graphically describes the plight of married women; C. Hamilton (1981) *Marriage as a trade*, London, Women's Press.

12 L. Davidoff (1983) 'Class and gender in Victorian England', in J. L. Newton, M. P. Ryan and J. R. Walkowitz (eds) *Sex and class in women's history*, London, Routledge and Kegan Paul: 17–71.

13 Barker-Benfield has written an exhaustive account of the dreadful fate waiting a Victorian masturbator; G. Barker-Benfield (1976) *The horrors of a half-known life: male attitudes towards women and sexuality in nineteenth century America*, New York, Harper and Row: 174–88.

14 Webb, *The declining birth-rate*.

15 Ibid.

16 C. MacAlister (1914) *The dangers of venereal disease: an address delivered at the Liverpool Medical Institution, May 27, 1914*, London, National Council for Combating Venereal Diseases: 10.

17 A pregnant women infected by gonorrhoea was said to stand a much increased chance of infection spreading to her fallopian tubes and ovaries. She was at great risk of the disease altering the structure of her reproductive organs and rendering her sterile. PP Royal Commission on Venereal Diseases (1916) *Final report*, London, HMSO, Cd 8189: 86.

18 PP Local Government Board (1913) *Report on venereal diseases by Dr R. W. Johnstone*, London, HMSO, Cd 7029: 18.

19 L. Tickner (1987) *The spectacle of women*, London, Chatto and Windus: 214.

20 G. Jones (1986) *Social hygiene in twentieth century Britain*, London, Croom Helm: 8.

21 L. Bland (1982) ' "Guardians of the race", or "vampires upon the nation's health"? Female sexuality and its regulation in early twentieth-century Britain', in E. Whitelegg (ed.) *The changing experience of women*, Oxford, Martin Robertson: 373–88.

22 The National Council for Combating Venereal Diseases, was set up in 1914, changed its name to the British Social Hygiene Council (BSHC) in 1925. From 1918 to 1942, the Council received annual grants from central and local government to pursue its extensive propaganda work around venereal diseases and sex education. Its aim was to maintain moral standards; it refused to recognize prophylaxis as a way of overcoming venereal diseases as this would legitimize immorality. The Central Council for Health Education (CCHE), established in 1927 at the instigation of the Society of Medical Officers of Health, became a rival to the BSHC. In 1942, the CCHE assumed responsibility for the work carried out by the BSHC. The CCHE developed into the present-day Health Education Authority. See J. Austoker (1981) 'Biological education and social reform: the British Social Hygiene Council, 1924–42', unpublished MA dissertation, University of London.

23 A. Scoggins (1977) 'The influence of the British Social Hygiene Council on the development of social biology and its subsequent introduction into the educational curriculum', *Biology and Human Affairs*, 42: 93–100, 141–4; J. Lewis (1990) 'Public institution and private relationship', *Twentieth Century*

British History, 1: 233–63.

24 J. Brownlee (1868–1927) worked as both a practitioner and a teacher in fever hospitals in Glasgow. In 1914 he became Director of Statistics, Medical Research Committee. See P. E. M. Fine (1979) 'John Brownlee and the measurement of infectiousness: an historical study in epidemic theory', *Journal of the Royal Statistical Society A*, 142: 347–62. A. K. Chalmers (1856–1925) is best known for his campaign against infant mortality before the First World War. He was a founder of the National Conference on Infant Mortality which advocated antenatal care as a means of bringing down the infant death rate.

25 National Birth-Rate Commission (1916) *The declining birth-rate: its causes and effects*, London, Chapman and Hall: 15.

26 J. W. Brown, Major Greenwood and F. Wood (1920) 'The fertility of the English middle classes: a statistical study', *Eugenics Review*, 12: 158–211.

27 Mass Observation (1945) *Britain and her birth rate*, London, Curwen: 36.

28 The history of the British birth control movement is discussed in A. Leathard (1980) *The fight for family planning*, London, Macmillan, and R. Soloway (1982) *Birth control and the population question in England, 1877–1930*, Chapel Hill, University of North Carolina Press.

29 Corrado Gini (1884–1965), Italian statistician and demographer, was a well-known figure at the international meetings held to discuss population, birth control and eugenics in the interwar period. His special interest was 'exotic' societies. He directed several scientific expeditions to study demographic and anthropometric medical characteristics of ethnic groupings in Libya, Palestine, Mexico, Poland, Lithuania, Sardinia and Calabria. Despite his enthusiastic support for Mussolini, Gini was welcomed at postwar international gatherings on population. His biography in the *International encyclopaedia of the social sciences* omits any reference to his interwar political activities.

30 Gini's parabola of evolution drew on demographic data drawn from ancient Greece and Rome and strange, exotic peoples, and three contemporary theories of biological fertility: degeneration, Chalmers' and Brownlee's theory of germinal vitality, and the logistic curve, a biological law of population developed by the eminent American biologist Raymond Pearl. Pearl (1879–1940) based the logistic curve of population growth on experiments on fruit flies in milk bottles. He claimed that reproductive vigour was a function of available space. Using the example of Algeria before and after French colonization, Pearl also argued that a major disaster could stimulate fertility. Little wonder, then, that Mussolini awarded Pearl a medal in 1929; he had demonstrated that imperialism acted as a novel treatment of infertility! Pearl and Gini were both involved in the International Union for the Scientific Study of Populations. Set up in 1927 with Pearl as President, it quickly became a platform for fascist demography. In the 1930s Gini, who published extensively in both English and American eugenic and demographic journals, was banned from some of their meetings because he used them to deliver eulogies on Mussolini's pronatalist policies. For a discussion

of the admixture of biology, demography and politics exemplified by Pearl, see S. Kingsland (1985) *Modeling nature: episodes in the history of population ecology*, Chicago, Chicago University Press: 57–107; S. Kingsland (1984) 'Raymond Pearl: on the frontier in the 1920s', *Human Biology*, 56: 1–18; S. Kingsland (1982) 'The refractory model: the logistic curve and the history of population ecology', *Quarterly Review of Biology*, 57: 29–52; E. Fee (1987) *Disease and discovery: a history of the John Hopkins School of Hygiene and Public Health, 1916–39*, Baltimore, John Hopkins University Press; G. Allen (1980) 'The work of Raymond Pearl: from eugenics to population control', *Science for the people*, 12: 22–8; K. Ludmerer (1969) 'American geneticists and the eugenics movement: 1905–23', *Journal of the History of Biology*, 2: 337–62; B. Glass (1986) 'Geneticists embattled: their stand against rampant eugenics and racism in America during the 1920s and 1930s, *Proceedings of the American Philosophical Society*, 130: 130–54. For more information on biological 'laws' of population growth which were expounded before the Second World War, see E. T. Hiller (1930) 'A culture theory of population', *Journal of Political Economy*, 5: 523–50; Population Division, United Nations (1956) 'History of population theories', in J. Spengler and O. D. Duncan (eds) *Population theory and policy*, Glencoe, Illinois, Free Press: 5–54.

31   C. Gini (1925) 'Decline in the birth-rate and the "fecundability" of woman', *Eugenics Review*, 17: 258.

32   The calculation of the birth rate requires two kinds of data: first, the total population of the country, which is estimated from the decennial census and adjusted for annual births and deaths; second, the number of live births each year, obtained from the registers of births. The latter is divided by the former.

There are two types of reproduction rates: gross and net. The gross reproduction rate shows the average number of baby girls who would be born to one woman during her child-bearing period if she were subject successively to the specific birth rates prevailing in the year in question. The net reproduction rate refines the gross by making allowances for the obvious fact that not all the potential mothers born in the year in question will survive through the whole of their child-bearing period. This refinement is achieved by allowing for specific mortality rates for the given year.

Not all the data needed in the calculation of reproduction rates were collected in England. Before the Population Statistics Act 1938, English reproduction rates were calculated using substitute data from countries that collected the necessary data: Ukraine and Sweden.

33   R. R. Kuczynski (1932) *Fertility and reproduction: methods of measuring the balance of births and deaths*, New York, Falcon Press: 3.

34   E. Grebenik (1959) 'The development of demography in England', in P. M. Hauser and O. D. Duncan (eds) *The study of population: an inventory and appraisal*, Chicago, University of Chicago Press: 190–202; E. Grebenik (1986) 'Demographic research in Britain 1936–86', unpublished paper presented at a conference of the British Society for Population Studies, September.

35   Some forecasts were more pessimistic than others; see D. Glass (1940)

Population policies and movements, Oxford, Clarendon Press: 468–72.

36 D. V. Glass (1936) *The struggle for population*, Oxford, Oxford University Press; A. M. Carr-Saunders (1936) *World population*, Oxford, Oxford University Press; R. R. Kuczynski (1936) *The measurement of populations*, Oxford, Oxford University Press.

37 The most comprehensive study of eugenics in the twentieth century is D. J. Kevles (1985) *In the name of eugenics*, Harmondsworth, Pelican.

38 For a brief history of the PIC see D. Glass (1978) *Population Investigation Committee: a record of research and publications 1936–1978*, London, Population Investigation Committee at the London School of Economics; C. M. Langford (1988) *The Population Investigation Committee: a concise history to mark its fiftieth anniversary*, London, Population Investigation Committee at the London School of Economics.

39 The deliberations of the Population Policies Committee were finally published in 1948: Political and Economic Planning (1948) *Population policy in Great Britain*, London, PEP. For a description of the Committee's prewar work, see F. Lafitte (1939) 'The work of the Population Policies Committee', *Eugenics Review*, 31: 47–56.

40 Notes of the quarter (1950) *Eugenics Review*, 42: 1–4.

41 Population Investigation Committee (1939) *Questionnaire on fertility: instructions and notes*, London, PIC: 15. It is instructive to compare this comment with the survey carried out by the Women's Health Enquiry Committee into the health and lives of working-class women in the 1930s. Women were asked to complete a two-part questionnaire. The first contained questions about social conditions, and the second questions about health. Adequate space was allowed for lengthy answers to these questions and women were encouraged to, and often did, give supplementary accounts of their health on the backs of the forms. The Women's Health Enquiry Committee failed to elicit comparative data from middle-class women. See M. Spring Rice (1981) *Working-class wives*, London, Virago.

42 Population Investigation Committee Archives (henceforth PIC) PIC VIII/1 (PIC papers, London School of Economics).

43 PIC, Minutes of the Medical Sub-Committee.

44 L. Harris (1984) 'State and economy in the Second World War', in McLennan, Held and Hall *State and society*: 50–76.

45 Public Records Office, Kew (henceforth PRO) T221/85.

46 E. Lewis Faning (1949) *Family limitation and its influence on human fertility over the past 50 years: Papers of the Royal Commission on Population*, vol. 1. An investigation carried out by the Royal College of Obstetricians and Gynaecologists, London, HMSO.

47 Contemporary Medical Archives (henceforth CMAC) SA EUG/C57 (Wellcome Institute, London).

48 Lewis Faning, *Family limitation*: 21.

49 PP Royal Commission on Population (1949) *Report*, London, HMSO: 32.

50 Carr-Saunders, *World population*: 275.

51 O. Harkavy (1969) 'American foundations and the population problem', in B.

Berelson (ed.) *Family planning programs: an international survey*, New York, Basic Books: 241–51. For a first-hand account of the development of demography in America, see F. W. Notestein (1982) 'Demography in the United States: a partial account of the development of the field', *Population and Development Review*, 8: 651–87.

52 Frank Notestein has been described as one of the architects of modern demography. He exercised considerable influence over its development in the USA, from the Office of Population Research, Princeton University and, later, the Population Council; see N. B. Ryder (1984) 'Frank Wallace Notestein (1902–1983)', *Population Studies*, 38: 5–20. For a discussion of the US role in transforming demography into an applied political science, see D. Hodgson (1983) 'Demography as a social science and a policy science', *Population and Development Review*, 9: 11–34; J. Caldwell and O. Caldwell (1986) *Limiting population growth and the Ford Foundation contribution*, London, Pinter.

53 For an exhaustive account of US institutions involved in population policies and programmes after the war, see J. Kasun (1988) *The war against population: the economics and ideology of population control*, San Francisco, Ignatus Press.

54 B. Suitter (1973) *Be brave and angry: chronicles of the International Planned Parenthood Federation*, London, IPPF: 23.

55 CMAC SA FPA A18/2.

56 K. Kumar (1987) *Utopia and anti-utopia in modern times*, Oxford, Blackwell: 381.

57 CMAC SA FPA A17/103.

58 The papers of the Statistics Committee of the Royal Commission on Population (held in the PRO) offer an exhaustive critique of reproduction rates.

59 A good example of the way in which psychoanalysis began to intrude in theories of fertility is provided by Slater and Woodside, who believed that the influence of neurosis on reduced fertility should be acknowledged in population policies; see E. Slater and M. Woodside (1951) *Patterns of marriage*, London, Cassell.

60 G. Rowntree and R. Pierce (1961) 'Birth control in Britain', *Population Studies*: 4.

61 Ibid.: 9.

62 The data on subfecundity were analysed for use by a committee that had been set up to reorganize the Family Planning Association: CMAC SA FPA A5/65.

63 R. Symonds and M. Carder (1973) *The United Nations and the population question, 1945–70*, London, Chatto and Windus: xvi.

64 Kumar, *Utopia*: 388.

65 *Observer*, 5 September 1965.

66 Paul Demeny, quoted in J. Cleland and C. Wilson (1987) 'Demand theories of the fertility transition: an iconoclastic view', *Population Studies*, 41: 5.

67 In the 1980s the theory of demographic transition began to be reassessed by demographers, labour historians and feminists. For an overview of the cri-

tique see N. Folbre (1983) 'Of patriarchy born: the political economy of fertility decisions', *Feminist Studies*, 9: 261–84; R. I. Woods (1987) 'Approaches to the fertility transition in Victorian England', *Population Studies*, 41: 283–311; K. Ittmann (1991) 'Demography and working-class history: challenging the modernization model', *International Labor and Working-Class History*, 39: 49–60.

68 For a trenchant critique of the determination of postwar investigators to prove widespread use of contraception and thereby refute biological explanations of infertility, see D. G. Sloan (1983) 'The extent of contraceptive use and the social paradigm of modern demography', *Sociology*, 17: 380–7.

69 An enormous amount has been written on population programmes in the developing world. Some accounts support the politics and practices of the programme planners. See for example Symonds and Carder, *The United Nations and the population question*; Suitter, *Be brave and angry*; E. Moss (1978) *The Population Council: a chronicle of the first twenty-five years 1952–1977*, New York, Population Council; Caldwell and Caldwell *Limiting population growth*. Others are highly critical of the coercive nature of these programmes, their lack of sensitivity to women's needs and their focus on fertility rather than redistribution of wealth as a solution to population problems. See for example B. Hartman (1987) *Reproductive rights and wrongs: the global politics of population control and contraceptive choice*, New York, Harper and Row; M. Mamdani (1972) *The myth of population control: family, caste and class in an Indian Village*, New York, Monthly Review Press; Kasun, *The war against population*.

70 J. Borgeois-Pichat (1983) 'The demographic transition in Europe', in Council of Europe, *Proceedings of the European population conference, 1982, Strasbourg 21–24 September 1982*, Strasbourg, Council of Europe: 234.

71 Moss, *The Population Council*: 67.

72 B. Berelson (1966) 'KAP studies on fertility', in B. Berelson (ed.) *Family planning and population programs*, Chicago, University of Chicago Press: 655–68.

73 Leathard, *The fight for family planning*: 79.

74 Quoted in D. Glass (1968) 'Family planning programmes and action in western Europe', in E. Szabady (ed.) *World Views on population problems*, Budapest, Akademia Kiado: 105–25.

75 CMAC SA FPA A13/73.

76 P. Demeny (1988) 'Social science and population policy', *Population and Development Review*, 14: 467.

77 In March 1962 David Glass, a member of the PIC's staff from its earliest days and its Chairman 1959–78, wrote to the Population Council as follows: 'I must confess that I am becoming rather tired of writing around, cap in hand, for small sums for demographic research. I have been doing this for a number of years – indeed, ever since the war – and although we do good research and produce a good journal [*Population Studies*], there appears to be no build up so far as getting long term funds is concerned'. PIC III/3b.

78 PIC III/3b.

79   D. Glass (1976) 'Preface', in C. Langford, *Birth control and marital fertility in Great Britain*, London, PIC: x.

80   CMAC SA FPA 13/73.

81   Langford, *Birth control and marital fertility*.

82   A. Bramwell (1989) *Ecology in the 20th century*, New Haven, Yale University Press: 61.

83   The National Health Service (Family Planning) Act 1967 conferred permissive powers on local health authorities to give birth control advice, without regard to marital status, on social and medical grounds.

84   PIC III/6.

85   PP Select Committee on Science and Technology (1971) *First report: session 1970–71, Population of the United Kingdom*, London, HMSO.

86   M. Woolf (1971) *Family intentions*, London, HMSO; M. Woolf and S. Pegden (1976) *Families five years on*, London, HMSO; A. Cartwright and W. Wilkins (1976) 'Changes in family building plans', *Studies on Medical and Population Subjects*, 33, London, HMSO; A. Cartwright (1976) *How many children?* London, Routledge and Kegan Paul; A. Cartwright (1978) *Recent trends in family building and contraception*, London, HMSO; K. Dunnell (1979) *Family formations*, London, HMSO.

87   A. Cartwright (1970) *Parents and family planning services*, London, Routledge and Kegan Paul; M. Bone (1973) *Family planning services in England and Wales*, London, HMSO; M. Bone (1978) *The family planning services: changes and effects*, London, HMSO.

88   Economist Intelligence Unit (1969) 'The UK contraceptive market', *Retail business*, 138; Economist Intelligence Unit (1975) 'The UK contraceptive market', *Retail Business*, 218.

89   Bone, *The family planning services*.

90   Dunnell, *Family formations*: introduction.

91   C. Scott and V. C. Chidambaram (1985) 'World fertility survey: origins and achievements', in J. Cleland and J. Hobcraft (eds) *Reproductive change in developing countries: insights from the World Fertility Survey*, Oxford, Oxford University Press: 7–26.

92   Cleland and Hobcraft, 'Introduction', in Cleland and Hobcraft, *Reproductive change in developing countries*.

93   As the PIC put it, that 'the co-operation of two people, rather than just one, was required necessarily made the matter more difficult. Moreover, husbands may well be on average less easy to contact than wives. But interviewers reported back also their feeling that the simple fact of mentioning to wives that their husbands would be contacted as well – this was done in every case – of itself led to a diminished willingness even on the part of these wives to be interviewed.' Langford, *Birth control and marital fertility*: 4, n. 6.

94   See S. Pollock 'Sex and the contraceptive act', in Homans (ed.) *The sexual politics of reproduction*: 64–77.

95   J. Cantor (1973) 'Contraceptives on the NHS', *British Medical Journal*, ii: 117.

96   Between 1972 and 1975, the *British Medical Journal* was replete with edito-

rials, letters and articles on the British Medical Association's campaign to get the government to pay doctors for providing contraceptives.

97 *Guardian*, 23 April 1970: 2.
98 R. Newill (1986) 'Preface', in J. Bellina and J. Wilson, *The fertility handbook: a positive and practical guide*, Harmondsworth, Penguin.
99 A number of articles have appeared in medical journals which speculate on the causes of the increased visibility of infertility in the 1980s. They consider the role of a number of different factors: more people being involuntarily childless; changes in 'illness behaviour', that is, increased numbers of people seeking medical help; changing attitudes towards infertility which have made it less shameful; and the introduction of 'assisted' conception techniques which encouraged infertile people to come forward. None of the authors comes to a definite conclusion. See for example S. O. Aral and W. Coates (1983) 'The increased concern with infertility: Why now?' *Journal of the American Medical Association*, 250: 2327–31; H. Page (1988) 'The increasing demand for infertility treatment', *Health Trends*, 20: 115–18.
100 Not everyone experiencing infertility consults a doctor. A recent retrospective study of women in the age group 46–50, that is, past their child-bearing years, found that one in three of the women who had experienced infertility had not consulted a doctor: see A. Templeton, C. Fraser and B. Thompson (1990) 'The epidemiology of infertility in Aberdeen', *BMJ*, 301: 148–52.
101 M. Warnock (1985) *A question of life*, Oxford, Blackwell: 8.
102 T. Miles (1989) 'Health plea ignored in sex poll ban', *Observer*, 17 September: 4. Donald Acheson, who was the Chief Medical Officer at the Department of Health at the time that the survey was vetoed, said that Margaret Thatcher and other ministers were reluctant to get involved in the fight against Aids, fearing that there would be a public backlash against frank advertising. Indeed, no one in the Cabinet was prepared to take the threat of the disease seriously. As he put it, 'the buck was being passed round Whitehall like a hot potato': C. Mihill (1992) ' "Sensitive" Thatcher kept out of drive against Aids', *The Guardian*, 27 August: 6.
103 W. Brass (1989) 'Is Britain facing the twilight of parenthood?', in H. Joshi (ed.) *The changing population of Britain*, Oxford, Blackwell: 12–26.
104 Council of Europe (1976) *Population decline in Europe: implications of a declining or stationary population*, London, Edward Arnold; K. Davis, M. S. Bernstam and R. Ricardo-Campbell, eds (1986) 'Below-replacement fertility in industrial societies: causes, consequences, policies', *Population and Development Review*, supplement to vol. 12.
105 A much-quoted study into the incidence of infertility estimated that 17 per cent of couples in England, or one in six, experience primary or secondary infertility. This study took the number of people attending infertility or gynaecology clinics in a health district as a basis for deducing the incidence of infertility in the population as a whole. While its methodology is significant, there are good reasons for doubting the validity of its findings. First, it is dangerous to assume that the characteristics of patients attending hospitals are typical of the local or national population; this needs to be examined

with respect to class, age, ethnic group and so on. Second, the method assumes that the number of patients then being treated is a guide to past and future demand. This is highly questionable. Both the national focus on infertility and the high public profile of the gynaecologist in charge of the clinics in question – who seemed to be particularly successful at making women pregnant – may mean that a backlog of people who had known for some years that they had a fertility problem came forward to seek treatment. Third, care needs to be exercised in generalizing to other parts of the country, which may be different demographically. See M. G. R. Hull, et al. (1985) 'Population study of causes, treatment and outcome of infertility', *British Medical Journal*, 291: 1693–7. See also Templeton, Fraser and Thompson, 'The epidemiology of infertility in Aberdeen'.

106 N. Pfeffer and A. Coote (1991) *Is quality good for you?*, London, Institute of Public Policy Research.

107 Mass Observation, *Britain and her birth-rate*: 30–1.

CHAPTER 2   NORMS AND DEVIATIONS

1 Middlesex Hospital London: Mr Duncan's patients, 1901.
2 St Bartholomew's Hospital, London, Medical Register MR 16/59, female gynaecological cases, vol. vi: Mr Champneys and Mr Griffiths.
3 O. Moscucci (1990) *The science of woman: gynaecology and gender in England, 1800–1929*, Cambridge, Cambridge University Press: 103.
4 J. Matthews Duncan (1866) *Fecundity, fertility, sterility and allied topics*, Edinburgh, A. & C. Black: 43.
5 J. Matthews Duncan (1884) *On sterility in women: being the Gulstonian lectures delivered in the Royal College of Physicians in February 1883*, London, J. & A. Churchill: 12.
6 In the Edwardian period, two Scottish actuaries employed a clerk for six hours each day for ten months to check the accuracy of Duncan's statistics. See C. J. Lewis and J. Norman Lewis (1906) *Natality and fecundity: a contribution to national demography*, Edinburgh, Olives & Boyd. Duncan's influence was acknowledged as late as July 1944, when in their evidence to the Royal Commission on Population, two demographers, Kucyzynski and Glass, deprecated the habit of doctors to hand down without question his statistics on childlessness: PRO RG 24/9.
7 L. Jordanova (1989) *Sexual visions: images of gender in science and medicine between the eighteenth and twentieth centuries*, London, Harvester Wheatsheaf: 51.
8 H. Grant (1904) 'The diminishing birth rate', *British Medical Journal*, i: 578.
9 S.Gilman (1985) 'Black bodies, white bodies: toward an iconography of female sexuality in late-nineteenth century art, medicine and literature', *Critical Inquiry*, 12: 204–42.
10 These descriptions are taken from the case notes of patients who were admitted for investigation and treatment of sterility in the first decade of the

twentieth century to two prestigious London voluntary teaching hospitals: the Middlesex Hospital, and St Bartholomew's Hospital.

11 G. E. Herman (1903) *Diseases of women: a clinical guide to their diagnosis and treatment*, London: 1.

12 Gilman, 'Black bodies': 223.

13 H. McNaughton-Jones (1915) 'Sterility in women – a survey', *The Practitioner*, 95: 10.

14 R. A. Gibbons (1910) 'Sterility: its etiology and treatment', *The Lancet*, 3 September: 705.

15 F. Champneys (1906) 'Sterility', in T. C. Allbutt, W. S. Playfair and T. W. Eden (eds) *A system of gynaecology by many writers*, London, Macmillan: 110.

16 See E. Showalter (1987) *The female malady: women, madness and English culture, 1830–1980*, London, Virago.

17 Moscucci, *The science of woman*: 104–5.

18 Ibid.: 104.

19 Duncan, *On sterility in women*: 14.

20 Moscucci, *The science of woman*: 34.

21 P. Horrocks (1903) 'A lecture on sterility', *The Lancet*: 71.

22 PP Select Committee on Patent Medicines (1913) *Proceedings, evidence, appendices and index*, London, HMSO: 240.

23 E. Corner (1910) *Male diseases in general practice: an introduction to andrology*, London, Henry Frowde/Hodder and Stoughton: 55.

24 Ibid.: 61.

25 This is the only reference to the history of the anatomy of the human testes I have been able to find. Unfortunately, its title is more rewarding than its contents: W. B. Ober and C. Sciagura (1981) 'Leydig, Setoli and Reinke: three anatomists who were on the ball', *Pathology Annual*, 16, part 1: 1–13.

26 Corner, *Male diseases*: 59.

27 A. Cooper (1910) *The sexual disabilities of man and their treatment*, London, H. K. Levois.

28 S. Shuttleworth (1990) 'Medical discourse and popular advertising in the mid-Victorian era', in M. Jacobus, E. Fox Keller and S. Shuttleworth (eds) *Body/politics: women and the discourses of science*, London, Routledge: 47–68.

29 Corner, *Male diseases*: v.

30 C. Smart (1987) 'Law and the problem of paternity', in M. Stanworth (ed.) *Reproductive technologies: gender, motherhood and medicine*, Cambridge, Polity: 98–117.

31 The double standard is exemplified by the campaigns against venereal diseases waged during the second half of the nineteenth century. Prostitutes were policed, stigmatized and punished, whereas their male clients were let off lightly. Under the Contagious Diseases Acts, a woman who was suspected of being a prostitute was subjected to compulsory medical examination, and if found to have a venereal infection was imprisoned in a 'lock' hospital. The best study of nineteenth-century British prostitution is J. Walkowitz (1980) *Prostitution and Victorian society: women, class and*

state, Cambridge, Cambridge University Press.

32   PP Local Government Board (1913) *Report on Venereal Diseases by R. W. Johnstone*, Cd 7029, London, HMSO: 18; W. Osler (1917) 'The campaign against venereal disease', *British Medical Journal*, i: 694.

33   The gonococcus, the organism responsible for gonorrheal infection, had been identified in 1879 by Albert Neisser, a German dermatologist. Although syphilis featured more prominently than gonorrhea in the moral panic around venereal diseases, I have excluded it on the grounds that it does not prevent women from conceiving. It can, however, cause miscarriage and stillbirth. See A. M. Brandt (1985) *No magic bullet: a social history of venereal disease in the United States since 1880*, Oxford, Oxford University Press.

34   PP Royal Commission on Venereal Diseases (1914) *Report*, London, HMSO, Cd 7475: 42.

35   The Clinical Research Association Limited (1914) *The practitioner's guide to clinical research*, London: appendix.

36   For an illustrated guide of suffragette propaganda, see L. Tickner (1987) *The spectacle of women: imagery of the suffrage campaign*, 1907–14, London, Chatto and Windus.

37   Gibbons, 'Sterility': 705.

38   The best-known account of the complementarity of the sexes is that of P. Geddes and J. A. Thomson (1901) *The evolution of sex*, 2nd edn, London, W. Scott: 290.

39   Champneys, 'Sterility': 114.

40   M. J. Sandelowski (1990) 'Failures of volition: female agency and infertility in a historical perspective', *Signs*, 15: 475–99.

41   V. Bonney (1932) 'On sterility', *The Lancet*, i: 971.

42   S. Reiser (1981) *Medicine and the reign of technology*, Cambridge, Cambridge University Press: 80.

43   Champneys, 'Sterility': 111.

44   Cooper, *The sexual disabilities of man*: 11.

45   Ibid.: 18.

46   Shuttleworth, 'Medical discourse and popular advertising': 53.

47   C. Berkeley and V. Bonney (1915) *A guide to gynaecology in general practice*, London, Henry Frowde/Hodder and Stoughton: 111.

48   P. Horrocks (1903) 'A lecture on sterility', *The Lancet*, i: 71.

49   Editorial (1921) *British Medical Journal*, ii: 1076.

50   L. Davidoff (1983) 'Class and gender in Victorian England', in J. L. Newton, M. P. Ryan and J. R. Walkowitz (eds) *Sex and class in women's history*, London, Routledge and Kegan Paul: 19.

51   L. Kidd (1914) 'Answers', *British Medical Journal*, i: 516.

52   C. Lawrence (1985) 'Incommunicable knowledge: science, technology and the clinical art in Britain, 1850–1914', *Journal of Contemporary History*, 20: 503–20.

53   I. Loudon (1984) 'The concept of the family doctor', *Bulletin of the History of Medicine*, 58: 347–62.

54   I have assumed that a majority of women who received free treatment for their involuntary childlessness in voluntary hospitals were working-class. It is virtually impossible to gauge a woman's social class from the hospital records I examined. Almost without exception, a woman's occupation was recorded as 'housewife', 'housework' or a similar term. Perhaps the dressers who completed the form assumed that all women who sought treatment for involuntary childlessness were housewives. Or women may have been reluctant to admit that they were employed in case they were denied treatment. On rare occasions, the husband's occupation was recorded, but too infrequently to draw any systematic conclusions about social class from it.

55   C. Berkeley and V. Bonney (1911) *A text-book of gynaecological surgery*, London, Henry Frowde/Hodder and Stoughton: 678.

56   W. R. Winterton (1961) 'The story of the London gynaecological hospitals', *Proceedings of the Royal Society of Medicine*, 54: 191–8.

57   M. A. Elston (1990) 'Women and antivivisection in Victorian England', in N. Rupke (ed.) *Vivisection in historical perspective*, London, Routledge: 259–94.

58   Berkeley and Bonney, *A text-book on gynaecological surgery*: 78.

59   Moscucci, *The science of woman*: 113–18.

60   If a woman was diagnosed as infected with a venereal disease, she became liable to detention for up to one year and to regular fortnightly inspection. She had no right of appeal and no recourse to *habeas corpus*. The Acts were introduced in order to provide 'clean' prostitutes to service members of the armed forces, and thereby maintain them in fighting health. See Walkwowitz, *Prostitution and Victorian society*; also F. B. Smith (1990) 'The Contagious Diseases Acts reconsidered', *Social History of Medicine*, 3: 197–216.

61   Davidoff, 'Class and gender in Victorian England': 26.

62   Elston, 'Women and antivivisection in Victorian England'.

63   E. Lewis Faning (1949) *Family limitation and its influence on human fertility during the past 50 years: Papers of the Royal Commission on Population*, vol 1. An investigation carried out by the Royal College of Obstetricians and Gynaecologists, London, HMSO: 90.

64   A good example of the way in which involuntarily childless women have been overlooked by oral historians is found in the work of Diana Gittins. She explored the factors that influenced women's fertility in the early part of the twentieth century by interviewing older women, all of whom were mothers. An underlying assumption is that none of the women experienced difficulties around conception; the first question on 'Children and family life' is 'Did you enjoy being pregnant?' See D. Gittins (1982) *Fair sex: family size and structure 1900–1939*, London, Hutchinson: 20.

65   E. Roberts (1984) *A woman's place: an oral history of working-class women 1890–1940*, Oxford, Blackwell: 103.

66   The 1921 Census considered the problem of orphaned and fatherless children; it asked women about the number of children for whom they were responsible.

67 Departmental Committee appointed by the Home Secretary to consider '(1) whether it is desirable to make legal provisions for the adoption of children in this country, and (2) if so, what form should provision take' (1920) *Minutes of evidence*, London, Home Office.

68 The history of adoption and fostering has not yet been written. See PP Home Office Committee of Child Adoption (1921) *Report*, London, HMSO, Cmd 1254; PP Departmental Committee on Adoption Societies and Agencies (1937) *Report*, London, HMSO, Cmd 5499; PRO MH 55/276; PRO MH 55/1635; PRO RG 24/3 RC 106.

69 PRO RG 24/3 RC 106.

70 A. Digby and N. Bosanquet (1988) 'Doctors and patients in an era of National Health Insurance and private practice, 1913–1938', *Economic History Review*, 2nd ser. xli: 78.

71 PP Select Committee on Patent Medicines (1914) *Proceedings of the committee: minutes of evidence and appendices*, London, HMSO: 232.

72 P. Thane (1978) 'Women and the Poor Law in Victorian and Edwardian England', *History Workshop Journal*, 6: 34.

73 Editorial (1904) *The Lancet*, i: 1171.

74 L. Hall (1989) 'Medical attitudes to the sexual disorders of the "normal" male in Britain, 1900–1950', unpublished Phd thesis, University of London: 11.

75 'The financial prospects of medicine', *British Medical Journal*, i: 1431.

76 British Medical Association (1909) *Secret remedies: what they cost and what they contain*, London, BMA; British Medical Association (1912) *More secret remedies: what they cost and what they contain*, London, BMA.

77 PP Local Government Board (1910) *Report as to the practice of medicine and surgery by unqualified persons in the United Kingdom*, Cd 5422, London, HMSO.

78 Select Committee on Patent Medicines, *Proceedings*: x.

79 Doctors were paid a capitation fee for each patient covered by the panel system. For an analysis of the impact of the scheme on doctors' incomes, see Digby and Bosanquet, 'Doctors and patients': 74–94.

80 Digby and Bosanquet, 'Doctors and patients': 74–94.

CHAPTER 3   IMAGES OF STERILITY

1 Patients' records, Kings College Hospital, 1930.

2 This case history is a combination of several letters in Marie Stopes' voluminous correspondence held at the Contemporary Medical Archives, Wellcome Institute, London. See CMAC PP/MCS.

3 L. Hall (1991) *Hidden anxieties: male sexuality, 1900–1950*, Cambridge, Polity: 37.

4 Ibid.: 50.

5 J. Weeks (1983) *Sex, politics and society: the regulation of sexuality since 1800*, London, Longman: 214–15.

6 This clause offended many women; it was dropped quietly a few months

later by politicians who feared the response of recently enfranchised women at the general election; see R. Davenport-Hines (1990) *Sex, death and punishment: attitudes to sex and sexuality in Britain since the Renaissance,* London, Fontana: 228–9.

7   M. W. Browdy (1924) 'Impotence and sterility in the male', *The Practitioner,* 113: 19.

8   K. Walker (1920) 'Sterility in the male', *British Medical Journal,* i: 10.

9   K. Walker (1925) 'Discussion on sterility and impotence in the male', *Proceedings of the Royal Society of Medicine,* 18: 56–64.

10   Hall, *Hidden anxieties:* 34.

11   Davenport-Hines, *Sex, death and punishment:* 247.

12   K. Walker (1929) 'The interpretation of tests of sterility and fertility in the male', *The Lancet,* ii: 995–6.

13   Walker, 'Discussion on sterility': 57.

14   K. Walker (1928) 'Diagnosis and treatment of sterility in the male', *British Medical Journal,* ii: 654.

15   The choice of a capon's comb as the bioassay of the male sex hormone was an unfortunate one; castrating day-old male chicks is a difficult procedure. During the 1930s, there was only one expert 'caponiser' in Britain: a Dr Greenwood who worked in the biologist F. H. Crew's unit at Edinburgh. Greenwood received financial support from both the Medical Research Council (henceforth MRC) and the Agricultural Research Council. He used the flock of capons to test the value of commercial preparations containing testes (MRC 1644/10, MRC papers, MRC, London). To understand why scientists used an avian model in the experimental approach to sexual differentiation in humans, see C. Sindong (1990) 'Clinical research and basic science: the development of the concept of end-organ resistance to a hormone', *Journal of the History of Medicine,* 45: 198–232.

16   Bulls' testes contain very small amounts of a hormone with comb-growth properties among what scientists call masses of inert material. In 1931, several scientists independently and almost simultaneously found that the urine of 'normal' men is a rich source of the hormone. In 1935, this substance was called 'testosterone'.

17   In 1927, it was established that both sperm-forming and secretory functions of the testes were controlled by the anterior pituitary gland. This discovery was followed by a controversy over whether the testicular secretion came from the seminiferous tubules or the Leydig cells. The argument was settled in 1936.

18   Almost all the investigations into the chemistry and properties of testosterone were carried out outside Britain, by, for example, Ernst Laqueur of the Netherlands; A. Butenandt of Germany; and Karl Miescher of Basle. See A. S. Parkes (1966) *Sex, science and society,* London, Oriel Press: 24.

19   Minutes of the MRC's Sex Hormones Committee (MRC 1068). The career of Vladimir Korenchevsky (1880–1959) testifies to the peculiar difficulties the British had with male sex hormones. Korenchevsky was an eminent doctor and scientist. He worked with two distinguished scientists: at the Pasteur

Institute with Professor Metchnikoff, and with I. P. Pavlov, best known for his behavioural experiments on dogs. When only 32 years old, he was appointed professor of experimental pathology in the Imperial Military Medical Academy. A White Russian, he resisted the Revolution and in 1920 fled Russia for England, where he became a British subject. The British establishment welcomed Korenchevsky with open arms; he was engaged in research at the Lister Institute, and supported by the MRC. However, he soon fell out of favour, in part because of his political activities, but largely because the work he carried out in relation to male sex hormones was anathema to the MRC. Korenchevsky was persuaded of a connection between male sex hormones and senility, an idea that was popular on the European continent but which the English seem to have found distasteful. Korenchevsky did have a few supporters; in 1945, with the aid of a donation from Lord Nuffield, he established the Oxford Gerontological Research Unit. See obituary (1959) 'Vladimir Korenchevsky', *British Medical Journal*, ii: 194; obituary (1959) 'Vladimir Korenchevsky', *The Lancet*: ii: 83.

20 M. Borell (1976) 'Organotherapy, British physiology, and discovery of the internal secretions', *Journal of the History of Biology*, 9: 235–68; D. Hamilton (1989) *The monkey gland affair*, London, Chatto and Windus; PRO HO 45/14719.

21 R. Greep (1978) 'Reproductive endocrinology: concepts and perspectives, an overview', *Recent Progress in Hormone Research*, 34: 9.

22 A good example of the research inspired by concern with the environment in which spermatogenesis took place is A. W. Badenoch (1945) 'Descent of the testis in relation to temperature', *British Medical Journal*, ii: 601–3.

23 Testicular biopsy was first advocated by Charny to distinguish cases of obstructive aspermia from non-obstructive: C. W. Charny (1940) *Journal of the American Medical Association*, 115: 1429.

24 After Hitler came to power, German doctors also began actively to investigate the parameters of male fertility (I am grateful to Paul Weindling for this information). However, judging from medical journals, German research was rarely reported in Britain until the postwar period.

25 Robert L. Dickinson was a New York gynaecologist and a pioneering sex researcher. He retired from active practice aged 55 and began to promote his philosophy as a voluntary officer of the CMH and through his own researches. His best-known works are *A thousand marriages* and *The single woman*, in which he analysed the reproductive histories of 5,000 New York City women who had been his patients. See W. B. Pomeroy (1972) *Dr Kinsey and the Institute for Sex Research*, New York, Harper and Row: 156–8. For an appreciation by his peers, heavy on anecdote and light on biographical detail, see F. A. Simmons (1953) 'Robert Latou Dickinson: an appreciation', *Fertility and Sterility*, 4: 1–9.

26 M. Borell (1987) 'Biologists and the promotion of birth control research, 1918–1938', *Journal of the History of Biology*, 20: 51–87.

27 Weeks *Sex, politics and society*: 184–6.

28 S. R. Tattersall (1919) 'A note on duplication in human spermatozoa', *The*

Lancet, ii: 201.

29   G. L. Moench and H. Holt (1931) 'Sperm morphology in relation to fertility', *American Journal of Obstetrics and Gynaecology*, 22: 203. In the 1940s, a new explanation of abnormally shaped sperm was advanced: sperm were normal when first detached from the germinal epithelium, but became misshapen through age. This theory was adapted from one that had been put forward in 1939 by two American biologists, Richard Blandau and William Young. From their research on guinea pigs they concluded that if an egg newly released from the ovary was not fertilized at once, it became increasingly unworthy of new life, and if fertilized subsequently was often 'blighted'. However, in contrast to 'ageing' ova which were still capable of fertilization, albeit creating 'blighted' ova, the potential of elderly sperm was cut short; they died. Age in gametes had a different significance according to whether they were of male or female origin.

30   Macomber's work is referred to by Walker. See Borell, 'Biologists and the promotion of birth control research': n. 37. Working in England, it has proved impossible to find out anymore about them.

31   John MacLeod and Ruth Z. Gold published their statistical study of the parameters of semen quality in a series of seven articles in *Fertility and Sterility*, vols 1–3. MacLeod was associated with the Male Sterility Clinic, Bellevue Hospital, New York, set up in 1932 by the renowned urologist Robert Sherman Hotchkiss, with financial support from Margaret Sanger. MacLeod's research was funded by Cornelius Vanderbilt Whitney.

32   Editorial (1938) 'Semen analyses in fertile men', *The Lancet*, ii: 1476.

33   Editorial (1943) 'The semen in sterility', *The Lancet*, i: 588–9.

34   J. Marion Sims (1868) 'Illustrations of the value of the microscope in the treatment of the sterile condition', *British Medical Journal*, ii: 465–6, 492–4.

35   S. Reiser (1981) *Medicine and the reign of technology*, Cambridge, Cambridge University Press, 140.

36   The *Catholic Medical Guardian*, the organ of the Guild of St Luke, St Cosmas and St Damien, reported the Holy Office's decisions to the 3,000 Catholic doctors practising in Britain. The Guild, which was founded in 1910, described itself as a brotherhood among Catholic doctors against materialism, state medicine and attacks on the unborn child.

37   See for example M. Huhner (1937) 'The importance of the Huhner test in cases of necrospermia', *British Journal of Obstetrics and Gynaecology of the British Empire*, 44: 334–6.

38   V. B. Green-Armytage (1936) 'Sterile mating', *The Lancet*, ii: 426.

39   H. A. Davidson (1949) 'Male subfertility: interim report' of 3,182 cases', *British Medical Journal*, ii: 1330.

40   K. Walker (1924) 'Discussion on sterility and impotence in the male', *Proceedings of the Royal Society of Medicine*, 18: 57.

41   Reiser, *Medicine and the reign of technology*: 158–73.

42   F. M. Huxley (1929) 'The treatment of sterility in women', *The Lancet*, ii: 138–9.

43   V. Bonney (1932) 'On sterility', *The Lancet*, i: 971–5.

44 This debate was conducted in the correspondence pages of the *British Medical Journal*. See H. Leith Murray (1930) 'Sterility in woman', *British Medical Journal*, i: 798; J. Connell (1930) *British Medical Journal*, i: 841; W. Blair Bell (1930) *British Medical Journal*, i: 882–3; T. C. Clare (1930) *British Medical Journal*, i: 927; K. Walker (1930) *British Medical Journal*, i: 978; W. Blair Bell (1930) *British Medical Journal*, i: 1073.

45 Clare 'Sterility in woman'.

46 T. N. A. Jeffcoate (1946) 'Male infertility', *British Medical Journal*, ii: 186.

47 S. Forsdike (1922) 'Sterility', *The Practitioner*, 108: 243.

48 Jeffcoate, 'Male infertility': 185.

49 C. K. Vartan, 'The investigation of sterility in women', *St Bartholomew's Hospital Journal*, July: 246.

50 M. Moore White (1940) 'Some investigations on the treatment of sterility', *Proceedings of the Royal Society of Medicine*, 33: 518.

51 R. Stevens (1966) *Medical practice in modern England: the impact of specialization and state medicine*, New Haven, Yale University Press: 56.

52 PRO RG 24/5.

53 Catholic nurses would complain to their priest who would then write in protest to the Ministry of Health. See for example PRO MH 58/406.

54 A. Digby and N. Bosanquet (1988) 'Doctors and patients in an era of national health insurance and private practice, 1913–1938', *Economic History Review*, 2nd ser. xli: 91.

55 Editorial (1939) 'Male sterility', *British Medical Journal*, i: 999.

56 M. Moore White (1939) 'Treatment of sterility', *British Medical Journal*, i: 62.

57 CMAC SA FPA A5/103.

58 C. M. McLane (1959) 'The American Society for the Study of Sterility: early history of the ASSS', *Fertility and Sterility*, 10: 117–21.

59 Borell, 'Biologists and the promotion of birth control research'. Baker also analysed semen specimens of men who feared that they might be sterile; J. R. Baker (1937) 'Further research on chemical contraception', *Eugenics Review*, 29: 109–12.

60 Margaret Jackson's clinic was set up in 1930 by the Exeter and District Women's Welfare Association. From the start it offered both advice on contraception and sterility. Jackson was one of the first English doctors to offer artificial insemination using donor semen. See M. H. Jackson (1944) 'A medical service for the treatment of involuntary childlessness', *Eugenics Review*, 36: 117–25.

61 CMAC SA FPA A7/16; Medical Research Council (henceforth MRC) MRC 2526/3 (Medical Research Council, London). C. Harvey and M. H. Jackson (1945) 'Assessment of male fertility by semen analysis', *The Lancet*, ii: 99–104, 134–7.

62 CMAC SA FPA A/120.

63 Royal College of Obstetricians and Gynaecologists Archives (henceforth RCOG) RCOG A4/2/16 (Royal College of Obstetricians and Gynaecologists, London).

64 RCOG D/9/7.

65 Editorial, 'The semen in sterility': 588–9.

66 CMAC SA FPA A3/20. Wiesner had once been highly respected as a scientist by the establishment. The MRC had sponsored his research into sex hormones; and at one stage the Royal College of Obstetricians and Gynaecologists had considered setting up a laboratory especially for him. Yet in 1946 the FPA refused to invite Wiesner to a conference on male sterility. According to Alan Parkes, to most scientists and many medical men he was *persona non grata*: CMAC SA FPA A6/3, I have not been able to find out what he did to be considered disreputable.

67 MRC 2526.

68 CMAC SA FPA A5/102; CMAC SA FPA A6/2.

69 A. Walton (1958) 'Artificial insemination in retrospect and prospect', *Journal of the Royal Agricultural Society of England*, 119: 63–9.

70 Davidson, 'Male subfertility': 1328–32.

71 The Society for the Study of Fertility was formed in June 1949. The founder members included clinicians and basic scientists actively involved in the FPA's work on standardization of tests of male fertility. None the less, at its first annual general meeting in June 1950 Margaret Jackson's proposal that the Society take over the FPA's campaigning work was turned down. Early on in its history, the Society decided against indulging – overtly – in semi-political activities in relation to fertility. The financial position of the Society was assured in 1953 when several drug companies gave it unexpectedly generous donations. I am grateful to Stuart Milligan, Department of Zoology, King's College, London, for allowing me to examine the Society's records.

72 E. Holland (1934) 'On infertile marriage', *The Practitioner*, 132: 312.

73 Deficient spermatogenesis; obstruction and occlusion in the male genital tract; hostility of prostato-vesicular secretions; faults of delivery and reception of semen; hostility of endocervical secretions; 'uterine blockage'; tubal obstruction and occlusion; impassability of ovario-tubal hiatus; and deficient oogenesis.

74 S. Meaker (1934) 'The modern approach to the problem of human sterility', *The Practitioner*, 132: 327.

75 Review (1946) *British Medical Journal*, i: 238.

76 E. K. Trimberger (1984) 'Feminism, men and modern love: Greenwich Village, 1900–1925', in A. Snitow, C. Stansell and S. Thompson (eds) *Desire: the politics of sexuality*, London, Virago: 169–89.

77 Davidson, 'Male subfertility': 1330.

78 E. C. Hill (1983) 'The Rubin test', *Journal of the American Medical Association*, 250: 2366–8.

79 I. C. Rubin (1925) 'Diagnostic value and therapeutic application of per-uterine insufflation of the fallopian tubes in cases of sterility', *Proceedings of the Royal Society of Medicine*, 19: 1–14.

80 A. Sharman (1954) 'Some lessons from 4,000 utero-tubal insufflations', *British Medical Journal*, i: 239.

81 The Science Museum, London, has a large collection of trade catalogues published by pharmaceutical and surgical instrument manufacturers.

82 A good example is V. Bonney (1924) 'On the inflation test for tubal patency and a simple instrument for carrying it out', *The Lancet*, ii: 1062–3.
83 W. Blair Bell (1930) 'Sterility in woman', *British Medical Journal*, i: 629–32.
84 S. Forsdike (1928) 'Diagnosis and treatment of sterility in women', *British Medical Journal*, ii: 648–52.
85 V. B. Green-Armytage (1936) 'Treatment of sterility', *The Lancet*, i: 373.
86 Sharman, 'Some lessons from 4,000 utero-tubal insufflations': 239–42; Editorial (1954) 'Utero-tubal insufflation', *British Medical Journal*, i: 265–6.
87 CMAC SA FPA A19/22A.
88 A wonderful example of this tendency is H. Speert (1958) *Obstetrics and gynaecology milestones: essays in eponymy*, New York, Macmillan.
89 I. C. Rubin (1925) 'Pre-uterine insufflation of fallopian tubes for sterility', *The Lancet*, ii: 756.
90 Forsdike, 'Diagnosis and treatment of sterility in women': 648–52.
91 C. K. Vartan (1938) 'Results of Mr C. K. Vartan's lipiodol injections for sterility in women', *St Bartholomew's Hospital Journal, August*: 276.
92 M. Moore White (1939) 'Treatment of sterility', *British Medical Journal*, i: 62–5.
93 Yad Vashem Archives, Jerusalem: 2080–404.
94 PP Departmental Committee on Sterilisation (1934) *Report*, Cmd 4485, London, HMSO: appendix VII, 105–8.
95 J. Macnicol (1989) 'Eugenics and the campaign for voluntary sterilization in Britain between the wars', *Social History of Medicine*, 2: 147–69.
96 W. Blair Bell, first president of the British College of Obstetricians and Gynaecologists, complained in 1931 that at least 60,000 women annually in England and Wales (10 per cent of all mothers) 'are more or less crippled as the result of childbearing'; see A. Oakley (1986) *The captured womb: a history of the medical care of pregnant women*, Oxford, Blackwell: 68.
97 Oakley, *The captured womb*: 108–10.
98 F. J. McCann (1912) 'The surgical treatment of sterility in women', *The Lancet*, i: 221–4.
99 V. B. Green-Armytage (1937) 'Tubo-uterine implantation for sterility', *British Medical Journal*, ii: 6–7.
100 Ibid.: 6.
101 Quoted in A. E. Clarke (1990) 'Controversy and the development of reproductive sciences', *Social Problems*, 37: 26. One measure of the explosion of interest in reproductive physiology is the number of experiments on non-human animals, which reached a peak in 1938 of 958,761. A similar pattern is seen in the numbers of laboratories registered for vivisection; see R. French (1975) *Antivivisection and medical sciences in Victorian society*, Cambridge, Mass., Princeton University Press: 392–412.
102 A. S. Parkes (1934) 'Coordination of the reproductive processes', *The Lancet*, i: 557.
103 Using numbers of papers published in learned journals, Vivien Seal has charted the interest in sex hormones from 1930 to 1960; a peak was reached around 1935. See V. Seal (1975) 'The relationship and links between aca-

demic research in steroid chemistry and the industrial development of steroid drugs', unpublished PhD thesis, Victoria University of Manchester.

104 For the history of ovariotomy, see O. Moscucci (1990) *The science of woman: gynaecology and gender in England*, 1800–1929, Cambridge, Cambridge University Press: 135–40.

105 G. Corner (1965) 'The early history of the oestrogenic hormones', *Journal of Endocrinology*, 31: iii-xvii.

106 The term 'hormone' was introduced in 1902 by Bayliss and Starling. They defined a hormone as 'any substance normally produced in the cells of some part of the body, and carried by the blood stream to distant parts which it affects for the good of the organism as a whole'. See F. G. Young (1970) 'The evolution of ideas about animal hormones', in J. Needham (ed.) *The chemistry of life: lectures in the history of biochemistry*, Cambridge, Cambridge University Press: 125–55.

107 E. A. Schafer (1907) 'The hormones which are contained in animal extracts: their physiological effects', *Pharmaceutical Journal*: 670.

108 Information on organotherapies is found in the textbooks and journals produced by manufacturers in order to inform clinicians how to prescribe their products; for example, Evans, Sons, Lescher & Webb Limited (1917) *Organo-therapeutic products*, Liverpool, Bacteriological Research Laboratories; and Endocrines Limited *The Organotherapeutic Review*, Wigmore Street, London, which was published from 1916 onwards. See also note 125 below.

109 *Chemist and Druggist Yearbook, 1939*: 72.

110 *Chemist and Druggist Yearbook, 1938*: 407.

111 *Chemist and Druggist Yearbook, 1937*: 107.

112 Medico-legal (1947) 'Institute of endocrinology', *British Medical Journal*, i: 744.

113 PRO MH 79/384.

114 Green-Armytage, 'Sterile mating': 427.

115 A. Giles (1928) 'Sterility in women', *British Medical Journal*, ii: 648.

116 Eardley Holland (1931) 'On sterility', *The Lancet*, ii: 931.

117 C. Lane-Roberts (1936) 'Treatment of sterility', *The Lancet*, i: 372–3.

118 Pharmaceutical Society of Great Britain (1939) *Report of the Committee of Enquiry*, London, Pharmaceutical Society: 19.

119 Armour & Co., for example, was a large meat processor, with a manufacturing plant situated adjacent to the Chicago abbatoirs. In its advertisements, Armour boasted that every year it was responsible for the slaughter of 16 million head of livestock. See *Chemist and Druggist Diary, 1937*: 247. British manufacturers of organotherapies used frozen meat, which was reputed to make inferior products.

120 PRO MH 79/384.

121 V. Swale Vincent (1922) 'Arris and Gale lecture on a critical examination of current views on internal secretions', *The Lancet*, ii: 313–20.

122 M. Borell (1978) 'Setting the standards for a new science: Edward Schafer and endocrinology', *Medical History*, 22: 282–90.

123 Bioassays are now integral to clinical science and are taken for granted. Yet the idea that a substance can be evaluated by a physiological action on non-human animals, humans, tissue or vegetables marks a conceptual shift away from determining the quality of medicines according to their chemical composition. Bioassays test potency. The concept of potent substances emerged towards the end of the nineteenth century; they form a very diverse group in terms of origin and purpose, including the then new 'biologicals' – vaccines, sera, toxins and hormones – and the synthetics: the isolated, synthesized, active principles of old medicines – morphine from opium, valium from valerian, etc. – and new ones such as salvarsan. For a discussion of the technical aspect of bioassays see D. J. Finney (1952) *Statistical method in biological assay*, High Wycombe, Charles Griffin & Co.

124 H. R. Harrower (1923) 'The physiologist and the clinician', *The Organo-therapeutic Review: a Journal of applied pluriglandular therapy*, 1: 17.

125 Good examples are found in *The Journal of Organotherapy: A Record of Progress in the Study of the Internal Secretions and Metabolism*, published from 1916 onwards by C. W. Carnick & Co, an American manufacturer of organo-therapeutics, and distributed by its London agent, Brooks and Warburton Limited. The information on both organotherapies and sex hormones published in this journal is much more accessible than that contained in learned journals.

126 V. Swale Vincent (1925) 'Uses and abuses of endocrine therapy', *British Medical Journal*, ii: 1053. In keeping with the strategy adopted in its campaign against patent medicines waged in the Edwardian period, the British Medical Association attacked organotherapies because of the poor quality of their ingredients; they were inaccurately standardized and their manufacturers made extravagant claims. The BMA did not object to organotherapies because they were inactive. See RCOG B/02/3.

127 The history of the isolation of sex hormones has been written largely from the point of view of physiologists and other scientists. See Corner, 'The early history of the oestrogenic hormones'; A. Parkes (1966) *Sex, science and society*, Newcastle upon Tyne, Oriel Press; Young 'The evolution of ideas about animal hormones', D. Long Hall (1975) 'Biology, sex hormones and sexism in the 1920s', in M. Wartofsky and C. Could (eds) *Women and philosophy*, New York, Putnam: 81–95; D. Long Hall and T. F. Glick (1976) 'Endocrinology: a brief introduction', *Journal of the History of Biology*, 9: 229–33. M. Borell (1976) 'Organotherapy, British physiology and discovery of the internal secretions', *Journal of the History of Biology*, 9: 235–268; D. Long Hall (1976) 'The critic and the advocate: contrasting British views on the state of endocrinology in the early 1920', *Journal of the History of Biology*, 9: 269–85; Greep 'Reproductive endocrinology'; M. Borell (1976) 'Origins of the hormone concept: internal secretions and physiological research, 1889–1905', unpublished PhD dissertation, Yale University; Borell, 'Setting the standards for a new science'; A. S. Parkes (1985) *Off-beat biologist*, Cambridge, Galton Foundation; D. E. Long (1989) 'Physiological identity of American sex researchers between the two World Wars', in G. L. Geison

(ed.) *Physiology in the American context*, Bethesda, American Physiological
Society: 263–78; A. E. Clarke (1989) 'Research materials and reproductive
science in the United States, 1910–1940', in Geison (ed.) *Physiology in the
American context*: 323–50; N. Oudshoorn (1990) 'On the making of sex
hormones: research materials and the production of knowledge', *Social
Studies of Science*, 20: 5–33, N. Oudshoorn 'On measuring sex hormones:
the role of biological assays in sexualizing chemical substances, *Bulletin of
Medical History*, 64: 243–61; D. E. Long (1990) 'Moving reprints: a historian
looks at sex research publications of the 1930s', *Journal of the History of
Medicine*, 45: 452–68.

128   This bioassay was developed by George Papanicolaou when he was work-
      ing at Cornell Medical School. Papanicolaou correlated the pattern of smears
      of vaginal discharge with changes in the uterus and ovaries of virginal guinea
      pigs. The results of his study were published in *Science* in July 1917.
      Papanicolaou used this technique in the study of the sexual cycle of other
      non-human mammals. For a period of twenty-one years starting in 1920, he
      examined daily the vaginal discharge of his wife! In the mid-1930s, he set up
      a private clinic where he investigated the endocrines of sterile women. D.
      Erskine Carmichael (1973) *The Pap smear: life of George N. Papanicolaou*,
      Springfield, Illinois, Chartes C. Thomas. Bioassays of sex hormones crys-
      tallized contemporary ideas about masculinity and femininity; see also
      Long Hall, 'Biology, sex hormones and sexism in the 1920s'; Oudshorn, 'On
      measuring sex hormones'.

129   The success of strategies adopted in order to overcome difficulties in obtain-
      ing a plentiful supply of raw materials had a major influence on the institu-
      tional development of sex hormones. See Oudshoorn, 'On the making of sex
      hormones'.

130   One of the first of these is the now notorious diethylstilboestrol, stilboestrol
      or DES, a synthetic oestrogen. In the late 1960s, this drug was found to have
      produced genital abnormalities and sterility in the sons and daughters of
      pregnant women who were given it in order to prevent threatened miscar-
      riage. It also caused vaginal cancer in some of their daughters and has
      recently been implicated in the etiology of cancer of the testicles. Editorial
      (1971) 'Stilboestrol and cancer', *British Medical Journal*, ii: 593–4; N. Pfeffer
      (1992) 'Lessons from history: the salutory tale of stilboestrol', in Alderson P.
      (ed.) *Consent to health treatment and research: differing perspectives*,
      London, SSRV, Institute of Education: 31–6.

131   For an account of how the corpus luteum hormone came to be called
      'progesterone', see Parkes, *Sex, science and society*: 43–6.

132   C. J. Thomas (1958) 'The pharmaceutical industry', in D. Burn (ed.) *The
      structure of British industry: a NIESR symposium*, Cambridge, Cambridge
      University Press: 331–76; J. B. Jefferys (1954) *Retail trading in Britain,
      1850–1950*, Cambridge, Cambridge University Press: 379–99; J. Liebenau
      (1984) 'Industrial R & D in pharmaceutical firms in the early twentieth
      century', *Business History*, 26: 331–46.

133   The use of the bioassay in toxicity testing involves administering a substance

to an animal in order to see if it has ill-effects. Medical Research Committee (1916) *Memorandum submitted to Mr Asquith's Reconstruction Committee by the Medical Research Committee upon a National Laboratory for Biological Standardization,* London, HMSO; Medical Research Committee (1919) *Memorandum by the Medical Research Committee on the supply, standardization and testing of biological preparations and of certain drugs for use in medical work,* London, HMSO; MRC 1101; PRO MH 81/52.

134   For the history of the MRC see A. Landsborough Thomson (1973) *Half a century of medical research,* vol. 1: *Origins and policy of the Medical Research Council (UK),* London, HMSO; A. Landsborough Thomson (1975) *Half a century of medical research,* vol. 2: *The programme of the Medical Research Council (UK),* London, HMSO; J. Austoker and L. Bryder, eds (1989) *Historical perspectives on the role of the MRC,* Oxford, Oxford University Press.

135   In Britain, this tendency resulted in the passage of the Therapeutic Substances Act 1925.

136   P. Stechl (1969) 'Biological standardisation of drugs before 1928', unpublished PhD dissertation, University of Wisconsin; PRO MH 58/117.

137   P. Hartley (1945) 'International biological standards: prospect and retrospect', *Proceedings of the Royal Society of Medicine,* 39: 45–58.

138   MRC 1523/13.

139   MRC Sex Hormone Committee Minutes.

140   MRC 1766/1.

141   E. C. Dodds (1937) 'The chemistry of oestrogenic compounds and methods of assay', in *The endocrines in theory and practice: articles published from the British Medical Journal,* London, H. K. Lewis: 162

142   The full range of commercial sex hormone preparations is described in an illustrated guide in H. E. Dale (1939) 'The chemistry of sex hormones', *Pharmaceutical Journal,* 140: 432–42.

143   RCOG B/02/3.

144   J. Haram (1939) 'Report of an endocrine clinic', *British Medical Journal,* i: 1243–5.

145   Professional bodies frowned upon direct association between doctors and manufacturers of medicines, even for the purpose of a clinical trial. It was considered not quite the correct thing to associate with 'trade'; doing so put doctors at risk of suspicion of having a pecuniary interest in a drug. The MRC was not very adept at negotiating this tricky relationship, largely because it also abhorred the idea of making profits out of medicines; MRC 1523.

146   F. H. K. Green (1954) 'The clinical evaluation of remedies', *The Lancet,* ii: 1085–90.

147   MRC Minutes of Therapeutic Trials Committee.

148   G. W. Corner (1951) 'Our knowledge of the menstrual cycle', *The Lancet,* i: 919–23.

149   T. N. A. Jeffcoate (1935) 'Sterility due to ovarian dysfunction', *British Medical Journal,* i: 345–50; Green-Armytage, 'Sterile mating': 427.

150   Bonney, 'On sterility': 974.

151 R. K. Callow (1938) 'The significance of the excretion of sex hormones in the urine', *Proceedings of the Royal Society of Medicine*, 31: 19–34.
152 MRC Oestrin Sub-Committee Minutes.
153 MRC 1523/23A.
154 A. Bourne (1947) 'Endocrines in gynaecology', *British Medical Journal*, i: 979–82.
155 Sales of aspirin were £959,000 or 3.0 per cent; penicillin £6,792 or 21 per cent; insulin £1,392 or 4.2 per cent; sulphonamides £3,382 or 10.4 per cent; and vitamins £1,179 or 3.7 per cent. Thomas, 'The pharmaceutical industry': 336.
156 Bourne, 'Endocrines in gynaecology': 81.

CHAPTER 4   POLITICS, HEALTH AND STERILITY

1 PRO MH 58/399.
2 PRO MH 58/399.
3 I have developed the arguments in this chapter in: N. Pfeffer (1990) 'Fertility control: health or population policy?', *Critical Public Health*, 2: 19–21; N. Pfeffer (1992) From private patients to privatisation', in M. Stacey (ed.) *Changing human reproduction: some social science perspectives*, London, Sage: 48–74.
4 L. Tickner (1987) *The spectacle of women: imagery of the suffrage campaign, 1907–14*, London, Chatto and Windus: 4.
5 A. Summers (1979) 'A home from home – women's philanthropic work in the nineteenth century', in S. Burman (ed.) *Fit work for women*, London, Croom Helm: 33–63.
6 G. Jones (1986) *Social hygiene in twentieth century Britain*, London, Croom Helm.
7 Pauline Mazumder describes the common ground held by Edwardian pressure groups: P. Mazumder (1980) 'The eugenists and the residuum: the problem of the urban poor', *Bulletin of the History of Medicine*, 54: 204–15.
8 In the USA and Germany, eugenics was concerned primarily with the politics of race rather than class.
9 C. Dyhouse (1981) 'Working-class mothers and infant mortality in England, 1895–1914', in C. Webster (ed.) *Biology, medicine and society, 1840–1940*, Cambridge, Cambridge University Press: 73–98.
10 For a discussion of the crisis in confidence in the British state that began in the 1880s see S. Hall (1984) 'The rise of the representative/interventionist state', in G. McLennan, D. Held and S. Hall (eds) *State and society in contemporary Britain*, Cambridge, Polity: 7–49; S. Hall and B. Schwarz (1985) 'State and society, 1880–1939', in M. Langan and B. Schwarz (eds) *Crises in the British state, 1880–1930*, London, Hutchinson: 7–32.
11 G. R. Searle (1971) *The quest for national efficiency*, Oxford, Blackwell.
12 Instruction of women in how to be good mothers has been covered exhaustively in A. Davin (1978) 'Imperialism and motherhood', *History Workshop*

Journal, 5: 9–65; J. Lewis (1980) *The politics of motherhood: child and maternal welfare in England, 1900–1939*, London, Croom Helm; Dyhouse, 'Working-class mothers'; C. Rowan (1985) 'Child welfare and the working-class family, in Langan and Schwarz (eds) *Crises in the British state*: 226–39; Deborah Dwork (1987) *War is good for babies and other young children: a history of the infant and child welfare movement in England, 1898–1918*, London, Tavistock.

13   B. Gilbert (1965) 'Health and politics: the British Physical Deterioration Report of 1904', *Bulletin of the History of Medicine*, 39: 143–53; P. Thane (1982) *The foundations of the welfare state*, London, Longman: 74–81.

14   Tickner, *Spectacle of women*: 65.

15   Thane, *Foundations of the welfare state*: 29.

16   Ibid.: 29–30.

17   L. Davidoff and B. Westover (1986) *Our work, our lives, our words: women's history and women's work*, Basingstoke, Macmillan Education: 13–14.

18   The National Insurance Act was the first time the state interfered in the treatment of tuberculosis; it provided £1.5 million for the erection of sanatoria. The Public Health Act 1913 was particularly aimed at tuberculosis. It required county councils to prepare schemes for prevention and treatment. A scheme implied appointment of a Tuberculosis Officer, nurses for home visiting, a voluntary after-care committee, and the provision of dispensaries and sanatoria.

19   J. Turner (1988) ' "Experts" and interests: David Lloyd George and the dilemmas of the expanding state, 1906–19', in R. MacLeod (ed.) *Government and expertise: specialists, administrators and professionals, 1860–1919*, Cambridge, Cambridge University Press: 203–23.

20   For a brief, critical overview of the different explanations of the origins of the welfare state in Britain, see Thane, *Foundations of the welfare state*: 288–301.

21   Quoted in Davidoff and Westover, 'From Queen Victoria to Jazz age', in *Our work, our lives, our words*: 20.

22   The Women's Co-operative Guild was set up in 1883 as a self-governing organization within the Co-operative Movement that dealt with the position of married women. Before the First World War, it was a vigorous campaigning organization of some 32,000 women. The movement then was concerned with the virtually non-existent maternal and infant care for poorer women. As part of its campaign, the Guild sought and published the famous, moving accounts of working-class women's experiences of childbirth and child-rearing in M. Llewellyn Davies (1978) *Maternity: letters from working women*, London, Virago.

23   S. Pedersen (1989) 'The failure of feminism in the making of the British welfare state', *Radical History Review*, 43: 86–110.

24   Davin, 'Imperialism and motherhood': 13.

25   Simon Szreter describes the background to the 1911 Census in S. R. S. Szreter (1983) 'The decline of marital fertility in England and Wales c. 1870–1914: a critique of the theory of social class differentials through an examination of

the date for the constituent male occupations', unpublished PhD dissertation, University of Oxford; and S. R. S. Szreter (1984) 'The genesis of the Registrar-General's social classification of occupations', *British Journal of Sociology*, 35: 522–46.

26 PP *Hansard* (1910) xviii: col. 297.

27 S. Szreter (1991) 'The GRO and the public health movement in Britain, 1837–1914', *Social History of Medicine*, 4: 435–64.

28 Tickner, *Spectacle of women*: 214.

29 Ibid.: 159.

30 D. Kevles (1986) *In the name of eugenics: genetics and the uses of human heredity*, Harmondsworth, Pelican: 9.

31 F. Galton (1869) *Hereditary genius: an enquiry into its laws and consequences*, London: 131.

32 For a discussion of the way in which eugenic ideas influenced English thought and social policy, see G. Jones (1980) *Social Darwinism and English thought: the interaction between biological and social theory*, Brighton, Harvester; Jones, *Social hygiene in twentieth century Britain*; D. A. Mackenzie (1981) *Statistics in Britain 1865–1930: the social construction of scientific knowledge*, Edinburgh, Edinburgh University Press.

33 Quoted in Mackenzie, *Statistics in Britain*: 18.

34 The eugenics movement appealed strongly to the professional middle classes; see G. R. Searle (1981) 'Eugenics and class', in C. Webster (ed.) *Biology, medicine and society, 1840–1940*, Cambridge, Cambridge University Press: 217–42.

35 G. R. Searle (1983) 'Socialism and Malthusianism in late Victorian and Edwardian Britain', in J. Dupaquier. A. Fauve-Chamoux and E. Grebenik (eds) *Malthus past and present*, London, Academic Press: 341–56.

36 National Birth-Rate Commission (1920) *Problems of population and parenthood*, London, Chapman and Hall: 418.

37 R. A. Soloway (1989) 'Eugenics and pronatalism in wartime Britain', in R. Wall and J. Winter (eds) *The upheaval of war in Europe, 1914–18*, Cambridge, Cambridge University Press: 369–87.

38 Editorial (1916) 'Birth-rate in war time', *British Medical Journal*, i: 105.

39 PP Local Government Board (1913) *Report on venereal diseases by Dr R. W. Johnstone*, Cd 7029, London, HMSO.

40 J. Weeks (1983) *Sex, politics and society: the regulation of sexuality since 1800*, London, Longman: 215.

41 Dwork, *War is good for babies*: 211.

42 A flurry of legislation during and immediately after the First World War gave official recognition to many of the demands of campaigners for the safeguarding of infant life: the Notification of Birth Extensions Act 1915 made the notification of birth compulsory; the Milk and Dairies Consolidation Act 1915 enabled local authorities to establish milk depots for the sale of milk for infants at cost price; and the Midwives Act 1916 made midwives' training more rigorous.

43 Weeks, *Sex, politics and society*: 188.

44 R. E. Dowse and J. Peel (1965) 'The politics of birth control', *Political Studies*, 13: 183.

45 Historians of the birth control movement seem to love military metaphors: for example, A. Leathard (1980) *The fight for family planning: the development of family planning services in Britain, 1921–1974*, London, Macmillan; Soloway calls his final chapter documenting the birth controller's victory 'The walls of the citadel fall' (R. Soloway (1982) *Birth control and the population question in England 1877–1930*, Chapel Hill, University of North Carolina Press).

46 Pedersen, 'Failure of feminism': 91.

47 E. Cronin and P. Weiler (1991) 'Working-class interests and the politics of social democratic reform in Britain, 1900–1940', *International Labor and Working-class History*, 40: 52.

48 This point is also relevant to American Catholicism; see P. J. Donaldson (1988) 'American Catholicism and the international family planning movement', *Population Studies*, 42: 367–73.

49 M. Hornsby-Smith (1978) *Roman Catholics in England: studies in social structure since the Second World War*, Cambridge, Cambridge University Press: 21.

50 Perhaps the troubled relationship between Britain and Ireland accounts for the suprising dearth of sociological analysis of British Catholicism. The best book on the subject is P. Coman (1977) *Catholics and the welfare state*, London, Longman.

51 The influence of the catholic vote in the interwar period is discussed in R. E. Dowse and J. Peel (1965) 'The politics of birth-control', *Political Studies*, 13: 179–97.

52 A. E. C. W. Spencer (1966) 'The demography and sociography of the Roman Catholic community of England and Wales', in L. Bright and S. Clements (eds) *The committed church*, London, Darton, Longman and Todd: 60–85.

53 These strategies are borrowed from a discussion of the attitude of liberal democratic governments to abortion since the Second World War in J. Lovenduski and J. Outshoorn (1986) 'Introduction: the new politics of abortion', in J. Lovenduski and J. Outshoorn (eds) *The new politics of abortion*, London, Sage: 2.

54 M. Mitchell (1985) 'The effects of unemployment on the social condition of women and children in the 1930s', *History Workshop Journal*, 19: 105–27.

55 The redoubtable Eleanor Rathbone is the best-known figure in this campaign; see J. Macnicol (1980) *The movement for family allowance, 1918–1945: a study in social policy development*, London, Heinemann; E. Rathbone (1986) *The disinherited family* (with an introductory essay by Suzie Fleming), Bristol, Falling Wall Press.

56 R. Stevens (1966) *Medical practice in modern England: the impact of specialization and state medicine*, New Haven, Yale University Press: 45.

57 See A. Oakley (1986) *The captured womb: a history of the medical care of pregnant women*, Oxford, Blackwell: 62–85; J. Lewis (1990) 'Mothers and maternity policies in the twentieth century', in J. Garcia, R. Kilpatrick

and M. Richards (eds) *The politics of maternity care: services for child-bearing women in twentieth-century Britain*, Oxford, Oxford University Press: 15–29.

58 Quoted in J. Lewis (1979) 'The ideology and politics of birth control in inter-war England', *Women's Studies International Quarterly*, 2: 40.

59 Leathard *The fight for family planning*: 13.

60 Quoted in Lewis, 'The ideology and politics of birth control': 40.

61 B. Brookes (1988) *Abortion in England, 1900–1967*, London, Croom Helm.

62 Dowse and Peel, 'The politics of birth-control': 184–6.

63 Mitchell, 'The effects of unemployment': 105.

64 J. Gyford (1985) 'The politicisation of local government', in M. Loughlin, M. Gelfand and K. Young (eds) *Half a century of municipal decline, 1935–85*, London, Allen and Unwin: 82–3.

65 CMAC FPA A8/12.

66 PRO MH 52/177.

67 PRO MH 55/1503.

68 The Women's Health Enquiry Committee was formed in 1933 by representatives of women's organizations. The Committee investigated the general conditions of health among women, especially working-class women. See M. Spring Rice (1981) *Working-class wives: their health and conditions*, London, Virago: 199.

69 CMAC SA FPA NK/90.

70 PRO RG 24/3.

71 J. Lewis (1990) 'Public institution, private relationship: marriage and marriage guidance, 1920–1968', *Twentieth Century British History*, 1: 233–63.

72 A. Digby and N. Bosanquet (1988) 'Doctors and patients in an era of national health insurance and private practice, 1913–1938', *Economic History Review*, 2nd ser. xli: 87.

73 Spring Rice, *Working-class wives*: 38.

74 Digby and Bosanquet, 'Doctors and patients': 89.

75 Ibid.: 85.

76 E. Lewis Faning (1949) *Family limitation and its influence on human fertility during the past 50 years: Papers of the Royal Commission on Population*, vol. 1. An investigation carried out by the Royal College of Obstetricians and Gynaecologists, London, HMSO: 90.

77 His findings were published in one of the three books that began the depopulation scare; D. Glass (1936) *The struggle for population*, Oxford, Oxford University Press; it was revised and enlarged in D. Glass (1940) *Population policies and movements in Europe*, Oxford, Oxford University Press.

78 For a discussion of pronatalist policies introduced in Europe during the interwar period, see Glass, *The struggle for population*; Glass, *Population policies*. On Nazi Germany see T. Mason (1976) 'Women in Nazi Germany: part I', *History Workshop Journal*, 1: 74–113; part 2: *History Workshop Journal*, 2: 5–32; G. Bock (1984) 'Racism and sexism in Nazi Germany: motherhood, compulsory sterilization and the state', in R. Bridenthal, A.

Grossman and M. Kaplan (eds) *When biology became destiny: women in Weimar and Nazi Germany*, New York, Monthly Review Press: 271–96; F. Kudlien (1990) 'The German response to the birth-rate problem during the Third Reich', *Continuity and Change*, 5: 225–47; M. Burleigh and W. Wippermann (1991) *The racial state: Germany 1933–1945*, Cambridge, Cambridge University Press. On Italy see A. De Grand (1976) 'Women under Italian fascism', *Historical Journal*, 19: 947–88; L. Caldwell (1986) 'Reproducers of the nation: women and the family in fascist policy', in D. Forgacs (ed.) *Rethinking Italian fascism*, London, Lawrence and Wishart: 110–41.

79   Glass, *Population policies*: 302.
80   R. Proctor (1988) *Racial hygiene: medicine under the Nazis*, Cambridge, Mass., Harvard University Press: 121.
81   The archives of the Population Investigation Committee include a scrapbook of newspaper cuttings on German and Allied birth rates published in Britain between June 1939 and December 1942.
82   Proctor, *Racial hygiene*: 121.
83   R. J. Lifton (1986) *The Nazi doctors: a study of the psychology of evil*, London, Macmillan: 43.
84   P. Weindling (1989) *Health, race and German politics between national unification and Nazism, 1870–1945*, Cambridge, Cambridge University Press: 551.
85   E. Holland (1938) 'Medical aspects of decline of population', *British Medical Journal*, i: 471.
86   For a discussion of the racial policies espoused by Mussolini see A. M. Canepa (1979) 'Half-hearted cynicism: Mussolini's racial politics', *Patterns of Prejudice*, 13: 18–27.
87   The history of the British eugenics movement, British fascism, and other bodies organized around biological politics, has been written as though their ideas bore no relation to one another. Perhaps this was the case, but in view of the strong links between eugenics and fascism in Nazi Germany, the question is undoubtedly worthy of further exploration.
88   D. Paul (1984) 'Eugenics and the left', *Journal of the History of Ideas*, 45: 567–90.
89   The debate on the political complexion of the Eugenics Society is found in M. Freeden (1979) 'Eugenics and progressive thought: a study in ideological affinity', *Historical Journal*, 22: 645–71; G. R. Searle (1979) 'Eugenics and politics in Britain in the 1930s', *Annals of Science*, 36: 159–69; G. Jones (1982) 'Eugenics and social policy between the wars', *Historical Journal*, 25: 717–28; Paul 'Eugenics and the left'.
90   C. P. Blacker (1952) ' "Eugenic" experiments conducted by the Nazis on human subjects', *Eugenics Review*, 44: 9–19.
91   Burleigh and Wippermann, *The racial state*: 98.
92   Since the 1940s, historians have failed to agree on whether Nazi Germany is an aberration or a more extreme version of modern industrialized nations. Some argue that the brand of eugenic and racist ideas and policies found in

Nazi Germany is unique; others claim with equal force that Nazi Germany
serves as a clear warning of the sickness that threatens all modern civilization. A good summary of these arguments in relation to Nazi Germany, and
the interests they serve, is to be found in Burleigh and Wippermann *The
racial state*: 7–22.

93 For an introduction to the concept of reactionary modernism see J. Herf
(1984) *Reactionary modernism: technology, culture, and politics in Weimar
and the Third Reich*, Cambridge, Cambridge University Press. Herf belongs
to the school that believes reactionary modernism was confined to Nazi
Germany.

94 Formed in 1910, three years after the Eugenics Education Society was set up,
the Guild of St Luke, St Cosmas and St Damian disseminated pro-life propaganda among the roughly 3,000 Catholic doctors and dentists in the British
Empire. In contrast, the membership of the Eugenics Society was never
large; even in its peak years (1911 and 1932/3) there were never more than
800 members and usually considerably fewer. The Guild stood out against
materialism, state medicine and attacks on the unborn child. It held meetings
where doctors discussed from a Catholic perspective topics ranging over
infanticide, eugenics, rejuvenation, birth control, obstetric emergencies, psychoanalysis, the Turin shroud and creation versus evolution. Its quarterly
journal *The Catholic Medical Journal* reprinted items from the medical press,
criticizing them from the point of view of Catholic theology. Its circulation
was at least 1,000.

95 Another version of this accusation was that if sterility existed, it was deliberate, or a side-effect of scientific contraceptives. The amount of energy
expended by birth controllers on disproving this claim is evident in the
papers of the Royal Commission of Population and numerous references to
the subject in contemporary medical journals. It is ultimately to women's
disadvantage that they succeeded in discrediting talk about side-effects of
contraceptives.

96 PRO RG 24/10 Ev 48 C and D.

97 CMAC SA FPA A5/108.

98 M. Hadley Jackson (1942) 'Sterility', *The Lancet*, i: 477.

99 D. Riley (1987) 'Some peculiarities of social policy concerning women in
wartime and postwar Britain', in M. R. Higonnet, J. Jensen and S. Michel (eds)
Behind the lines: gender and the two world wars, New Haven, Yale University Press: 260–71.

100 Denise Riley explores the relationships among social policies around
women's employment, facilities for childcare and theories of developmental psychology. Her thoughtful and thought-provoking analysis provides
a careful critique of pronatalism. She demonstrates how pronatalism focused
on children's emotional needs after the war, justifying women's return to the
domestic sphere in order to vacate jobs for men. However, she gives undue
emphasis to the association of maternalism and pronatalism during the war;
before and during it, it was soaked in medical and biological concerns.
See D. Riley (1983) *War in the nursery: theories of child and mother*,

London, Virago.

101 This topic is discussed exhaustively in J. Costello (1986) *Love, sex and war, 1939–1945*, London, Pan.

102 PRO MH 55/1503.

103 A. Sharman (1943) 'Sterility and the state', *British Medical Journal*, ii: 282.

104 M. Hadley Jackson (1942) 'Declining population and the preservation of the race', *British Medical Journal*, ii: 55.

105 CMAC SA FPA A5/103.

106 Lord Horder (1943) 'Sterility', *The Lancet*, i: 664; Lord Horder 'Advice on sterility', *British Medical Journal*, i: 644.

107 At one time or another, the following doctors were members of the *ad hoc* committee: Aleck Bourne, Christie Brown, Hans Davidson, Eric Crook, Fouracre Barns, Lord Horder, Annis Gillies, Kathleen Harding, Margaret Jackson, Robert Kellar, Cedric Lane-Roberts, Linton Snaith, Joan Malleson, Mary Mayeur, William Nixon, Margaret Moore White; Percival, Albert Sharman, John Stallworthy, and Kenneth Walker. CMAC FPA A5/102–7.

108 M. Hadley Jackson (1943) 'Contraception and sterility', *The Lancet*, ii: 691.

109 CMAC SA FPA A3/20.

110 R. H. P. Hick (1943) 'Advice on sterility', *British Medical Journal*, i: 707.

111 An analysis of questions submitted to the *British Medical Journal* by general practitioners between 1943 and 1946 drew attention to their apparent ignorance on matters related to sex; see R. T. Bevan (1948) 'What the medical practitioner wants to know', *British Medical Journal*, i: 294.

112 Digby and Bosanquet, 'Doctors and patients': 80.

113 See for example British Medical Association (1931) *The problem of the out-patient*, London, BMA.

114 Digby and Bosanquet, 'Doctors and patients': 90.

115 R. Stevens (1966) *Medical practice in modern England: the impact of specialization and state medicine*, New Haven, Yale University Press: 56.

116 Stevens, *Medical practice in modern England*: 41.

117 Ibid.: 58.

118 F. Honigsbaum (1989) *Health, happiness, and security: the creation of the National Health Service*, London, Routledge: 119.

119 J. Malleson (1943) 'Advice on sterility', *British Medical Journal*, i: 769.

120 ' "Motherhood clinics" all over the country for childless couples', *Daily Mirror*, 22 May 1943.

121 CMAC SA FPA A3/20, Blacker to Malleson, 9 August 1943.

122 J. Malleson (1943) 'Contraception and sterility', *British Medical Journal*, ii: 587.

123 PRO MH 58/406.

124 PRO MH 58/399.

125 PRO MH 58/406.

126 E. Holland 'Why I went to the MRC', RCOG A4/5/1.

127 Ibid.

128 MRC 2526.

129 The Committee carried out an exhaustive review of abortion, stillbirth, infant

mortality and involuntary childlessness: Royal Commission on Population (1950) *Reports of the Biological and Medical Committee*, London, HMSO.

130   PRO RG 24/5, 24/9.

131   PRO CAB 124/1037.

CHAPTER 5   A CRUTCH IN THE CROTCH

1   This account is an amalgam of letters written by six patients of Margaret Jackson who wrote in support of AID during the 1940s. See CMAC SA/EUG/D6.

2   H.J.L. Fitch (1965) 'Childless marriages', *The Guardian*, 28 April.

3   K. Kumar (1987) *Utopia and anti-utopia in modern times*, Oxford, Blackwell: 100. The idea that involuntarily childless women and men are unworthy of sympathy in a world threatened by overpopulation became so persuasive that in the 1970s authors of popular books on infertility apologized for mentioning the problem. For example: 'It is a fairly common reaction of many people to question whether investigation into infertility is justified in an over-populated country, particularly under a free Health Service . . . This book aims at defending the position of the infertility specialist and of those married people who want children but find they cannot have them'; R. Newill (1974) *Infertile marriage*, Harmondsworth, Penguin: 9–10. Similarly: 'It is nowadays unfashionable to talk about increasing the world's population by even one child . . . Yet no woman, who desperately desires a baby . . . gives any thought at all to overpopulation and overcrowding, under-nutrition or any of these matters'; E. Philipp (1975) *Childlessness: its causes and what to do about them*, London, Arrow Books: 7.

4   This point is worth emphasising. Recently, infertile women have stood accused of posing a threat to fertile women by submitting to the new reproductive technologies and supporting their development. Yet it could be argued that from the end of the Second World War until the 1970s the reverse obtained: fertile women colluded with science and medicine in order to gain access to effective contraception, and in so doing contributed to the diminishment of the significance of involuntary childlessness. It is also worth remembering that the technology of contraception has not always received a favourable press. During the interwar period, for example, it was represented by Conservatives and Catholics as the embodiment of evil; birth controllers sought data that would counter the claim that contraception causes promiscuity, venereal infection and sterility. After the war, increasingly the new technology of contraception was accepted as pro-women and anodyne. The tragedy of these representations is that they persistently serve to create an apartheid of fertile and infertile women. They suggest that the interests of the two groups are in opposition, and instead of uniting in sympathy, pit them against one another.

5   Carol Smart defines paternity as the legal status of men who are deemed to

have fathered certain children. Paternity alone does not automatically confer rights of custody or control over children unless the father is married to the mother of the children. Fatherhood is defined as the actual biological or genetic relationship between a man and his 'offspring'. A man's role in parenting, which may occur independently of a biological link, is called social fatherhood. See C. Smart (1989) ' "There is of course the distinction dictated by nature": law and the problem of paternity', in M. Stanworth (ed.) *Reproductive technologies*, Cambridge, Polity: 98.

6 A. Roberts (1945) *British Medical Journal*, i: 199.
7 PP Home Office and Scottish Home Department (1960) *Report of the Departmental Committee on Human Artificial Insemination* (the Feversham Committee), Cmnd 1105, London, HMSO: 9.
8 PRO MH 58/403.
9 Editorial (1947) 'Artificial insemination', *British Medical Journal*, i: 605–6.
10 H. Brewer (1935) 'Eutelegenesis', *Eugenics Review*, 27:121.
11 H. Brewer (1937) 'Eutelegenesis and sterility', *Eugenics Review*, 28: 343–5.
12 M. Barton, K. Walker and B. P. Wiesner (1945) 'Artificial insemination', *British Medical Journal*, i: 40–2.
13 The Marriage Guidance Council – recently renamed Relate – is a national organization that provides counselling for women and men experiencing marital difficulties; see J. Lewis, D. Clark and D. Morgan (1992) *Whom God hath joined together: the work of Marriage Guidance*, London, Routledge.
14 Commission appointed by His Grace the Archbishop of Canterbury (1948) *Artificial human insemination*, London, SPCK: 33.
15 During the Second World War, for example, F. I. Seymour, secretary of the New York-based National Research Foundation for Eugenic Alleviation of Sterility, generously offered to assist Britain's postwar reconstruction endeavours by establishing a clinic in London where the semen of men living in the USA would be collected and used to inseminate British women. The so-called 'Seymour Plan' was rejected. Instead of millions of sperms, the British government accepted millions of dollars from the USA under the 'Marshall Plan'. See CMAC SA EUG/D6.
16 PRO MAF 124/1.
17 A. Walton (1958) 'Artificial insemination in retrospect and prospect', *Journal of the Royal Agricultural Society of England*, 119: 63–9. In order to ensure that all farmers would have access to the semen of superior bulls after the war, in 1944 the Ministry of Agriculture introduced legislation which established a national AI breeding programme.
18 One of the more enduring ideas in English culture, is that the 'blood' tie holds ideological supremacy; all kinds of social obligations and support flow from biological relationships. However, it is not biology but paternity that ties a child to a kinship network. Paradoxically, paternity is established through a legal, not a biological process; according to the law, where a child is conceived outside of marriage, the mother is left holding an apparently fatherless baby; in this instance, an appeal to biology is insufficient to establish a legal claim on inheritance and legitimacy. Although in some other

cultures social fatherhood – taking responsibility for the care of children – is recognized as grounds for assumption of paternity, in the English system of kinship it is regarded as a weak tie. Marriage confers a legal relationship between a man and a woman's children; children born within marriage are the legal responsibility of the husband, unless he goes to great lengths to prove otherwise. See Smart, ' "There is of course a distinction" ': 101.

19 I discussed the way in which the public outrage provoked by AID stigmatized infertile women in N. Pfeffer (1987) 'Artificial insemination, in-vitro fertilization and the stigma of infertility', in Stanworth (ed.) *Reproductive technologies*: 81–97.

20 J. R. A. Todhunter (1944) 'Artificial insemination', *British Medical Journal*, i: 25.

21 F. M. R. Walshe (1945) 'Artificial insemination', *British Medical Journal*, i: 165.

22 J. S. M. Connell (1944) 'Artificial insemination', *British Medical Journal*, i: 95.

23 R. Harper (1944) 'Artificial insemination', *British Medical Journal*, ii: 512–13.

24 C. Gordon-Watson (1945) 'Artificial insemination', *British Medical Journal*, i: 236.

25 L. G. Parsons (1945) 'Artificial insemination', *British Medical Journal*, i: 96.

26 J. Phelan (1944) 'Artificial insemination', *British Medical Journal*, ii: 802.

27 F. Murray (1947) 'Artificial insemination', *British Medical Journal*, i: 826.

28 J. A. Rooth (1945) 'Artificial insemination', *British Medical Journal*, i: 165.

29 V. Zachary Cope (1945) 'Artificial insemination', *British Medical Journal*, i: 276.

30 F. M. R. Walshe (1945) 'Artificial insemination', *British Medical Journal*, i: 276–7.

31 L. J. Bendit (1943) 'Artificial insemination', *British Medical Journal*, ii: 404.

32 E. H. Strange (1944) 'Artificial insemination', *British Medical Journal*, ii: 578 & 772.

33 A. Leitch (1943) 'Artificial insemination', *British Medical Journal*, ii: 434.

34 PRO MH 58/403. Tom Driberg MP persistently pressed the government to set up an enquiry into AID.

35 Public Morality Council (1947) *Artificial human insemination: report of a conference held under the auspices of the Public Morality Council*, London, Heinemann Medical Books; Archbishop's Commission, *Artificial human insemination*. For a full discussion of the Catholic position on AID, see *New Catholic encyclopaedia* (1967), Washington, The Catholic University of America.

36 CMAC SA EUG D7.

37 PRO MH 58/403.

38 See Memorandum prepared for Council Meeting, 24 March, 1945, RCOG A2/ 4; also PRO MH 58/403.

39 Margaret Jackson was a leading birth controller; her clinic in Exeter provided poor women with an exemplary service. She was also interested in sterility, and together with Clare Harvey carried out important research into male infertility. She discussed her approach to AID in M. Hadley Jackson (1957)

'Artificial insemination (donor)', *Eugenics Review*, 48: 203–7. Because she kept in regular contact with couples who had AID, encouraging them to write to her at least once a year, her records have provided data for a retrospective study of the experience of AID. See R. Snowden, G. D. Mitchell and E. M. Snowden (1983) *Artificial reproduction: a social investigation*, London, Allen and Unwin.

40 CMAC SA FPA A3/2.

41 Archbishop's Commission, *Artificial human insemination*: 13.

42 Public Morality Council, *Artificial human insemination*: 44.

43 The Eugenics Society set up the Committee in March 1958 in order to collect evidence for and possibly collaborate with the government's Departmental Committee. See CMAC SA EUG D6, D7: Minutes of AID Investigation Committee, 3 December 1958.

44 Feversham Committee, *Report*: 7.

45 H. McLeave (1958) 'Fathers anonymous', *News Chronicle and Daily Dispatch*, 4 February.

46 Feversham Committee, *Report*: 17.

47 PRO MH 58/403.

48 British Medical Association (1959) 'Memorandum of evidence submitted to the Departmental Committee set up by the Home Office', *British Medical Journal*, supplement, i: 289.

49 R. Stevens (1966) *Medical practice in modern England: the impact of specialization and state medicine*, New Haven, Yale University Press: 166.

50 R. Forbes (1944) 'The medico-legal aspects of artificial insemination', *Medico-legal and Criminological Review*, 12: 138–52.

51 PRO MH 58/403. Despite the passage of nearly fifty years, during which ideas about informed consent have been transformed, the wording of the Medical Defence Union's form is remarkably similar to that recommended for use in IVF clinics in the 1990s. The 1945 form stated: 'We—and—being desirous of having a child and having been advised that this is impossible to achieve by normal sexual intercourse between us hereby request and authorize you to inseminate artificially . . .'. The Interim Licensing Authority (discussed in chapter 6) used the following format: 'We—[full name of woman] and—[full name of man] of—being unlikely to have a child by other means, have requested the—Centre, through its medical and scientific staff, to assist the woman to give birth to a child by the man.' According to many IVF practitioners, many patients found the consent form incomprehensible. See N. Pfeffer (1991) 'Are British IVF forms adequate?', *Bulletin of Medical Ethics*, 69: 28–31.

52 D. Riley (1983) *War in the nursery*, London, Virago.

53 P. Taylor (1958) *Daily Sketch*, 16 January.

54 L. Segal (1988) 'Look back in anger: men in the 50s', in R. Chapman and J. Rutherford (eds) *Male order: unwrapping masculinity*, London, Lawrence and Wishart: 68–96.

55 J. Weeks (1981) *Sex, politics, and society: the regulation of sexuality since 1800*, London, Longman: 239.

56 Homosexuals emerged as scapegoats in the tense international climate. The US State Department, under the influence of McCarthyism, had itself purged employees who were homosexual, on the grounds that they were security risks by reason of their 'lack of emotional stability', the 'weakness of their moral fibre' and their susceptibility to blandishments and blackmail. Following the defection to Russia of the British spies Guy Burgess and Donald McLean in 1950, there is evidence of American pressure on the British government to put its own house in order. See Weeks, *Sex, politics, and society*: 240I–1.

57 Feversham Committee, *Report*: 20.

58 CMAC SA EUG N66

59 C. Pincher (1957) 'Muller's warning', *Daily Express*, 27 November.

60 J. Hajnal (1960) 'Artificial insemination and the frequency of incestuous marriages', *Journal of the Royal Statistical Society A*, 123: 182–94.

61 C. Smart (1984) *The ties that bind: law, marriage and the reproduction of patriarchal relations*, London, Routledge and Kegan Paul: 23–41.

62 BMA, 'Memorandum of evidence': 291.

63 RCOG (1958) Minutes of Finance and Executive Committee, Minute Book 10, 12 December 1958.

64 CMAC SA FPA A3/23.

65 P. Coman (1977) *Catholics and the welfare state*, London, Longman: 49–50.

66 PRO HO 342/45.

67 Feversham Committee, *Report*: 10.

68 *Daily Express*, 20 January 1958 (anonymous).

69 Sol Bender, a consultant obstetrician and gynaecologist, used this term in a paper on infertility investigations submitted to the *British Medical Journal* in 1952. It was omitted. See S. Bender (1979) 'Infertility', *British Medical Journal*, ii: 1117.

70 B. Sandler (1952) 'The investigation and treatment of sterility', *The Medical Press*, 227: 8. Dr Bernard Sandler worked with Green-Armytage, Mary Barton and Margaret Jackson before opening the first clinic for the investigation of both male and female infertility at the Manchester Jewish Hospital in 1947. I am grateful to Dr Sandler for giving me copies of all the many papers he published on infertility during his long career, together with many important documents on AID.

71 J. McLeod (1956) 'Human semen', *Fertility and Sterility*, 7: 368–410.

72 T. Laqueur (1990) *Making sex: body and gender from the Greeks to Freud*, Cambridge, Mass., Harvard University Press: 171.

73 Although now sadly out of print, this book repays efforts made to obtain it: R. Herschberger (1948) *Adam's rib*, New York, Harper and Row: 71–2.

74 See for example critical comments in T. N. A. Jeffcoate (1946) 'Male infertility', *British Medical Journal*, ii: 187–91.

75 R. H. Glass and R. J. Ericsson (1979) 'Spontaneous cure of male fertility', *Fertility and Sterility*, 31: 305.

76 N. Pfeffer and A. Woollett (1983) *The experience of infertility*, London, Virago: 61.

77 See for example C. Harvey and M. Hadley Jackson (1957) 'Intermittent methyltestosterone therapy in male subfertility', *The Lancet*, i: 711–13.
78 Any questions (1963) 'Scrotal temperature and fertility', *British Medical Journal*, i: 937.
79 Quoted in H. Davidson (1955) 'The role of the male', unpublished paper: CMAC SA FPA A19/22A.
80 Jeffcoate, 'Male infertility': 190.
81 L. Stuart Scott (1968) 'Infertility in men', *Hospital Medicine*, 3: 646.
82 M. Freund (1966) 'Standards for the rating of human sperm morphology', *International Journal of Fertility*, 11 (supplement): 97–180.
83 During the 1950s many papers were published exploring this question: for example, C. G. Hartman (1957) 'How do sperm get into the uterus?', *Fertility and Sterility*, 8: 403–27.
84 On 24 August 1955, four British experts met to discuss the method and standard of semen to be used in testing of contraceptives for inclusion in the British *Pharmacopoeia*; see CMAC SA FPA A7/16.
85 Scott, 'Infertility in men': 644–52.
86 T. Mann (1964) *The biochemistry of semen and of the male reproductive tract*, London, Methuen: 85.
87 Physicochemical methods of semen analysis were used to examine a wide range of physical, chemical and metabolic characteristics of semen related to the physiological function of the sperm and the seminal plasma, including: light-scattering and light-absorption power; electrical conductivity and impedance changes; specific gravity; osmotic pressure; hydrogen concentration; buffering capacity; occurrence of semen—specific metabolites; and the rate of anaerobic and aerobic metabolic processes of semen. Mann, *Biochemistry of semen*: 82–4.
88 W. W. Williams (1961) 'The enigma of male infertility', *International Journal of Fertility*, 6: 316.
89 The same situation obtained in the USA. A survey of 147 doctors known to be working with marital infertility found that only nine applied a type of sperm stain by which presence of spermatic pathology might reasonably be identified; see Williams 'The enigma of male infertility': 311.
90 CMAC SA FPA A5/102–7.
91 CMAC SA FPA A3/25.
92 In 1981–2, Anne Woollett and I interviewed over thirty women who had gone through infertility investigations; almost without exception, they described the post-coital test as a very negative experience. Male partners often failed to co-operate, refusing to have sexual intercourse in order to comply with medical demands, and so they had to miss the appointment. One woman summed her experience up as follows: 'I really hated the post-coital test. It was horrid waking up at seven knowing you have to have sex. You've got to get the stuff into you and then get yourself to the hospital. He hated it and I hated making him do it' (Pfeffer and Woollett, *The experience of infertility*: 102).
93 G. T. Kovacs, G. B. Newman and G. L. Henson (1978) 'The *post coital* test:

what is normal', *British Medical Journal*, i: 818.

94   In order to measure exactly the interval between ejaculation and commence-ment of observation, the husband was given a stopwatch to hold in his hand. On three occasions, the researchers were able to make their observations within ninety seconds of ejaculation. See A. J. Sobrero and J. McLeod (1962) 'The immediate postcoital test', *Fertility and Sterility*, 13: 184–9.

95   A comprehensive review of contemporary practice around the post-coital test is found in V. Davajan, R. M. Nakamura and K. Kharma (1970) 'Sperma-tozoan transport in cervical mucus', *Obstetrics and Gynaecology Survey*, 24: 1–43.

96   A. Grant (1958) 'Cervical hostility: incidence, diagnosis and prognosis', *Fer-tility and Sterility*, 9: 321–3.

97   Pfeffer and Woollett, *The experience of infertility*: 105.

98   M. Barton and B. Wiesner (1946) 'The receptivity of cervical mucus to spermatozoa', *British Medical Journal*, ii: 606–10.

99   There is a dearth of negative medical terms to describe male reproductive pathology, and an excess for 'women's troubles'. For a discussion of the gendered language of reproductive pathology see N. Pfeffer (1985) 'The hidden pathology of the male reproductive system', in H. Homans (ed.) *The sexual politics of reproduction*, Aldershot, Gower: 30–44.

100 For an exhaustive account of ancient and modern ideas about the impor-tance of female orgasm to conception, see Laqueur, *Making sex*.

101 Parkes' autobiography documents the history of reproductive physiology in the twentieth century, albeit from a rather idiosyncratic perspective: A. S. Parkes (1985) *Off-beat biologist*, Cambridge, Galton Foundation.

102 A. Parkes (1974) 'Sexuality and reproduction', *Perspectives in Biology and Medicine*, 17: 407.

103 Family Planning Association (1951) *For childless wives: a doctor advises*, London, FPA: 8.

104 T. N. A. Jeffcoate (1954) 'The management of infertility', *Journal of Obstetrics and Gynaecology of the British Empire*, 61: 184.

105 This survey was carried out by Dr Bernard Sandler, who kindly lent me a copy of the results.

106 M. Hadley Jackson (1952) 'Clinical methods of determining ovulation', *The Practitioner*, 168: 154.

107 The twenty-five tests of ovulation identified were: pregnancy; evidence of corpus luteum based on histologic examination of the ovaries; direct inspec-tion of ovaries *in vivo* by laparotomy; direct inspection of the ovaries *in vivo* by culdoscopy; histologic readings of endometrial biopsies; cytologic read-ing of vaginal smears; basal body temperature; pregnanediol in urine; pro-gesterone in blood; quantitative glycogen concentration in endometrium; cyclic vaginal bleeding; intermenstrual pain; qualitative evaluation of glyco-gen concentration in endometrium; arborization of cervical mucus; gonadotrophic hormone in urine; oestrogenic fractions in urine; histologic reading of endocervical biopsies; physical and chemical properties of the cervical mucus; premenstrual symptoms and signs; psychosexual cyclic fluc-

tuations; ph, viscosity and specific gravity of urine; electrolytes in serum; total serum protein and albumin in serum; electric test of Burr; and cytologic reading of exfoliated cells of mucus membrane. See G. H. Arronet (1957) 'Studies on ovulation in the normal menstrual cycle', *Fertility and Sterility*, 8: 301–22.

108 Editorial (1960) 'Oestrogen excretion in gynaecological disorders', *British Medical Journal*, i: 46–7.

109 In 1951, a survey of eighty-seven members of the American Society for the Study of Sterility found that the BBT was the most popular test of ovulation: 96 per cent of respondents said they used it routinely, although only 80 per cent said it was valuable. The other tests used in order of popularity (and value) were: endometrial biopsy 68 per cent (92 per cent); cervical mucus study 51 per cent (48 per cent); mittelschmerz (mid-cycle pain) 43 per cent (42 per cent); vaginal smear cytology 29 per cent (31 per cent); ovarian hyperemia test 17 per cent (56 per cent); pregnanediol assay 16 per cent (63 per cent). See S. H. Sturgis and W. T. Pommerenke (1951) 'The clinical signs of ovulation: a survey of opinions. A report of the sub-committee on ovulation, Research Correlating Committee, American Society for the Study of Sterility', *Fertility and Sterility*, 1: 13.

110 M. Barton and B. P. Wiesner (1945) 'Waking temperature in relation to female fecundity', *British Medical Journal*, ii: 663–8.

111 R. A. Klein and B. J. Schuman (1953) *How to have a baby*, London, Peter Nevill: 64.

112 Jackson 'Clinical methods of determining ovulation': 154.

113 It was common for women to 'improve' their charts before they showed them to their doctor, for example, by demonstrating that they had a reasonably active sex life.

114 Jeffcoate, 'The management of infertility': 184.

115 One woman told Anne and me: 'I broke two thermometers and I don't think it was an accident. I've stopped taking my temperature. I got to loathe waking up in the morning and reaching out for the thermometer so I stopped it' (Pfeffer and Woollett, *The experience of infertility*: 77).

116 S. Bender (1952) 'End-results in primary sterility', *British Medical Journal*, ii: 409–13.

117 T. Barns, H. Campbell and L. Snaith (1953) 'The failure of therapy in the management of infertility', *Journal of Obstetrics and Gynaecology of the British Empire*, 60: 671–9.

118 T. N. A. Jeffcoate (1954) 'The management of infertility', *Journal of Obstetrics and Gynaecology of the British Empire*, 61: 181–5.

119 See the bitter exchange on the effectiveness of treatments of male infertility between Peter Bishop, of the Chelsea Hospital for Women, and Margaret Moore White and Mary Barton, who had large private practices: P. M. F. Bishop (1951) 'Conception and oligozoospermia', *British Medical Journal*, i: 882; M. Moore White and M. Barton (1951) 'Conception and oligozoospermia', *British Medical Journal*, i: 1142; P. M. F. Bishop (1951) 'Conception and oligozoospermia', *British Medical Journal*, i: 1392.

120 Jeffcoate, 'The management of infertility'.
121 A. Sharman (1947) 'Some aspects of human infertility', *British Medical Journal*, ii: 83–7.
122 Jeffcoate, 'The management of infertility'.
123 V. B. Green-Armytage (1949) 'The lessons and virtues of salpingography: an improved technique', *Journal of Obstetrics and Gynaecology of the British Empire*, 43: 23–6.
124 B. Carter (1963) 'Three decades of an infertility clinic', *Journal of Obstetrics and Gynaecology of the British Empire*, 70: 971–5.
125 A. Sharman (1962) 'Primary infertility', *British Medical Journal*, i: 719.
126 For a review of some of these findings, see J. F. P. Wyper (1962) 'Pregnancy after primary infertility investigations', *British Medical Journal*, ii: 274–6.
127 A. S. Parkes (1971) 'The Society for the Study of Fertility, 1950–1971', *Journal of Reproduction and Fertility*, 25: 315–27.
128 Minutes of the Society for the Study of Fertility.
129 W. W. Williams (1958) 'The purpose of the International Fertility Association', *International Journal of Fertility*, 3: 343–8.
130 C. M. McLane (1959) 'The American Society for the Study of Sterility: early history of the ASSS', *Fertility and Sterility*, 10: 117–24.
131 For example, in 1945 both the FPA and the American Society for the Study of Sterility were engaged in an attempt to establish a consensus on the parameters of male fertility. See CMAC SA FPA A6/2; W. W. Williams (1946) 'Routine semen examinations and their interpretation, *Proceedings of the American Society for the Study of Sterility*.
132 Sturgis and Pommerenke 'The clinical signs of ovulation: a survey of opinions'.
133 R. Stevens (1966) *Medical practice in modern England: the impact of specilization and state medicine*, New Haven, Yale University Press: 96.
134 Ibid.: 160.
135 A good example of the tendency of gynaecologists to define 'women's complaints' as emotional and not physical conditions, best suited to treatment in general practice, is a paper published in 1958 in which the authors concluded that 'emotional tension outweighs physical malfunction and disease as a cause of illness in women who attend a gynaecology clinic'. The subsequent correspondence suggests a consensus among gynaecologists and GPs on this finding. GPs were said to be best equipped to deal with these women, as they take care of the patient for the whole of her life; see N. Morris and D. O'Neill (1958) 'Out-patient gynaecology', *British Medical Journal*, i: 1038–9.
136 RCOG A3/7.
137 RCOG Council Minute Book 6: 23.
138 A. Leathard (1980) *The fight for family planning: the development of family planning services in Britain, 1921–1974*, London, Macmillan: 78–9.
139 CMAC SA EUG D 24.
140 Leathard, *The fight for family planning*: 74.
141 Royal Commission on Population (1950) *Report of the Biological and Medi-*

cal Committee, London, HMSO: 48–9.

142   CMAC SA FPA A3/23.

143   D. Maxwell (1954) 'The infertile marriage', *British Medical Journal*, i: 813.

144   Stevens, *Medical practice in modern England*: 162.

145   D. Owens and M. J. Read (1979) *The provision, use and evaluation of medical services for the subfertile: an analysis of the experience of involuntarily childless couples*, University College Cardiff, SRU Working Paper no. 4: 6.

146   CMAC SA FPA A5/102–7.

147   FPA Working Party (1962) *Family planning and family planning clinics today*, unpublished survey, Family Planning Association; CMAC SA FPA A5/64: 20.

148   CMAC SA FPA A3/23.

149   FPA, *Family planning and family planning clinics today*, ch. 3: 1.

150   A. Leathard (1985) *District health authority family planning services in England and Wales*, London, Family Planning Association: 23.

151   J. Higgins (1988) *The business of medicine: private health care in Britain*, Basingstoke, Macmillan: 18.

152   Consultants who work full-time in the National Health Service are those dependent on its staff and facilities, for example, radiotherapy and pathology. See Stevens, *Medical practice in modern England*: 198.

153   Stevens, *Medical practice in modern England*: 202–3.

154   Owens and Read, *The provision, use and evaluation of medical services for the subfertile*: 8.

CHAPTER 6   BANK ACCOUNTS AND BABIES

1   G. C. L. Lachelin, H. A. Brandt, G. I. M. Swyer, V. Little and E. O. R. Reynolds (1972) 'Sextuplet pregnancy', *British Medical Journal*, i: 787–90.

2   F. Corless (1991) 'Mum who swapped house for a baby', *Daily Mirror*, 19 August.

3   There is a marked difference between medical attitudes to sex hormones in Britain and USA; see for example, F. B. McCrea and G. E. Markle (1984) 'The estrogen replacement controversy in the USA and UK: different answers to the same question?', *Social Studies of Science*, 14: 1–26.

4   A. Bourne (1947) 'Endocrines in gynaecology', *British Medical Journal*, i: 79.

5   L. Williams (1954) 'The sex hormones in gynaecology', in J. Munro Kerr, R. W. Johnstone and M. H. Phillips (eds) *Historical review of British obstetrics and gynaecology*, Edinburgh, Livingstone: 390.

6   Family Planning Information Service (1982) *Current estimate of contraceptive use in the UK*, Fact Sheet C2, London, FPA.

7   B. Zondek (1966) 'An interview', *Journal of Reproduction and Fertility*, 12: 13.

8   In 1954, the eminent American gynaecologist Edward Tyler claimed that thyroid therapy was popular among his colleagues who did not wish, or did

not have the time, to subject patients to routine infertility examinations. Instead, he would prescribe thyroid and ask the patient to return after a given period of time, sometimes up to a year, in the hope that she would conceive in the interval: E. Tyler (1954) 'The thyroid myth in infertility', *Fertility and Sterility*, 4: 223.

9   T. M. Fullenlove, J. O. Haman and A. J. Williams (1956) 'Roentgen therapy in anovulation and sterility', *Fertility and Sterility*, 7: 18–27.

10   The history of the isolation and development of gonadotrophins is also described by one of the key workers in H. McLean Evans (1969) 'An interview', *Journal of Reproduction and Fertility*, 19: 1–49.

11   In 1927, with Ascheim, Zondek discovered a gonadotrophic substance in the urine of pregnant women which they exploited in the first hormonal diagnostic test of pregnancy: Zondek, 'An interview': 7. In Britain, the MRC supported trials of the Ascheim – Zondek diagnostic test for pregnancy. It established a Pregnancy Diagnosis Station in Edinburgh, where Berthold Wiesner carried out research into gonadotrophins.

12   The MRC's annual reports describe in detail its support of research into both sex hormones and gonadotrophins.

13   H. E. Dale (1939) 'The chemistry of sex hormones', *Pharmaceutical Journal*, 142: 432–42. After the war, in the USA, whole unfractionated pituitary extracts were available from Searle as 'Gonadophysin', and Squibb as 'Pituitary-anterior pituitary extract'; HCG was available from Winthrop as 'Prolan' and 'Prolan B', Schering as 'Pranturon', Leo as 'Gonadex' and 'Physex', Ayerst as 'APL', Parke Davis as 'Antuitrin-S', Squibb as 'Follutein'; PMS was made by Cutter as 'Gonadin', Upjohn as 'Gonadogen', Schering as 'Anteron', and Lovens Kemiska as 'Antex'. Parke Davis also sold mixtures such as 'Synapoidin'. See H. L. Kotz and W. Herman (1961) 'A review of the endocrine induction of human ovulation', *Fertility and Sterility*, 12: 375–94.

14   Kotz and Herman, 'A review of the endocrine induction': 379.

15   During the war, the MRC and the Agricultural Research Council (ARC) collaborated in experiments on increasing the fertility of sheep: MRC Annual Report 1939/40, Cmd 6163: 28–30.

16   For details of papers reporting good results with mixtures of PMS and HCG see Kotz and Herman 'A review of the endocrine induction': 384.

17   The development of satisfactory bioassays of gonadotrophins proved very difficult. The response elicited by a gonadotrophin varies according to the test material: ovaries act differently from testicles, and ovaries of rabbits differently from those of mice. For an overview of the technical difficulties in the development of gonadotrophins see J. B. Brown (1986) 'Gonadotrophins', in V. Insler and B. Lunenfeld (1986) *Infertility: male and female*, Edinburgh, Churchill Livingstone: 359–96. J. B. Brown from Edinburgh was one of the original members of the Gonadotrophin Club; others were E. Diczfalusy from Stockholm, A. C. Crooke and W. R. Butt from Birmingham, and B. Lunenfeld from Geneva.

18   C. Gemzell (1962) 'Induction of ovulation with human pituitary gonadotrophins', *Fertility and Sterility*, 13: 153.

19   The MRC organized the collection of human pituitaries, which were sent first to the Department of Biochemistry, Cambridge University, where growth hormones were extracted. There is some concern that gonadotrophins prepared from pituitary glands taken from corpses may have caused Creutzfeld-Jakob disease (CJD), a fatal neurological condition. Although there are reported cases of deaths from CJD in women who received pituitary gonadotrophins, at the time of writing this book none have been reported in Britain, although deaths have occurred, and are occurring, in people who received growth hormones extracted from human pituitaries. No doubt it is possible that women may have died of the disease without their doctors recognizing it. See L. J. Dumble and R. D. Klein (1992) 'Creutzfeld-Jakob legacy for Australian women treated with human pituitary gonadotrophins', *The Lancet*, 340: 847–8.

20   Brown, 'Gonadotrophins': 359.

21   See for example A. C. Crooke, P. V. Bertrand, W. R. Butt and R. Morris (1968) 'Joint action of human follicle-stimulating hormone and chorionic gonadotrophin in women with failure of ovulation', *The Lancet*, ii: 180–4.

22   At the time of writing this book, Ares-Serono was testing genetically engineered gonadotrophins.

23   H. Sjostrom and R. Nilsson (1972) *Thalidomide and the power of the drug companies*, Harmondsworth, Penguin.

24   PP *Hansard*, 29 November 1965, vol. 721, col. 125.

25   A. C. Crooke, W. R. Butt, P. V. Bertrand and R. Morris (1967) 'Treatment of infertility and secondary amenorrhoea with follicle-stimulating hormone and chorionic gonadotrophin', *The Lancet*, ii: 636–7.

26   M. Jeffries (1966) 'Happiness drug plea to women', *Evening News*, 29 June.

27   Brown 'Gonadotrophins': 360.

28   C. Gemzell and P. Roos (1966) 'Pregnancies following treatment with human gonadotrophins', *American Journal of Obstetrics and Gynaecology*, 94: 490.

29   A staff correspondent (1965) 'FSH: optimism is tempered by caution', *Medical News*, 6 August.

30   Staff correspondent, 'FSH: optimism'. The view that a woman's susceptibility – rather than, say, the doctor's skills, the potency of the drugs or method of administration – is responsible for the unpredictability of human gonadotrophins seems to have won the day. At a Serono Seminar held in Harrogate in April 1991, Michael Hull, of the Department of Obstetrics and Gynaecology at Bristol University, claimed that the main determinant of outcome is the state of the ovary itself and the number of follicles ready to respond to any gonadotrophins delivered; as he put it, 'the selection and control of gonadotrophin therapy is dictated by the state of the ovaries': M. Hull (1991) 'Gonadotrophins in anovulatory infertility', *Conceive*, 20a: 3.

31   At the time of writing this book, doctors had still not found a way of preventing ovarian hyperstimulation; nor had they agreed on the best way to manage the syndrome. See B. H. Smith and I. D. Cooke (1991) 'Ovarian hyperstimulation: actual and theoretical risks', *British Medical Journal*, i: 127–8.

32 Radioimmunoassays depend on the use of radioactive tracers, proteins with a specific binding site which seek out and latch on to the hormone being measured. By measuring the amount of radioactivity in the test material, it is possible to gauge the amount of hormone present in it.

33 Editorial (1986) 'First class facilities for Serono Labs (UK) Ltd', *Conceive*, 5.

34 Editorial (1988) 'The Serono Fertility Monitoring Service', *Conceive*, 13: 3.

35 A useful critical review of the value of ultrasound in infertility investigations and treatments is W. G. M. Ritchie (1985) 'Ultrasound in the evaluation of normal and induced ovulation', *Fertility and Sterility*, 43: 167–80.

36 D. Gullick (1972) ' "Sorcerers" apprentices', *British Medical Journal*, i: 111.

37 Gemzell and Roos, 'Pregnancies following treatment with human gonadotrophins': 492.

38 D. Martin (1965) 'Birth-drug wife had 7 babies', *Daily Mirror*, 4 August.

39 The number of quadruplets born in England and Wales in 1966–70 was six; 1971–5, nineteen; 1976–80, twenty-four. Quintuplets showed an increase from one set in 1966–70 to four in 1971–5 and four again in 1976–80. The increase is due to gonadotrophins, not assisted conception technologies, which since 1980 are the principal cause of higher order multiple pregnancies. Because these are statistics of birth and not conception, the data probably underestimate the number of women who conceived a multiple pregnancy as a result of gonatrophins (multiple pregnancies suffer a high rate of pregnancy loss). See B. J. Botting, A. J. Macfarlane and F. V. Price, eds (1990) *Three, four and more: a study of triplet and higher order births*, London, HMSO: 19.

40 CMAC SA FPA B10/53.1 contains press cuttings on gonadotrophins.

41 Shirley Tart (1976) 'Fertile mind of Midland test tube "missionary" ', *Wolverhampton Express*, 5 March.

42 Ibid.

43 Ibid.

44 Ibid.

45 Ibid.

46 Gemzell and Roos 'Pregnancies following treatment with human gonadotrophins': 492.

47 R. Edwards and P. Steptoe (1981) *A matter of life: the sensational story of the world's first test-tube baby*, London, Sphere: 93.

48 See M. H. Pappworth (1990) 'Human guinea pigs – a history', *British Medical Journal*, 301: 1456–60.

49 During the 1970s, research ethics committees began to be set up in order to evaluate the ethics of medical research proposals, although the safeguards they currently offer research subjects are considered inadequate; see J. Neuberger (1992) *Ethics and health care: the role of research ethics committees in the United Kingdon*, London, King's Fund Institute.

50 This argument is powerfully and elegantly made in relation to reproductive technologies in B. Katz Rothman (1984) 'The meaning of choice in reproductive technology', in R. Arditti, R. Duelli Klein and S. Minden (eds) *Test-tube women: what future for motherhood?*, London, Pandora: 23–34.

51	For a discussion of the troubling similarities between the two drugs, see R. Klein and R. Rowland (1989) 'Hormonal cocktails: women as test-sites for fertility drugs', *Women's Studies International Forum*, 12: 333–48.

52	Leon Speroff, Robert H. Glass and Nathan G. Kase (1979) *Clinical gynecologic endocrinology and infertility*, Baltimore, The William & Wilkins Company.

53	Leading article (1966) 'Induction of ovulation', *British Medical Journal*, i: 1436–7.

54	Medical Research Council (1964) *Report for the year 1962–1963*, Cmnd 2382, London, HMSO: 50.

55	Preliminary communication (1963) 'Effect of clomiphene on urinary oestrogens in men, *British Medical Journal*, i: 798–9.

56	Today's drugs (1968) 'Clomiphene citrate', *British Medical Journal*, i: 364.

57	Editorial (1967) 'Clomiphene for ovulation', *British Medical Journal*, ii: 435.

58	P. Bishop (1967) 'Clomiphene for ovulation', *British Medical Journal*, ii: 617–18; P. Bishop (1967) 'Clomiphene for ovulation', *British Medical Journal*, ii: 802.

59	A. Byrne (1967) '39 babies from fertility pill', *Sunday Times*, 16 July.

60	Leading article (1969) 'Human gonadotrophins in the treatment of infertility', *The Lancet*, i: 1082–3.

61	Today's drugs, 'Clomiphene citrate': 364.

62	CMAC SA FPA B10/53.1.

63	A. Klopper and M. Hall (1971) 'New synthetic agent for induction of ovulation: preliminary trials in women', *British Medical Journal*, i: 152–4. Tamoxifen failed as a treatment of anovulation. It went on to be used as adjuvant chemotherapy in breast cancer. Its effectiveness in preventing the occurrence of breast cancer is currently being tested in the USA. For a dicussion of the controversy surrounding Tamoxifen see C. Faulder (1992) 'Better safe than sorry', *Bulletin of Medical Ethics*, 75: 29–33.

64	Today's drugs 'Clomiphene citrate': 363.

65	S. J. Behrman and R. W. Kistner (1975) *Progress in infertility*, 2nd edn, Moston, Little, Brown & Co: xiii.

66	See for example, Martin, 'Birth-drug wife had 7 babies'; Byrne, '39 babies from fertility pill'.

67	Martin, 'Birth-drug wife had 7 babies'.

68	For a discussion of the conflict between the government and antinatalist interests in the early 1970s see D. McKie (1973) 'Family planning and the NHS', *The Lancet*, i: 715.

69	P. Coman (1977) *Catholics and the welfare state*, London, Longman: 100.

70	For a discussion of the pressure groups mobilized around abortion in the 1960s and 1970s, see D. Marsh and J. Chambers (1981) *Abortion politics*, London, Junction Books.

71	British political parties are still reluctant to admit to having a policy on population. In 1990, I asked the Conservative, Labour, Liberal and Green political parties whether they had a population policy. Only the Greens replied in the affirmative. Conservative Central Office seemed not to understand what I meant and directed me to census data; The Labour Party sent me the relevant pages on women's health from a paper outlining its health policy; the Liberals did not reply. See N. Pfeffer (1990) 'Fertility control: health or population policy', *Critical Public Health:* 19–21.

72   I was alerted to the political significance of a distinction between 'population' and 'health' by the discovery that after the oil crisis of the 1970s, governments of developing countries which expelled international agencies promoting birth control in terms of keeping down population growth then introduced similar programmes under the rubric of 'health'.

73   PP Select Committee on Science and Technology (1972) *Fifth report: population policy*, London, HMSO: 24–36.

74   Rudolf Klein (1989) *The politics of the National Health Service*, London, Longman: 56.

75   A good example of the impact of the legislation on abortion and the introduction of a family planning service in the National Health Service is an investigation carried out in the mid-1970s, which found more liberal attitudes towards abortion, contraception and sterilization in general practitioners, gynaecologists and surgeons practising in Aberdeen, Scotland; see J. Aitken-Swan (1977) *Fertility control and the medical profession*, London, Croom Helm.

76   Royal College of Obstetricians and Gynaecologists (1972) *Unplanned pregnancy*, London, RCOG.

77   In the first half of the 1970s, on behalf of GPs, the British Medical Association fought hard and long over this issue. The *British Medical Journal* of that period contains numerous articles and letters that record their campaign.

78   For example, in Bristol, the Abortion Act increased the waiting list for inpatient gynaecological treatment at National Health Service hospitals from 240 patients in 1964 to 708 in 1971. See A. H. John and B. Hackman (1972) 'Effects of legal abortion on gynaecology', *British Medical Journal*, ii: 99–102.

79   R. Klein (1975) 'Is there a case for private practice?', *British Medical Journal*, ii: 591–3.

80   Klein *The Politics of the National Health Service*: 117–24.

81   J. P. Nicholl, N. R. Beeby and B. T. Williams (1989) 'Comparison of the activity of short stay independent hospitals in England and Wales, 1981 and 1986', *British Medical Journal*, i: 239–42. Similar data are not available for National Health Service hospitals.

82   Panel on Human Artificial Insemination (1973) 'Report', *British Medical Journal*, supplement, i: 3–5.

83   M. Brudenell, A. McLaren, R. Short and M. Symonds, (eds) (1976) *Artificial insemination: proceedings of the fourth study group of the Royal College of Obstetricians and Gynaecologists 1976*, London, RCOG.

84   Royal College of Obstetricians and Gynaecologists (1979) *Artificial insemination*, London, RCOG.

85   G. W. Pennington and S. Naik (1975) 'Artificial insemination (donor)', *British Medical Journal*, ii: 225–6.

86   Editorial (1975) 'Artificial insemination (donor)', *British Medical Journal*, iv: 2.

87   AI Sub-committee (1977) *Confidential enquiry into extent to which artificial insemination by a donor (AID) is practised in the United Kingdom (up to the end of 1977)*, London, RCOG.

88   H. Welford (1980) 'How AID can help', *Parents*, 48: 66.

89   In 1992, BPAS decided to cease arranging AID.

90   Editorial (1979) 'Artificial insemination for all?', *British Medical Journal*, ii: 458.

91   AI Sub-committee, *Confidential enquiry*: 10.

92   Editorial (1981) 'Artificial insemination at private clinics', *The Lancet*, i: 1325–6.

93   Editorial, 'Artificial insemination (donor)': 2–3.

94   C. Smart (1984) *The ties that bind: law, marriage and the reproduction of patriarchal relations*, London, Routledge & Kegan Paul: 135.

95   Brudenell et al., *Artificial insemination*: 56.

96   Ibid.: 57.

97   Royal College of Obstetricians and Gynaecologists, *Artificial insemination*.

98   The interviewer was a senior social worker employed by the hospital to prepare a social report on the couples' suitability for AID; see R. S. Ledward, L. Crawford and E. M. Symonds (1979) 'Social factors in patients for artificial insemination by donor (AID)', *Journal of Biosocial Science*, 11: 473–9.

99   B. Sandler (1976) '25 years of AID', *Doctor*, 20 May: 14.

100 B. Sandler (1983) 'Donor insemination: an ethical alternative for childless couples', *Current Practice*, 5 August: 16–19.

101 At a symposium on the ethics of AID and embryo transfer held in 1973, the gynaecologist Elliot Phillips described a study of the blood groups of the apparent father, mother and child, which showed that the mother's husband could not be the child's biological father in 30 per cent of the children examined. The findings were relevant to the town in which the study was carried out. See CIBA Foundation symposium, no. 17 (1973) *Law and ethics of AID and embryo transfer*, London, Association of Scientific Publishers: 63.

102 For a review of changing patterns and attitudes towards illegitimacy in Britain, see D. Gill (1977) *Illegitimacy, sexuality and the status of women*, Oxford, Blackwell.

103 D. H. Wilson (1979) 'AID for lesbians', *British Medical Journal*, ii: 669.

104 A. Massam (1979) 'Doctors, lesbians and right to a child', *Evening Standard*, 26 June.

105 The operation of a double standard in relation to the fertility of married and unmarried women during the 1970s is described in S. MacIntyre (1976) ' "Who wants babies?" The social construction of instincts', in D. Leonard Barker and S. Allen (eds) *Sexual divisions and society: process and change*, London, Tavistock: 150–73.

106 The gynaecologists questioned worked in the North East Thames Regional Health Authority, which was the first in the country to fund a regional prenatal screening programme for neural tube defects. Yet the incidence of

births with neural tube defects in this region is well below the national average. From her analysis of the different interests served by the introduction of prenatal screening in Britain, Wendy Farrant concludes that gynaecologists, geneticists and the medical supply industry have enjoyed considerable benefits from it, and women and people with disabilities very few. See W. Farrant (1985) 'Who's for amniocentesis? The politics of prenatal screening' in H. Homans (ed) *The sexual politics of reproduction*, Aldershot, Gower: 96–122.

107   It is also obvious in renal dialysis, where stringent criteria of suitability are applied: criteria which are more severe than in other countries. People in Britain are turned away to die who, if they lived somewhere else, would be successfully treated. It is remarkable that this refusal to provide sufficient resources to save lives does not raise a storm of political protest. It demonstrates the positive advantages that central policy-makers derive from the doctrine of medical autonomy. See Klein, *The politics of the National Health Service*: 85.

108   These techniques have been described in detail from a number of different perspectives. For a flavour of the different perspectives see PP Committee of Inquiry into Human Fertilisation and Embryology (1984) *Report*, Cmnd 9314, London, HMSO; R. Winston (1987) *Infertility: a sympathetic approach*, London, Optima; R. D. Klein (1989) *Infertility: women speak about their experiences of reproductive medicine*, London, Pandora; Pat Spallone (1989) *Beyond conception: the new politics of reproduction*, London, Macmillan.

109   Edwards and Steptoe, *A matter of life*: 91.

110   Robert Edwards, quoted in an obituary to Patrick Steptoe: A. Veitch (1988) 'A man who made thousands of babies', *The Guardian*, 23 March: 19.

111   S. Franklin (1990) 'Deconstructing "desperateness": the social construction of infertility in popular representations of new reproductive technologies', in M. McNeil, I. Varcoe and S. Yearley (eds) *The new reproductive technologies*, London, Macmillan: 214.

112   S. Herbert (1987) 'The right to a baby', *The Guardian*, 28 October.

113   R. Winston (1984) 'The quads: nothing to apologise for', *Observer*, 13 May.

114   The enormous increase in output of papers on psychological aspects of infertility can be gauged from R. J. Edelmann (1989) *Infertility; in vitro fertilization: psychological aspects and counselling. A bibliography, prepared on behalf of the British Infertility Counselling Association*, Guildford, Department of Psychology, University of Surrey.

115   Social scientists are making a valuable critical contribution to our understanding of the impact of assisted conception technologies on kinship. See for example M. Strathern (1992) 'The meaning of assisted kinship', in M. Stacey (ed.) *Changing human reproduction: social science perspectives*, London, Sage: 148–69; E. Haimes (1992) 'Gamete donation and the social management of genetic origins', in Stacey (ed.) *Changing human reproduction*: 119–47.

116   O. Gillie (1988) 'Test-tube baby pioneer dies of cancer, aged 74', *Independent*, 23 March.

117   O. Sattaur (1984) 'New conception threatened by old morality', *New Scientist*, 17 September: 12–17.

118   Organizations set up in order to campaign in favour of human embryo research and support patients undergoing infertility treatment tend to favour acronyms suggestive of a controversial struggle against the forces of reaction. Good examples are PROSPECT, STRIVERS, GOAL, FACT, and ISSUE.

119   There are numerous examples of this tactic, but see Sattaur, 'New conception'.

120   Committee of Inquiry into Human Fertilisation *Report*: 1–3.

121   Sociologists have challenged the neglect of their discipline in the debate. Professor Margaret Stacey in particular has promoted the importance of the potential contribution of sociologists. See M. Stacey (1988) 'The manipulation of the birth process: research implications', paper prepared for the WHO European Advisory Committee for Health Research, Department of Sociology, University of Warwick; 'Introduction', in M. Stacey (ed.), *Changing human reproduction*: 1–8.

122   For a discussion of the salience of human embryo research during the 1980s, see F. Yoxen (1990) 'Conflicting concerns? The political context of recent embryo research policy in Britain', in McNeil et al., *The new reproductive technologies*: 173–99. This debate generated an enormous literature on the ethics of research on and manipulation of human embryos: see for example P. Singer and D. Wells (1984) *Reproduction revolution: new ways of making babies*, Oxford, Oxford University Press.

123   R. Pollack Petchesky (1987) 'Foetal images: the power of visual culture in the politics of reproduction', in M. Stanworth (ed.) *Reproductive technologies*, Cambridge, Polity: 57–80

124   S. Franklin (1991) 'Fetal fascinations: new dimensions to the medical-scientific construction of fetal personhood', in S. Franklin, C. Lury and J. Stacey (eds) *Off-centre: feminism and cultural studies*, London, HarperCollins Academic: 201.

125   For an analysis of the development of the term 'pre-embryo' see. C Crowe (1990) 'Whose mind over whose matter? Women, *in vitro* fertilisation and the development of scientific knowledge', in McNeil et al. (eds) *The new reproductive technologies*: 27–57.

126   Local factors are crucial to understanding the variation in rules regulating research on and manipulation of human embryos. In 1989, for example, human embryo research was forbidden in Germany; in Denmark, a moratorium had been imposed on human embryo research; in Italy, no legal restrictions were imposed on human embryo research. See J. Gunning (1990) *Human IVF, embryo research, fetal tissue for research and treatment, and abortion: international information*, London, HMSO.

127   The term pre-embryo is found only in the literature of enthusiasts of human embryo research, such as PROGRESS and the Voluntary Licensing Authority (VLA) and later Interim Licensing Authority (ILA).

128   F. Price (1989) 'Establishing guidelines: regulation and the clinical management of infertility', in R. Lee and D. Morgan (eds) *Birthright: law and ethics*

at the beginning of life, London, Routledge: 37–54.

129   The tension between gynaecologists pioneering new approaches to infertility treatment in private medical practice and the gynaecological establishment emerged again in a controversy over the number of embryos which it was safe to transfer into women. Claiming the right to clinical freedom, Ian Craft argued in favour of replacing as many embryos as he considered appropriate; the VLA insisted on a maximum of three. Peer group pressure had to work very hard to persuade him to accept this restriction on his clinical freedom; see F. V. Price (1990) 'The management of uncertainty in obstetric practice: ultrasonography, *in vitro* fertilisation and embryo transfer', in McNeil et al.; *The new reproductive technologies*: 123–53.

130   C. J. Pauerstein and C. A. Eddy (1979) 'The role of the oviduct in reproduction; our knowledge and our ignorance', *Journal of Reproduction and Fertility*, 55: 223–9; K. J. Betteridge (1981) 'An historical look at embryo transfer', *Journal of Reproduction and Fertility*, 62: 1–13; S. Fishel (1986) 'IVF – historical perspective', in S. Fishel and E. M. Symonds (eds) *In vitro fertilisation: past, present, future*, Oxford, IRL Press: 1–16; E. Yoxen (1990) 'Historical perspectives on human embryo research', in A. Dyson and J. Harris (eds) *Experiments on embryos*, London, Routledge: 27–41.

131   Editorial (1937) 'Conception in a watch glass', *New England Journal of Medicine*, 217: 678.

132   Edwards and Steptoe, *A matter of life*: 78. Unlike many of the gynaecological establishment, Steptoe believed in the application of science to medicine. He was responsible for the formation of the British Fertility Society in 1972, and through it became President of the International Federation of Fertility Societies in 1977.

133   The story of Steptoe and Edwards' collaboration is taken from Steptoe and Edwards, *A matter of life*.

134   Gillie, 'Test-tube baby pioneer dies of cancer'.

135   Quoted in Spallone, *Beyond conception*: 91.

136   Edwards and Steptoe, *A matter of life*: 83.

137   P. Alderson and N. Pfeffer (1992) 'The problems of being bioethical', *New Scientist*, 11 April: 46–7.

138   P. Steptoe (1978) 'Medicine and the media', *British Medical Journal*, ii: 565.

139   Voluntary Licensing Authority for Human in vitro Fertilization and Embryology (1986) *First report*, London, VLA: 26–9.

140   Interim Licensing Authority for Human in vitro Fertilization and Embryology (1992) *Statistical analysis of the United Kingdon IVF and GIFT data*, London, Human Fertilization and Embryology Authority.

141   Professor Robert Winston provided these figures at the annual general meeting of the National Association for the Childless, September 1988.

142   Allerton Medicare plc (1988) *Offer for subscription under the Business Expansion Scheme*, Manchester, Havers Securities.

143   C. J. Chandler (1987) 'GIFT in the District General Hospital', *Conceive*, 7.

144   See Edwards and Steptoe, *A matter of life*. Bourn Hall was chosen because it was close to the Cambridge laboratories of Edwards.

145 These data were kindly supplied to me by Madeleine Hodgkin.

146 P. R. Brinsden (n.d.) *Infertility and IVF: patient information booklet*, Cambridge, Bourn Hall.

147 'Bourn Hallam expertise in worldwide demand by infertility units', *Bourn Hallam Update*, February 1991: 2.

148 J. Higgins (1988) *The business of medicine: private health care in Britain*, Basingstoke, Macmillan Education: 85–6.

149 J. Parson (1987) 'Funding an assisted conception unit in an NHS hospital', *Conceive*, 7.

150 I am indebted to Mary-Claire Mason who collected this information.

151 For example, St Bartholomew's Hospital, London (Barts), a prestigious teaching hospital, has a joint operation with the AMI Portland Clinic, a private hospital for women specializing in gynaecology and obstetrics. The Portland supports Barts by paying part of the salary of a consultant gynaecologist, and for two embryologists, who work at both units.

152 In 1990, for example, the live birth rate per cycle of IVF at larger centres performing more than 400 IVF treatment cycles per year was 14.2 per cent; at medium centres, defined as those performing 100–400 IVF treatment cycles per year, the live birth rate was 11.1 per cent; at smaller centres, defined as those performing fewer than 100 IVF treatment cycles per year, the live birth rate was 7.9 per cent. See Human Fertilization and Embryology Authority (1992) *Annual report*, London, HFEA: 9.

153 Interim Licensing Authority for human in vitro fertilization and embryology (1991) *The sixth report*, London, Interim Licensing Authority: 12.

154 R. Klein and P. Day (199) *Inspecting the inspectors*, York, Joseph Rowntree Memorial Trust: 4.

155 Lesley Doyal examines the question of unequal access to assisted conception technology in terms of race, class and geography in L. Doyal (1987) 'Infertility - a life sentence? Women and the National Health Service', in Stanworth (ed.) *Reproductive technologies*: 174–90. In their annual reports, the VLA and ILA expressed concern about inequalities in access to assisted conception technology.

156 Interim Licensing Authority, *Sixth report*: 20.

157 Pfeffer and Woollett, *The experience of infertility*: 2.

158 For a trenchant crique of this tendency, see R. Smith (1992) 'The ethics of ignorance', *Journal of Medical Ethics*, 18: 117–118, 134.

159 The concern expressed over higher-order multiple pregnancies prompted a major study into the problems associated with them, which is uncomfortable to read: B. J. Botting et al. (eds) *Three, four and more*.

160 A.Phillips (1987) 'Rise in multiple births puts other babies at risk', *Independent*, 16 June.

161 R. M. L. Winston (1987) 'In vitro fertilisation: practice, prospects and problems', in P. Byrne (ed.) *Medicine in contemporary society: King's College studies, 1986–87*, London, King Edward's Hospital Fund: 73.

162 Winston, 'The quads: nothing to apologise for'.

163 N. Pfeffer and A. Quick (1989) *Infertility services: a desperate case*, London,

Greater London Association of Community Health Councils.

164 Royal College of Obstetricians and Gynaecologists, Working Party on Further Specialization within Obstetrics and Gynaecology (1982) *Report*, London, RCOG.

165 The survey was carried out for Frank Dobson MP, then Labour Shadow Health Minister: D. Mathieson (1986) *Infertility services in the NHS; what's going on? A report prepared for Frank Dobson MP*, London, House of Commons: 8.

166 National Association for the Childless Scotland (1989) *The organisation and management of infertility*, NAC Scotland.

167 The survey was repeated by Harriet Harman MP, Dobson's successor: H. Harman (1990) *Trying for a baby: a report on the inadequacy of NHS infertility service*, London, House of Commons.

168 M. Wagner and P. St Clair (1989) 'Are in-vitro fertilisation and embryo transfer of benefit to all?', *The Lancet*, ii: 1027–30.

169 The debate about the appropriate place of assisted conception technology is captured in the correspondence provoked by an editorial on treatment for infertility published in the *British Medical Journal* in 1987. See R. J. Lilford and M. E. Dalton (1987) 'Effectiveness of treatment for infertility', *British Medical Journal*, 295: 155–56; R. Winston and R. Margara (1987) 'Effectiveness of treatment for infertility', *British Medical Journal*, 295: 608–9.

170 R. Mallett (1988) 'Clinics' "waste time on infertility tests"', *Hospital Doctor*, 5 May: 25.

171 Modern assessment of semen begins with preliminary screening: sperm concentration; volume; number and grade of motile sperm; number of live sperm; morphology; presence of leucocytes and pathogenic organisms; agglutination; liquefaction. It is followed by secondary screening: sperm staining; measures of sperm progression using techniques such as Doppler laser velocimetry, spectrometry, photographic and video recordings; post-coital tests; cross-hostility tests; tests for antibodies. The following tests may be used to measure fertilizing capacity: zona free hamster test; zona fixation test; acrosome staining; monoclonal antibodies; exposing sperm to hypo-osmotic conditions; post-capacitational motility assessments; decondensation of the nucleus. Additionally, seminal plasma may be tested for the presence of zinc and other enzymes. See B. D. Ray (1987) 'Study of laboratory practices in a human in vitro fertilisation programme', unpublished MSc thesis, University of Bath: 225–6.

172 Women were not the first to be put through an ordeal in order to measure male fertility. In the hamster test, a female hamster is superovulated and then 'sacrificed' in order to obtain her eggs, which after treatment are used to test the fertilizing capacity of human sperm.

173 A good exploration of this tendency is, L. Meerabeau (1991) 'Husbands' participation in fertility treatments: they also serve who only stand and wait', *Sociology of Health and Illness*, 13: 396–410.

174 Before the ILA's *Sixth report*, published in 1991, the reasons why some centres succeed in making a higher than average proportion of women preg-

nant, wheras others have a very low success rate, were not made explicit. In 1989, the average live birth rate per treatment cycle was 11.1 per cent; however, five clinics achieved less than a 6 per cent live birth rate per treatment cycle. According to the ILA, there were good clinical reasons for these lower success rates, for example, preparedness to treat older women and couples with so-called 'male factor infertility'; see ILA (1991) *Sixth report*: 14–15. There is no doubt, though, that other clinics lack the necessary expertise. According to the ILA, 'there is a definite learning curve and the best results are obtained from those centres with well-qualified and established teams' (*Sixth report*: 5). There is no recognized training course for embryologists, who vary according to background and training.

175 M. G. R. Hull, H. A. Eddowes, U. Fahy, M. I. Abuzeid, M. S. Mills, D. J. Cahill, C. F. Fleming, P. G. Wardle, W. C. L. Ford and A. McDermott (1992) 'Expectations of assisted conception for infertility', *BMJ*, 304: 1465–9.

176 Rand K. Titmuss (1942) *Parent's revolt: a study of the declining birth-rate in acquisitive societies*, London, Secker and Warburg.

177 My attention was drawn to the extent of the financial sacrifices made by some involuntarily childless women and men by a group of infertility counsellors who saw debt counselling as central to their work.

178 J. Watson (1989) 'Clinic urged to scrap offer of test-tube babies on credit', *Scotland on Sunday*, 12 November.

179 A good example is an article published in *The Guardian* on the birth of the first baby born as a result of the technique of pre-uterine self-incubation. Headed 'New hope for the infertile', the article does not mention efficacy or safety; instead, it emphasizes the cheapness of this technique compared to that of other approaches to IVF. See A. Dunn (1989) "Birth brings new hope to the infertile', *The Guardian*, 30 September: 6.

180 WHO (Regional office for Europe) (1990) 'Recommendations on the management of services for in vitro fertilisation', *BMJ*, 305: appendix.

Index